DICKENS AS AN EDUCATOR

First published 1913
This edition published by Lector House in 2024

ISBN: 978-93-6138-752-4

Lector House LLP
Registered Office: H. No. 96, Block C, Tomar Colony,
Burari, Delhi – 110084, India
info@lectorhouse.com
www.lectorhouse.com

DICKENS AS AN EDUCATOR

JAMES LAUGHLIN HUGHES

2024

LECTOR HOUSE LLP

DICKENS AS AN EDUCATOR

BY

JAMES L. HUGHES

INSPECTOR OF SCHOOLS, TORONTO
AUTHOR OF FROEBEL'S EDUCATIONAL LAWS
MISTAKES IN TEACHING, ETC.

EDITOR'S PREFACE.

The following pages are sufficient to establish the claim of Mr. Hughes for Dickens as an educational reformer—the greatest that England has produced. It will be admitted that he has done more than any one else to secure for the child a considerate treatment of his tender age. "It is a crime against a child to rob it of its childhood." This principle was announced by Dickens, and it has come to be generally recognised and adopted. Gradually it is changing the methods of primary instruction and bringing into vogue a milder form of discipline and a more stimulative teaching—arousing the child's self-activity instead of repressing it.

The child is born with animal instincts and tendencies, it is true, but he has all the possibilities of human nature. The latter can be developed best by a treatment which takes for granted the child's preference to adopt what is good rather than what is bad in social customs and usages.

The child, it is true, is uneven in his proclivities, having some bad ones and some good ones. The true pedagogy uses the good inclinations as a lever by which to correct bad ones. The teacher recognises what is good in the child's disposition and endeavours to build on it a self-respect which may at all times be invoked against temptations to bad conduct. Child depravity sometimes exists, but it can generally be traced to injudicious methods of education in the family, the school, or the community. Dickens has laid so much emphasis on defects of method in these three directions that he has made the generation in which he lived and the next succeeding one sensitively conscious of them. He has even caricatured them with such vehemence of style as to make our ideals so vivid that we see at once any wrong tendency in its very beginning.

Walter Scott, in his schoolmasters, has caricatured pedantry; so has Shakespeare. But Dickens has discovered a variety of types of pedantry and made them all easily recognisable and odious to us. More than this, he has attacked the evil of cramming, the evil of isolation from the family in the boarding school for too young children, and the evil of uninteresting instruction. Whatever is good and reasonable for the child to know should be made interesting to the child, and the teacher is to be considered incompetent who can not find in the life histories of his class threads of daily experience and present interest to which he can attach every point that the regular lesson contains.

Dickens has done a great work in directing the attention of society to its public institutions—especially to its orphan asylums and poorhouses. The chill which the infant gets when it comes in direct contact with the formality of a state institution, or even a religious institution, without the mediation of the family, is portrayed so well that every reader of Dickens feels it by sympathy. So, too, in those families of public men or women or in those of the directors of industry or commerce who crush out the true family life by bringing home their unrelaxing business manners and trying to regulate the family as they regulate the details of a great business house—the reading world has imbibed a sympathy for the rights of the home. Free childhood and the culture of individuality has become a watchword.

Above all, Dickens has introduced a reform as to the habit of terrorizing children. Corporal punishment has diminished to one fourth of its former amount, and Charles Dickens is the prophet to whom the reform owes its potency. In fact, the habit of finding in the good tendencies of the child the levers with which to move him to the repression of his bad impulses has placed in the hands of the professional teacher the means of governing the child without appeal to force except in the rarest cases.

The tendency to caricature an evil has its dangers, of course, and Dickens, like all the other educational reformers, has often condemned as entirely unworthy of toleration what has really in it some good reason for its existence. It was the abuse that needed correction. Reform instead of revolution should have been recommended, but the reformer often gets so heated in his contest with superficial evil that he attacks what is fundamentally good. He cuts down the tree when it needed only the removal of a twig infested with caterpillars. This defect of the reformer renders necessary a new reformer, and thus arises a pendulum swing of educational method from one extreme to another.

Dickens shares with all reformers some of their weaknesses, but he does not share his most excellent qualities with many of them. He stands apart and alone as one of the most potent influences of social reform in the nineteenth century, and therefore deserves to be read and studied by all who have to do with schools and by all parents everywhere in our day and generation.

W. T. Harris.

Washington, D. C.,*October 12, 1900.*

AUTHOR'S PREFACE.

This book has two purposes: to prove that Dickens was the great apostle of the "new education" to the English-speaking world, and to bring into connected form, under appropriate headings, the educational principles of one of the world's greatest educators, and one of its two most sympathetic friends of childhood.

Dickens was the most profound exponent of the kindergarten and the most comprehensive student of childhood that England has yet produced. He was one of the first great advocates of a national system of schools, and his revelations of the ignorance and the intellectual and spiritual destitution of the children of the poor led to the deep interest which ultimately brought about the establishment of free schools in England.

He was essentially a child trainer rather than a teacher. In the twenty-eight schools described in his writings, and in the training of his army of little children in institutions and homes, he reveals nearly every form of bad training resulting from ignorance, selfishness, indifference, unwise zeal, unphilosophic philosophy, and un-Christian theology. No other writer has attacked so many phases of wrong training, unjust treatment, and ill usage of childhood.

He is the most distinctive champion of the rights of childhood. He struck the bravest blows against corporal punishment, and against all forms of coercive tyranny toward the child in homes, institutions, and schools, even condemning the dogmatic will control of such a placid, Christian woman as Mrs. Crisparkle. He demanded a free, real, joyous childhood, rich in all a child's best experiences and interests, so that "childhood may ripen in childhood." He pleaded for the development of the individuality of each child. He taught the wisdom of giving a child proper food, and he showed the vital importance of real sympathy with the child, not mere consideration for him. He was the English father of true reverence for the child.

But Dickens studied the methods of cultivating the minds of children, as well as their character development. He exposed the evils of cramming more vigorously than any other writer. He taught the essential character of the imagination in intellectual and spiritual development. He showed the need of correlation of studies, and of apperceptive centres of feeling and thought in order to comprehend, and assimilate, and transform into definite power the knowledge and thought that is brought to our minds.

It is said by some, who see but the surface of the work of Dickens, that his work is done. Much of the good work for which he lived has been done, but much more remains to be done. Men are but beginning the work of child study and of rational education. The twentieth century will understand Dickens better than the nineteenth has understood him. His profound philosophy is only partially comprehended yet, even by the leaders in educational work. Teachers and all students of childhood will find in his true feeling and rich thought revelation and inspiration.

CONTENTS

DICKENS AS AN EDUCATOR.

CHAPTER I.

THE PLACE OF DICKENS AMONG EDUCATORS.

Dickens was England's greatest educational reformer. His views were not given to the world in the form of ordinary didactic treatises, but in the form of object lessons in the most entertaining of all stories. Millions have read his books, whereas but hundreds would have read them if he had written his ideals in the form of direct, systematic exposition. He is certainly not less an educator because his books have been widely read.

The highest form of teaching is the informal, the indirect, the incidental. The fact that his educational principles are revealed chiefly by the evolution of the characters in his novels and stories, instead of by the direct philosophic statements of scientific pedagogy or psychology, gives Dickens higher rank as an educator, not only because it gives him much wider influence, but because it makes his teaching more effective by arousing deep, strong feeling to give permanency and propulsive force to his great thoughts.

Was Dickens consciously and intentionally an educator? The prefaces to his novels; the preface to his Household Words; the educational articles he wrote; the prominence given in his books to child training in homes, institutions, and schools; the statements of the highest educational philosophy found in his writings; and especially the clearness of his insight and the profoundness of his educational thought, as shown by his condemnation of the wrong and his appreciation of the right in teaching and training the child, prove beyond question that he was not only broad and true in his sympathy with childhood, but that he was a careful and progressive student of the fundamental principles of education.

Dickens deals with twenty-eight schools in his writings, evidently with definite purposes in each case: "Minerva House," in Sketches by Boz; "Dotheboys Hall," in Nicholas Nickleby; Mr. Marton's two schools, Miss Monflather's school, and Mrs. Wackles's school, in Old Curiosity Shop; Dr. Blimber's school and "The Grinders'" school, in Dombey and Son; Mr. Creakle's school, Dr. Strong's school, Agnes's school, and the school Uriah Heep attended, in David Copperfield; the school at which Esther was a day boarder and Miss Donney's school, in Bleak House; Mr. McChoakumchild's school, in Hard Times; Mr. Wopsle's great aunt's school, in Great Expectations; the evening school attended by Charley Hexam,

Bradley Headstone's school, and Miss Peecher's school, in Our Mutual Friend; Phœbe's school, in Barbox Brothers; Mrs. Lemon's school, in Holiday Romance; Jemmy Lirriper's school, in Mrs. Lirriper's Lodgings; Miss Pupford's school, in Tom Tiddler's Ground; the school described in The Haunted House; Miss Twinkleton's seminary, in Edwin Drood; the schools of the Stepney Union; The Schoolboy's Story; and Our School.

In addition to these twenty-eight schools, he describes a real school in American Notes, and makes brief references to The Misses Nettingall's establishment, Mr. Cripples's academy, Drowvey and Grimmer's school, the Foundation school attended by George Silverman, Scrooge's school, Pecksniff's school for architects, Fagin's school for training thieves, and three dancing schools, conducted by Mr. Baps, Signor Billsmethi, and Mr. Turveydrop. He introduces Mr. Pocket, George Silverman, and Canon Crisparkle as tutors, and Mrs. General, Miss Lane, and Ruth Pinch as governesses. Mrs. Sapsea had been the proprietor of an academy in Cloisterham. One of the first sketches by "Boz" was Our Schoolmaster, and his books are full of illustrations of wrong training of children in homes, in institutions, and by professional child trainers such as Mrs. Pipchin.

Clearly Dickens intended to reveal the best educational ideals, and to expose what he regarded as weak or wrong in school methods, and especially in child training.

Dickens was the first great English student of the kindergarten. His article on Infant Gardens, published in Household Words in 1855, is one of the most comprehensive articles ever written on the kindergarten philosophy. It shows a perfect appreciation of the physical, intellectual, and spiritual aims of Froebel, and a clear recognition of the value of right early training and of the influence of free self-activity in the development of individual power and character.

Dickens is beyond comparison the chief English apostle of childhood, and its leading champion in securing a just, intelligent, and considerate recognition of its rights by adulthood, which till his time had been deliberately coercive and almost universally tyrannical in dealing with children. He entered more fully than any other English author into sympathy with childhood from the standpoint of the child. Other educators and philanthropists have shown consideration for children, but Dickens had the perfect sympathy with childhood that sees and feels *with* the child, not merely *for* him.

Dickens attacked all forms of coercion in child training. He discussed fourteen types of coercion, from the brutal corporal punishment of Squeers and Creakle in schools, of Bumble and the Christian philanthropist with the white waistcoat in institutions, and of the Murdstones and Mrs. Gargery in homes, to the gentle but dwarfing firmness of the dominant will of placid Mrs. Crisparkle. He condemned all coercion because it prevents the full development of selfhood, and makes men negative instead of positive.

Among the many improvements made in child training none is more complete than the change in discipline. For this change the world is indebted chiefly to Froebel and Dickens. Froebel revealed the true philosophy, Dickens gave it wings;

Froebel gave the thought, Dickens made the thought clear and strong by arousing energetic feeling in harmony with it.

Thought makes slow progress without a basis of feeling. Dickens opened the hearts of humanity in sympathy for suffering childhood, and thus gave Froebel's philosophy definiteness and propulsive power. The darkest clouds have been cleared away from child life during the past fifty years. Teachers, managers of institutions for the care of children, and parents are now severely punished by the laws of civilized countries for offences against children that were approved by the most enlightened Christian philosophy at the time of Froebel and Dickens as necessary duties essential in the proper training of childhood.

Dickens helped to break the bonds of the doctrine of child depravity. This doctrine had a most depressing influence on educators. It was not possible to reverence a child so long as he was regarded as a totally depraved thing. Froebel and Dickens did not teach that a child is totally divine, but they did believe that every child possesses certain elements of divinity which constitute selfhood or individuality, and that if this selfhood is developed in conscious unity with the Divine Fatherhood the child will attain to complete manhood. This thought gives the educator a new and a higher attitude toward childhood. The child is no longer a thing to be repressed, but a being to be developed. Men are not persistently dwarfed now by deliberate efforts to define a blighting consciousness of weakness; they are stimulated to broader effort and higher purpose by a true self-consciousness of individual power. The philosophy that trains men to recognise responsibility for the good in their nature is infinitely more productive educationally than that which teaches men responsibility for the evil in their nature.

Dickens taught that loving sympathy is the highest qualification of a true teacher. He showed this to be true by both positive and negative illustrations. Mr. Marton, the old schoolmaster in Old Curiosity Shop, was a perfect type of a sympathetic teacher. Dr. Strong was "the ideal of the whole school, for he was the kindest of men." Phœbe's school was such a good place for the little ones, because she loved them. Like Mr. Marton, she had not studied the new systems of teaching, but loving sympathy gave her power and made her school a place in which the good in human hearts grew and blossomed naturally.

"You are fond of children and learned in the new systems of teaching them," said Mr. Jackson.

"Very fond of them," replied Phœbe, "but I know nothing of teaching beyond the pleasure I have in it, and the pleasure it gives me when they learn. Perhaps your overhearing my little scholars sing some of their lessons has led you so far astray as to think me a good teacher? Ah, I thought so! No, I have only read and been told about that system. It seems so pretty and pleasant, and to treat them so like the merry robins they are, that I took up with it in my little way."

She had heard of the kindergarten and had caught some of its spirit of sympathy with the child, but she did not understand its methods. Jemmy Lirriper received perfectly sympathetic treatment from Mrs. Lirriper and the Major; Agnes loved her little scholars; Esther, who sympathized with everybody, loved her pupils, and was beloved by them; and the Bachelor, who introduced Mr. Marton to his second school, was a genuine boy in his comprehensive sympathy with real, boyish boyhood.

So throughout all his books Dickens pleads for kindly treatment for the child, and for complete sympathy with him in his childish feelings and interests. He gave the child the place of honour in literature for the first time, and he aroused the heart of the Christian world to the fact that it was treating the child in a very un-Christlike way. He pleaded for a better education for the child, for a free childhood, for greater liberty in the home and in the school, for fuller sympathy especially at the time when childhood merges into youth and when the mysteries of life have begun to make themselves conscious to the young mind and heart. The poorer the child the greater the need he revealed.

Canon Crisparkle, Esther Summerson, Mr. Jarndyce, Joe Gargery, Rose Maylie, Allan Woodcourt, Betty Higden, Mr. Sangsby, the Old Schoolmaster, the Bachelor, Mrs. Lirriper, Major Jackmann, Doctor Marigold, Agnes Wickfield, Mr. George, and Mr. Brownlow are types of the people with whom Dickens would fill the world—men and women whose hearts were overflowing with true sympathy. Esther Summerson is the best type of perfect sympathy to be met with in literature. She expressed the central principle of Dickens's philosophy regarding sympathy when she said: "When I love a person very tenderly indeed my understanding seems to brighten; my comprehension is quickened when my affection is."

The need of sympathy with childhood was revealed by Dickens most strongly by the cruelty, the coercion, and the harshness of such characters as Squeers, Creakle, Bumble, the Murdstones, Mrs. Gargery, John Willet, Mrs. Pipchin, Mrs. Clennam, and the teachers in The Grinders' school.

Dickens's description of Dr. Blimber's school is the most profound criticism of the cramming system of teaching that was ever written. He treats the same subject also in Hard Times, Christmas Stories, and A Holiday Romance.

The vital importance of a free, rich childhood, the value of the imagination as the basis of intellectual and spiritual development, the folly of the Herbartian psychology relating to the soul, the error of regarding fact-storing as the chief aim of education, and the terrible evils resulting from the tyranny of adulthood in dealing with childhood are all treated very ably in Hard Times, the most advanced and most profound of Dickens's works from the standpoint of the educator.

The need of a real childhood, so well expressed in Froebel's maxim, "Let childhood ripen in childhood," is shown also in Nicholas Nickleby, Old Curiosity Shop, Martin Chuzzlewit, Barnaby Rudge, Dombey and Son, Great Expectations, and Edwin Drood.

The true reverence for individual selfhood is shown in Dombey and Son, David Copperfield, Bleak House, Hard Times, Little Dorrit, Our Mutual Friend, and Edwin Drood.

The wisdom of studying the subject of nutrition as one of the most important subjects connected with the development of children physically, intellectually, and morally, and the meanness or carelessness too frequently shown in feeding children, were taught in Oliver Twist, Old Curiosity Shop, Martin Chuzzlewit, Dombey and Son, David Copperfield, Bleak House, Great Expectations, Edwin Drood, Christmas Stories, and American Notes.

Play as an essential factor in education is treated in Martin Chuzzlewit, Dombey and Son, David Copperfield, and American Notes.

The folly of the old practice of attempting to educate by polishing the surface of the character, of training from without instead of from within, is revealed in Bleak House and Little Dorrit.

Bleak House discusses the contents of children's minds and the need of early experiences to form apperceptive centres of feeling and thought in a comprehensive and suggestive manner.

The need of practising the fundamental law of co-operation and the sharing of responsibilities and duties, as the foundation for the true comprehension of the law of community, is shown in Barnaby Rudge, David Copperfield, Dombey and Son, and Little Dorrit.

The need of child study is suggested in David Copperfield and Bleak House.

The value of joyousness in the development of true, strong character is discussed in Nicholas Nickleby, Barnaby Rudge, Old Curiosity Shop, Martin Chuzzlewit, Dombey and Son, David Copperfield, Hard Times, Little Dorrit, Great Expectations, and Edwin Drood.

Dickens was one of the first Englishmen to see the need of normal schools to train teachers, and to advocate the abolition of uninspected private schools and the establishment of national schools. He taught these ideals in the preface to Nicholas Nickleby, issued in 1839, so that he very early caught the spirit of Mann and Barnard in America, and saw the wisdom of their efforts to establish schools supported, controlled, and directed by the state.

He says, in his preface to Nicholas Nickleby:

> Of the monstrous neglect of education in England, and the disregard of it by the state as a means of forming good or bad citizens, and miserable or happy men, this class of schools long afforded a notable example. Although any man who had proved his unfitness for any other occupation in life, was free, without examination or qualification, to open a school anywhere; although preparation for the functions he undertook was required in the surgeon who assisted to bring a boy into the world, or might one day assist, perhaps, to send him out of it; in the chemist, the attorney, the butcher, the baker, the candlestick-maker; the whole round of crafts and trades, the schoolmaster excepted; and although schoolmasters, as a race, were the blockheads and impostors who might naturally be expected to spring from such a state of things, and to flourish in it, these Yorkshire schoolmasters were the lowest and most rotten round in the whole ladder. Traders in

> the avarice, indifference, or imbecility of parents, and the helplessness of children; ignorant, sordid, brutal men, to whom few considerate persons would have intrusted the board and lodging of a horse or a dog; they formed the worthy corner-stone of a structure which, for absurdity and magnificent high-handed *laissez-aller* neglect, has rarely been exceeded in the world.
>
> We hear sometimes of an action for damages against the unqualified medical practitioner, who has deformed a broken limb in pretending to heal it. But what about the hundreds of thousands of minds that have been deformed forever by the incapable pettifoggers who have pretended to form them?
>
> I make mention of the race, as of the Yorkshire schoolmasters, in the past tense. Though it has not yet finally disappeared, it is dwindling daily. A long day's work remains to be done about us in the way of education, Heaven knows; but great improvements and facilities toward the attainment of a good one have been furnished of late years.

This leaves no doubt in regard to the conscious purpose of Dickens in writing with definite educational plans.

Incidentally he discusses every phase of what is called the "new education." He was the first and the greatest English student of Froebel, and his writings gave wings to the profound thought of the greatest philosopher of childhood. Froebel revealed the truth that feeling is the basis of thought. In harmony with this great psychological principle, it may fairly be claimed that the works of Dickens so fully aroused the heart of the civilized world to the wrongs inflicted on childhood, and the grievous errors committed in training children, as to prepare the minds of all who read his books for the conscious revelation of the imperfections of educational systems and methods, and the imperative need of radical educational reforms.

The intense feeling caused by the writings of Dickens prepared the way for the thought of Froebel. Dickens studied Froebel with great care. He was not merely a student of theoretical principles, but he was a very frequent visitor to the first kindergarten opened in England. Madame Kraus-Boelte, who assisted Madame Rongé in the first kindergarten opened in London, says in a recent letter: "I remember very distinctly the frequent visits made by Mr. Dickens to Madame Rongé's kindergarten. He always appeared to be deeply interested, and would sometimes stay during the whole session."

The description of the schools of the Stepney Union in the Uncommercial Traveller shows how keenly appreciative Dickens was of all true new ideals in educational work. These were charity schools conducted on an excellent system. The pupils worked at industrial occupations half of their school hours, and studied the other half. They were taught music, and the boys had military drill and naval training. They had no corporal punishment in these schools.

Dickens approved most heartily of everything he saw in his frequent visits to the schools of the Stepney Union except the work of one of the younger teachers, who would, in his opinion, have been better "if she had shown more geniality." He commended the industrial work, the military training, the naval training, the music, the discipline without corporal punishment, and the intellectual brightness of the children. He pointed out at some length the difference in interest shown by the pupils in these schools and by the pupils in the school he himself attended when a boy, and drew the conclusion very definitely that shorter hours of study, with a variety of interesting operations, were much better for the physical and intellectual development of children than long hours spent in monotonous work.

The folly and wrong of trying to make children study beyond the fatigue point was never more clearly pointed out than by Dickens in the description of the school he attended when a boy, given as a contrast to the life and brightness and interest shown in the schools of the Stepney Union:

> When I was at school, one of seventy boys, I wonder by what secret understanding our attention began to wander when we had pored over our books for some hours. I wonder by what ingenuity we brought on that confused state of mind when sense became nonsense, when figures wouldn't work, when dead languages wouldn't construe, when live languages wouldn't be spoken, when memory wouldn't come, when dulness and vacancy wouldn't go. I can not remember that we ever conspired to be sleepy after dinner, or that we ever particularly wanted to be stupid, and to have flushed faces and hot, beating heads, or to find blank hopelessness and obscurity this afternoon in what would become perfectly clear and bright in the freshness of to-morrow morning. We suffered for these things, and they made us miserable enough. Neither do I remember that we ever bound ourselves, by any secret oath or other solemn obligation to find the seats getting too hard to be sat upon after a certain time; or to have intolerable twitches in our legs, rendering us aggressive and malicious with those members; or to be troubled with a similar uneasiness in our elbows, attended with fistic consequences to our neighbours; or to carry two pounds of lead in the chest, four pounds in the head, and several active bluebottles in each ear. Yet, for certain, we suffered under those distresses, and were always charged at for labouring under them, as if we had brought them on of our own deliberate act and deed.

It was therefore out of a full heart and an enriched mind that Dickens wrought the wonderful plots into which he wove the most advanced educational ideals of his time and of our time relating to the blighting influence of coercion, the divinity in the child, the recognition of freedom as the truest process and highest aim of education, the value of real sympathy, the importance of self-activity, the true reverence for the child leading to faith in it, the need of child study, the effect of joyousness on the child's development, the benefits of play, the influence of nutrition, the ideal of community, the importance of the imagination as a basis for the best intellectual growth, the narrowness of utilitarianism, the absolute need of apperceptive centres to which shall be related the progressive enlargement and enrichment of feeling and thought throughout the life of the individual, the arrest of development and the sacrifice of power and life due to cramming, and the weakness of all educational systems and methods that regard fact-storing as the highest work of the teacher.

It has been said by critics of Dickens that he exaggerated the defects and errors in the characters of those whom he described. Two things should be kept in mind, however. Dickens usually described the worst, not the best types, and he was justified in revealing a wrong principle or practice in the strongest possible light, in order to make it more easily recognisable and more completely repugnant to the aroused feeling and startled thought of humanity. He was writing with the definite purpose of making the world so thoroughly hate the wrong in education and child training as to lead to definite practical reforms.

Dickens himself did not admit the justness of the charge of exaggeration. His coarsest, most ignorant, and most brutal teacher is Squeers, yet he says "Mr. Squeers and his school are faint and feeble pictures of an existing reality, purposely subdued and kept down lest they should be deemed impossible. There are upon record trials at law in which damages have been sought as a poor recompense for lasting agonies and disfigurements inflicted upon children by the treatment of the master in these places, involving such offensive and foul details of neglect, cruelty, and disease as no writer of fiction would have the boldness to imagine. Since the author has been engaged upon these Adventures he has received, from private quarters far beyond the reach of suspicion or distrust, accounts of atrocities, in the perpetration of which upon neglected or repudiated children these schools have been the main instruments, very far exceeding any that appear in these pages."

Dickens discusses the charge of exaggeration in the preface to Martin Chuzzlewit. He says:

> What is exaggeration to one class of minds and perceptions, is plain truth to another. That which is commonly called a long-sight, perceives in a prospect innumerable features and bearings nonexistent to a shortsighted person. I sometimes ask myself whether there may occasionally be a difference of this kind between some writers and some readers; whether it is *always* the writer who colours highly, or whether it is now and then the reader whose eye for colour is a little dull?
>
> On this head of exaggeration I have a positive experience more curious than the speculation I have just set down. It is this: I have never touched a character precisely from the life, but some counterpart of that character has incredulously asked me: "Now really, did I ever really see one like it?"
>
> All the Pecksniff family upon earth are quite agreed, I believe, that Mr. Pecksniff is an exaggeration, and that no such character ever existed.

It is worth remembering, too, that it is impossible to exaggerate the description of the effects of the evils Dickens attacked. Coercion in any form blights and dwarfs the true selfhood of the child. The coercion of Mrs. Crisparkle's placid but unbending will, which she kept rigid from a deep conviction of Christian duty, is as clearly at variance with the elemental laws of individual freedom and growth by self-activity as the more dreadful forms of coercion practised by Squeers, Creakle, Bumble, or Murdstone.

Doctor Blimber's cramming is not exaggerated. It would be quite possible to find in England or the United States or Canada not only private but public institutions in which similar processes of illogical cramming are still practised. Words are still given before the thought, and as a substitute for thought. "Mathematical gooseberries" are yet produced "from mere sprouts of bushes," the "words and grammar" of literature are still given instead of the life and glory of the author's revelations, children yet are "made to bear to pattern somehow or other."

Whether Dickens exaggerated or not in regard to other spheres of work or of existence without work, he certainly did not exaggerate in regard to school conditions. He studied them faithfully, and described them truly. He saw wrongs more clearly than other men, and he made them stand out in their natural hideousness.

It is frequently asserted that Dickens portrayed wrong training more than right, that he was destructive rather than constructive. In a sense, this is correct. His mission was to startle men, so that they would be made conscious of the awful crimes that were being committed by teachers and parents in the name of duty, as conceived by the highest Christian civilization of his time. He knew that a basis of strong feeling must be aroused against a wrong before it can be overthrown and right practices substituted for it. The only sure foundation for any reform is an energetic feeling of dislike for present conditions. The chief work of Dickens was to lay bare the injustice, the meanness, and the blighting coercion practised on helpless children not only by "ignorant, sordid, brutal men called schoolmasters," but in a less degree by the best teachers and parents of his time. His was a noble work, and it was well done.

The grandest movement of the nineteenth century was the development of a profound reverence for the child, so deep and wide that his rights are beginning to be clearly recognised by individuals and by national laws, and that intelligent adulthood is studying him as the central element of power in the representation of God in the accomplishment of the progressive evolution of the race. Christ put "the child in the midst of his disciples"; men are learning to follow his example, and study the child as the surest way to secure industrial, social, and moral reforms. Froebel and Dickens were the men who revealed the child. They were the true apostles of childhood. It must not be supposed that Dickens was not conscious of the positive good while describing the evils. The expressions "child queller," "gospel of monotony," "bear to pattern," "taught as parrots are," etc., and the name "McChoakumchild," reveal the possession of the highest consciousness of child freedom, of individuality, and of child reverence yet given to humanity. So in all his wonderful pictures it would have been impossible for him to have so vividly described the wrong if he had not clearly understood the right. He had perfect sympathy with childhood, he was a great student of the child and of the existing methods of training and educating him, and his insights and judgment were so clear and true that, as Ruskin says, "in the last analysis he was always right."

If he had never written anything but his article on the kindergarten, published July, 1855, he would have proved himself to be an educational philosopher.

CHAPTER II.

INFANT GARDENS.

Dickens wrote the following article for Household Words in 1855. It reveals a surprising mastery of the vital principles of "the new education." He wrote the article to direct attention to the work of the Baroness Von Bülow, who had come to England to introduce the kindergarten system. Dickens's works show that he had long been a close student of Froebel's philosophy. The article must always take a front rank as a strikingly clear, comprehensive, and sympathetic exposition of the principles and processes of the kindergarten. Kindergartens were called "infant gardens" when first introduced into England.

> Seventy or eighty years ago there was a son born to the Pastor Froebel, who exercised his calling in the village of Oberweissbach, in the principality of Schwartzburg-Rudolstadt. The son, who was called Frederick, proved to be a child of unusually quick sensibilities, keenly alive to all impressions, hurt by discords of all kinds; by quarrelling of men, women, and children, by ill-assorted colours, inharmonious sounds. He was, to a morbid extent, capable of receiving delight from the beauties of Nature, and, as a very little boy, would spend much of his time in studying and enjoying, for their own sake, the lines and angles in the Gothic architecture of his father's church. Who does not know what must be the central point of all the happiness of such a child? The voice of its mother is the sweetest of sweet sounds, the face of its mother is the fairest of fair sights, the loving touch of her lip is the symbol to it of all pleasures of the sense and of the soul. Against the thousand shocks and terrors that are ready to afflict a child too exquisitely sensitive, the mother is the sole protectress, and her help is all-sufficient. Frederick Froebel lost his mother in the first years of his childhood, and his youth was tortured with incessant craving for a sympathy that was not to be found.
>
> The Pastor Froebel was too busy to attend to all the little fancies of his son. It was his good practice to be the peaceful arbiter of the disputes occurring in the village, and, as he took his boy with him when he went out, he made the child familiar with all the quarrels of the parish. Thus were suggested, week after week, comparisons between the harmony of Nature and the spite and scandal current among men. A dreamy, fervent love of God, a

fanciful boy's wish that he could make men quiet and affectionate, took strong possession of young Frederick, and grew with his advancing years. He studied a good deal. Following out his love of Nature, he sought to become acquainted with the sciences by which her ways and aspects are explained; his contemplation of the architecture of the village church ripened into a thorough taste for mathematics, and he enjoyed agricultural life practically, as a worker on his father's land. At last he went to Pestalozzi's school in Switzerland.

Then followed troublous times, and patriotic war in Germany, where even poets fought against the enemy with lyre and sword. The quick instincts, and high, generous impulses of Frederick Froebel were engaged at once, and he went out to battle on behalf of Fatherland in the ranks of the boldest, for he was one of Lützow's regiment—a troop of riders that earned by its daring an immortal name. Their fame has even penetrated to our English concert rooms, where many a fair English maiden has been made familiar with the dare-devil patriots of which it was composed by the refrain of the German song in honour of their prowess—"Das ist Lützow's fliegende, wilde Jagd." Having performed his duty to his country in the ranks of its defenders, Froebel fell back upon his love of nature and his study of triangles, squares, and cubes. He had made interest that placed him in a position which, in many respects, curiously satisfied his tastes—that of Inspector to the Mineralogical Museum in Berlin. The post was lucrative, its duties were agreeable to him, but the object of his life's desire was yet to be attained.

For the unsatisfied cravings of his childhood had borne fruit within him. He remembered the quick feelings and perceptions, the incessant nimbleness of mind proper to his first years, and how he had been hemmed in and cramped for want of right encouragement and sympathy. He remembered, too, the ill-conditioned people whose disputes had been made part of his experience, the dogged children, cruel fathers, sullen husbands, angry wives, quarrelsome neighbours; and surely he did not err when he connected the two memories together. How many men and women go about pale-skinned and weak of limb, because their physical health during infancy and childhood was not established by judicious management. It is just so, thought Froebel, with our minds. There would be fewer sullen, quarrelsome, dull-witted men or women if there were fewer children starved or fed improperly in heart and brain. To improve society—to make men and women better—it is requisite to begin quite at the beginning, and to secure for them a wholesome education during infancy and childhood. Strongly possessed with this idea, and feeling that the usual methods of education, by restraint and penalty, aim at the accomplishment of far too little, and by checking natural development even do positive mischief, Froebel determined upon the devotion of his entire energy, throughout his life, to a strong effort for the establishment of schools that should do justice and honour to the nature of a child. He resigned his appointment at Berlin, and threw himself, with only the resources of a fixed will, a full mind, and a right purpose, on the chances of the future.

At Keilhau, a village of Thuringia, he took a peasant's cottage, in which he proposed to establish his first school—a village boys' school. It was necessary to enlarge the cottage; and, while that was being done, Froebel lived on potatoes, bread, and water. So scanty was his stock of capital on which his enterprise was started, that, in order honestly to pay his workmen, he was forced to carry his principle of self-denial to the utmost. He bought each week two large rye loaves, and marked on them with chalk each day's allowance. Perhaps he is the only man in the world who ever, in so literal a way, chalked out for himself a scheme of diet.

After labouring for many years among the boys at Keilhau, Froebel—married to a wife who shared his zeal, and made it her labour to help to the utmost in carrying out the idea of her husband's life—felt that there was more to be accomplished. His boys came to him with many a twist in mind or temper, caught by wriggling up through the bewilderments of a neglected infancy. The first sproutings of the human mind need thoughtful culture; there is no period of life, indeed, in which culture is so essential. And yet, in nine out of ten cases, it is precisely while the little blades of thought and buds of love are frail and tender that no heed is taken to maintain the soil about them wholesome, and the air about them free from blight. There must be Infant Gardens, Froebel said; and straightway formed his plans, and set to work for their accomplishment.

He had become familiar in cottages with the instincts of mothers, and the faculties with which young children are endowed by Nature. He never lost his own childhood from memory, and being denied the blessing of an infant of his own, regarded all the little ones with equal love. The direction of his boys' school—now flourishing vigorously—he committed to the care of a relation, while he set out upon a tour through parts of Germany and Switzerland to lecture upon infant training and to found Infant Gardens where he could. He founded them at Hamburg, Leipzig, Dresden, and elsewhere. While labouring in this way he was always exercising the same spirit of self-denial that had marked the outset of his educational career. Whatever he could earn was for the children, to promote their cause. He would not spend upon himself the money that would help in the accomplishment of his desire, that childhood should be made as happy as God in his wisdom had designed it should be, and that full play should be given to its energies and powers. Many a night's lodging he took, while on his travels, in the open fields, with an umbrella for his bedroom and a knapsack for his pillow.

So beautiful a self-devotion to a noble cause won recognition. One of the best friends of his old age was the Duchess Ida of Weimar, sister to Queen Adelaide of England, and his death took place on the 21st of June, three years ago, at a country seat of the Duke of Meiningen. He died at the age of seventy, peaceably, upon a summer day, delighting in the beautiful scenery that lay outside his window, and in the flowers brought by friends to his bedside. Nature, he said, bore witness to the promises of revelation. So Froebel passed away.

> And Nature's pleasant robe of green,
> Humanity's appointed shroud, enwraps
> His monument and his memory.

Wise and good people have been endeavouring of late to obtain in this country a hearing for the views of this good teacher, and a trial for his system. Only fourteen years have elapsed since the first Infant Garden was established, and already Infant Gardens have been introduced into most of the larger towns of Germany. Let us now welcome them with all our hearts to England.

The whole principle of Froebel's teaching is based on a perfect love for children, and a full and genial recognition of their nature, a determination that their hearts shall not be starved for want of sympathy; that since they are by Infinite Wisdom so created as to find happiness in the active exercise and development of all their faculties, we, who have children round about us, shall no longer repress their energies, tie up their bodies, shut their mouths, and declare that they worry us by the incessant putting of the questions which the Father of us all has placed in their mouths, so that the teachable one forever cries to those who undertake to be its guide, "What shall I do?" To be ready at all times with a wise answer to that question, ought to be the ambition of every one upon whom a child's nature depends for the means of healthy growth. The frolic of childhood is not pure exuberance and waste. "There is often a high meaning in childish play," said Froebel. Let us study it, and act upon hints—or more than hints—that Nature gives. They fall into a fatal error who despise all that a child does as frivolous. Nothing is trifling that forms part of a child's life.

> That which the mother awakens and fosters,
> When she joyously sings and plays;

That which her love so tenderly shelters.
Bears a blessing to future days.

We quote Froebel again, in these lines, and we quote others in which he bids us

Break not suddenly the dream
The blessed dream of infancy;
In which the soul unites with all
In earth, or heaven, or sea, or sky.

But enough has already been said to show what he would have done. How would he do it?

Of course it must be borne in mind, throughout the following sketch of Froebel's scheme of infant training, that certain qualities of mind are necessary to the teacher. Let nobody suppose that any scheme of education can attain its end, as a mere scheme, apart from the qualifications of those persons by whom it is to be carried out. Very young children can be trained successfully by no person who wants hearty liking for them, and who can take part only with a proud sense of restraint in their chatter and their play. It is in truth no condescension to become in spirit as a child with children, and nobody is fit to teach the young who holds a different opinion. Unvarying cheerfulness and kindness, the refinement that belongs naturally to a pure, well-constituted woman's mind are absolutely necessary to the management of one of Froebel's Infant Gardens.

Then, again, let it be understood that Froebel never wished his system of training to be converted into mere routine to the exclusion of all that spontaneous action in which more than half of every child's education must consist. It was his purpose to show the direction in which it was most useful to proceed, how best to assist the growth of the mind by following the indications Nature furnishes. Nothing was farther from his design, in doing that, than the imposition of a check on any wholesome energies. Blindman's buff, romps, puzzles, fairy tales, everything in fact that exercises soundly any set of the child's faculties, must be admitted as a part of Froebel's system. The cardinal point of his doctrine is—take care that you do not exercise a part only of the child's mind or body; but take thorough pains to see that you encourage the development of its whole nature. If pains—and great pains—be not taken to see that this is done, probably it is not done. The Infant Gardens are designed to help in doing it.

The mind of a young child must not be trained at the expense of its body. Every muscle ought, if possible, to be brought daily into action; and, in the case of a child suffered to obey the laws of Nature by free tumbling and romping, that is done in the best manner possible. Every mother knows that by carrying an infant always on the same arm its growth is liable to be perverted. Every father knows the child's delight at being vigorously danced up and down, and much of this delight arises from the play then given to its muscles. As the child grows, the most unaccustomed positions into which it can be safely twisted are those from which it will receive the greatest pleasure. That is because play is thus given to the muscles in a form they do not often get, and Nature—always watchful on the child's behalf—cries, We will have some more of that. It does us good. As it is with the body, so it is with the mind, and Froebel's scheme of infant education is, for both, a system of gymnastics.

He begins with the newborn infant, and demands that, if possible, it shall not be taken from its mother. He sets his face strongly against the custom of committing the child during the tenderest and most impressible period of its whole life to the care and companionship of an ignorant nursemaid, or of servants who have not the mother's instinct, or the knowledge that can tell them how to behave in its presence. Only the mother should, if possible, be the child's chief companion and teacher during at least the first three years of its life, and she should have thought it worth while to prepare herself for the right fulfilment of her duties. Instead of tambour work, or Arabic, or any other useless thing that may be taught at girls' schools, surely it would be a great blessing if young ladies were to spend some of their time in an Infant Garden, that might be attached to every academy. Let them all learn from Froebel what are the requirements of a child, and be prepared for the wise performance of what is after all to be the most momentous business of their lives.

The carrying out of this hint is indeed necessary to the complete and general adoption of the infant-garden system. Froebel desired his infants to be taught only by women, and required that they should be women as well educated and refined as possible, preferring amiable unmarried girls. Thus he would have our maidens spending some part of their time in playing with little ones, learning to understand them, teaching them to understand; our wives he would have busy at home, making good use of their experience, developing carefully and thoughtfully the minds of their children, sole teachers for the first three years of their life; afterward, either helped by throwing them among other children in an Infant Garden for two or three hours every day, or, if there be at home no lack of little company, having Infant Gardens of their own.

Believing that it is natural to address infants in song, Froebel encouraged nursery songs, and added to their number. Those contributed by him to the common stock were of course contributed for the sake of some use that he had for each; in the same spirit—knowing play to be essential to a child—he invented games; and those added by him to the common stock are all meant to be used for direct teaching. It does not in the least follow, and it was not the case, that he would have us make all nursery rhymes and garden sports abstrusely didactic. He meant no more than to put his own teaching into songs and games, to show clearly that whatever is necessary to be said or done to a young child may be said or done merrily or playfully; and although he was essentially a schoolmaster, he had no faith in the terrors commonly associated with his calling.

Froebel's nursery songs are associated almost invariably with bodily activity on the part of the child. He is always, as soon as he becomes old enough, to do something while the song is going on, and the movements assigned to him are cunningly contrived so that not even a joint of a little finger shall be left unexercised. If he be none the better, he is none the worse for this. The child is indeed unlucky that depends only on care of this description for the full play of its body; but there are some children so unfortunate, and there are some parents who will be usefully reminded by those songs, of the necessity of procuring means for the free action of every joint and limb. What is done for the body is done in the same spirit for the mind, and ideas are formed, not by song only. The beginning of a most ingenious course of mental training by a series of playthings is made almost from the very first.

A box containing six soft balls, differing in colour, is given to the child. It is Froebel's "first gift." Long before it can speak the infant can hold one of these little balls in its fingers, become familiar with its spherical shape and its colour. It stands still, it springs, it rolls. As the child grows, he can roll it and run after it, watch it with sharp eyes, and compare the colour of one ball with the colour of another, prick up his ears at the songs connected with his various games with it, use it as a bond of playfellowship with other children, practise with it first efforts at self-denial, and so forth. One ball is suspended by a string, it jumps—it rolls—here—there—over—up; turns left—turns right—ding-dong—tip-tap—falls—spins; fifty ideas may be connected with it. The six balls, three of the primary colours, three of the secondary, may be built up in a pyramid; they may be set rolling, and used in combination in a great many ways giving sufficient exercise to the young wits that have all knowledge and experience before them.

Froebel's "second gift" is a small box containing a ball, cube, and roller (the last two perforated), with a stick and string. With these forms of the cube, sphere, and cylinder, there is a great deal to be done and learned. They can be played with at first according to the child's own humour: will run, jump, represent carts, or anything. The ancient Egyptians, in their young days as a nation, piled three cubes on one another and called them the three Graces. A child will, in the same way, see fishes in stones, and be content to put a cylinder upon a cube, and say that is papa on horseback. Of this element of ready fancy in all childish sport Froebel took full advantage. The ball, cube, and cylinder may be spun, swung, rolled, and balanced in so many ways as to display practically all their properties. The cube, spun upon the stick piercing it through opposite edges, will look like a circle, and so forth. As the child grows older, each of the forms may be examined definitely, and he may learn from observation to describe it. The ball may be rolled down an inclined plane and the acceleration of its speed observed. Most of the elementary laws of mechanics may be made practically obvious to the child's understanding.

The "third gift" is the cube divided once in every direction. By the time a child gets this to play with he is three years old—of age ripe for admission to an Infant Garden. The Infant Garden is intended for the help of children between three years old and seven. Instruction in it—always by means of play—is given for only two or three hours in the day; such instruction sets each child, if reasonably helped at home, in the right train of education for the remainder of its time.

An Infant Garden must be held in a large room abounding in clear space for child's play, and connected with a garden into which the children may adjourn whenever weather will permit. The garden is meant chiefly to assure, more perfectly, the association of wholesome bodily exercise with mental activity. If climate but permitted, Froebel would have all young children taught entirely in the pure, fresh air, while frolicking in sunshine among flowers. By his system he aimed at securing for them bodily as well as mental health, and he held it to be unnatural that they should be cooped up in close rooms, and glued to forms, when all their limbs twitch with desire for action, and there is a warm sunshine out of doors. The garden, too, should be their own; every child the master or mistress of a plot in it, sowing seeds and watching day by day the growth of plants, instructed playfully and simply in the meaning of what is observed. When weather forbids use of the garden, there is the great, airy room which should contain cupboards, with a place for every child's toys and implements; so that a habit of the strictest neatness may be properly maintained. Up to the age of seven there is to be no book work and no ink work; but only at school a free and brisk, but systematic strengthening of the body, of the senses, of the intellect, and of the affections, managed in such a way as to leave the child prompt for subsequent instruction, already comprehending the elements of a good deal of knowledge.

We must endeavour to show in part how that is done. The third gift—the cube divided once in every direction—enables the child to begin the work of construction in accordance with its own ideas, and insensibly brings the ideas into the control of a sense of harmony and fitness. The cube divided into eight parts will manufacture many things; and, while the child is at work helped by quiet suggestion now and then, the teacher talks of what he is about, asks many questions, answers more, mixes up little songs and stories with the play. Pillars, ruined castles, triumphal arches, city gates, bridges, crosses, towers, all can be completed to the perfect satisfaction of a child, with the eight little cubes. They are all so many texts on which useful and pleasant talk can be established. Then they are capable also of harmonious arrangement into patterns, and this is a great pleasure to the child. He learns the charm of symmetry, exercises taste in the preference of this or that among the hundred combinations of which his eight cubes are susceptible.

Then follows the "fourth gift," a cube divided into eight planes cut lengthways. More things can be done with this than with the other. Without strain on the mind, in sheer play, mingled with songs, nothing is wanted but a liberal supply of little cubes, to make clear to the children the elements of arithmetic. The cubes are the things numbered. Addition is done with them; they are subtracted from each other; they are multiplied; they are divided. Besides these four elementary rules they cause children to be thoroughly at home in the principle of fractions, to multiply and divide fractions—as real things; all in good time it will become easy enough to let written figures represent them—to go through the rule of three, square root, and cube root. As a child has instilled into him the principles of arithmetic, so he acquires insensibly the groundwork of geometry, the sister science.

Froebel's "fifth gift" is an extension of the third, a cube divided into twenty-seven equal cubes, and three of these further divided into halves, three into quarters. This brings with it the teaching of a great deal of geometry, much help to the lessons in number, magnificent accessions to the power of the little architect, who is provided, now, with pointed roofs and other glories, and the means of producing an almost infinite variety of symmetrical patterns, both more complex and more beautiful than heretofore.

The "sixth gift" is a cube so divided as to extend still farther the child's power of combining and discussing it. When its resources are exhausted and combined with those of the "seventh gift" (a box containing every form supplied in the preceding series), the little pupil—seven years old—has had his inventive and artistic powers exercised, and his mind stored with facts that have been absolutely comprehended. He has acquired also a sense of pleasure in the occupation of his mind.

But he has not been trained in this way only. We leave out of account the bodily exercise connected with the entire round of occupation, and speak only of the mental discipline. There are some other "gifts" that are brought into service as the child becomes able to use them. One is a box containing pieces of wood, or pasteboard, cut into sundry forms. With these the letters of the alphabet can be constructed; and, after letters, words, in such a way as to create out of the game a series of pleasant spelling lessons. The letters are arranged upon a slate ruled into little squares, by which the eye is guided in preserving regularity. Then follows the gift of a bundle of small sticks, which represent so many straight lines; and, by laying them upon his slate, the child can make letters, patterns, pictures; drawing, in fact, with lines that have not to be made with pen or pencil, but are provided ready made and laid down with the fingers. This kind of Stick-work having been brought to perfection, there is a capital extension of the idea with what is called Pea-work. By the help of peas softened in water, sticks may be joined together, letters, skeletons of cubes, crosses, prisms may be built; houses, towers, churches may be constructed, having due breadth as well as length and height, strong enough to be carried about or kept as specimens of ingenuity. Then follows a gift of flat sticks, to be used in plaiting. After that there is a world of ingenuity to be expended on the plaiting, folding, cutting, and pricking of plain or coloured paper. Children five years old, trained in the Infant Garden, will delight in plaiting slips of paper variously coloured into patterns of their own invention, and will work with a sense of symmetry so much refined by training as to produce patterns of exceeding beauty. By cutting paper, too, patterns are produced in the Infant Garden that would often, though the work of very little hands, be received in schools of design with acclamation. Then there are games by which the first truths of astronomy, and other laws of Nature, are made as familiar as they are interesting. For our own parts, we have been perfectly amazed at the work we have seen done by children of six or seven—bright, merry creatures, who have all the spirit of their childhood active in them, repressed by no parent's selfish love of ease and silence, cowed by no dull-witted teacher of the A B C and the pothooks.

Froebel discourages the cramping of an infant's hand upon a pen, but his slate ruled into little squares, or paper prepared in the same way, is used by him for easy training in the elements of drawing. Modelling in wet clay is one of the most important occupations of the children who have reached about the sixth year, and is used as much as possible, not merely to encourage imitation, but to give some play to the creative power. Finally, there is the best possible use made of the paint-box, and children engaged upon the colouring of pictures and the arrangement of nosegays are further taught to enjoy, not merely what is bright, but also what is harmonious and beautiful.

We have not left ourselves as much space as is requisite to show how truly all such labour becomes play to the child. Fourteen years' evidence suffices for a demonstration of the admirable working of a system of this kind; but as we think there are some parents who may be willing to inquire a little further into the subject here commended earnestly to their attention, we will end by a citation of the source from which we have ourselves derived what information we possess.

At the educational exhibition in St. Martin's Hall last year, there was a large display of the material used and results produced in Infant Gardens which attracted much attention. The Baroness von Marenholtz, enthusiastic in her advocacy of the children's cause, came then to England, and did very much to procure the establishment in this country of some experimental Infant Gardens. By her, several months ago—and at about the same time by M. and Madame Rongé who had already established the first English Infant Garden—our attention was invited to the subject. We were also made acquainted with M. Hoffman, one of Froebel's pupils, who explained the system theoretically at the Polytechnic Institution. When in this country, the Baroness von Marenholtz published a book called Woman's Educational Mission, being an explanation of Frederick Froebel's System of Infant Gardens. We have made use of the book in the preceding notice, but it appeared without the necessary illustrations, and is therefore a less perfect guide to the subject than a work published more recently by M. and Madame Rongé: A Practical Guide to the English Kindergarten. This last book we exhort everybody to consult who is desirous of a closer insight into Froebel's system than we have been able here to give. It not only explains what the system is, but, by help of an unstinted supply of little sketches, enables any one at once to study it at home and bring it into active operation. It suggests conversations, games; gives many of Froebel's songs, and even furnishes the music (which usually consists of popular tunes—Mary Blane, Rousseau's Dream, etc.) to which they may be sung. Furthermore, it is well to say that any one interested in this subject, whom time and space do not forbid, may see an Infant Garden in full work by calling, on a Tuesday morning between the hours of ten and one, on M. and Madame Rongé, at number 32 Tavistock Place, Tavistock Square. That day these earliest and heartiest of our established infant gardeners have set apart, for the help of a good cause, to interruptions and investigations from the world without, trusting, of course, we suppose, that no one will disturb them for the satisfaction of mere idle curiosity.

CHAPTER III.

THE OVERTHROW OF COERCION.

Dickens, in the preface to Nicholas Nickleby, states that, as Pickwick Papers had given him an audience, he determined to carry out a long-cherished plan and write for the purpose of driving out of existence a class of bad private schools, of which certain schools in Yorkshire were the worst types. He drew a picture of low cunning, avarice, ignorance, imposture, and brutality in Squeers that astounded his audience, and led to the closing of most of the Yorkshire private schools and to the overthrow of tyranny in schools throughout the civilized world. Tyranny and corporal punishment still exist, but not in the best schools. Not one child weeps now on account of corporal punishment for every hundred who wailed bitterly for the same reason when Froebel and Dickens began their loving work. Year by year the good work goes on. Men are learning the better ways of guiding and governing childhood. We can not yet say when men and women in the homes and schools everywhere shall understand the child and their own powers so thoroughly that there shall be no more corporal punishment inflicted, but we do know that the abatement of the terrible brutality began with the revelations of Froebel and Dickens. Froebel taught the new philosophy, Dickens sent it quivering through the hearts and consciences of mankind.

Members of the highest classes in England have been imprisoned near the close of the nineteenth century for improper methods of punishing children that would have excited no comment when Dickens described Squeers a little more than half a century earlier. In the report to the British Government, at the close of his remarkable half-century of honourable and very able educational work, Sir Joshua Fitch said: "In watching the gradual development of the training colleges for women from year to year, nothing is more striking than the increased attention which is being paid in those institutions to the true principles of infant teaching and discipline. The circular which has recently been issued by your lordships, and which is designed to enforce and explain these principles, would, if put forth a few years ago, have fallen on unprepared soil, and would indeed have seemed to many teachers both in and out of training colleges to be scarcely intelligible. Now its counsels will be welcomed with sympathy and full appreciation."

Dickens describes Squeers as a man "whose appearance was not prepossessing."

> He had but one eye, and the popular prejudice runs in favour of two. The eye he had was unquestionably useful, but decidedly

> not ornamental: being of a greenish gray, and in shape resembling the fanlight of a street door. The blank side of his face was much wrinkled and puckered up, which gave him a very sinister appearance, especially when he smiled, at which times his expression bordered closely on the villainous. His hair was very flat and shiny, save at the ends, where it was brushed stiffly up from a low protruding forehead, which assorted well with his harsh voice and coarse manner.

He then proceeds to reveal the character of Squeers by a series of incidents:

> Mr. Squeers was standing in a box by one of the coffee-room fireplaces. In a corner of the seat was a very small deal trunk, tied round with a scanty piece of cord; and on the trunk was perched—his lace-up half-boots and corduroy trousers dangling in the air—a diminutive boy, with his shoulders drawn up to his ears, and his hands planted on his knees, who glanced timidly at the schoolmaster, from time to time, with evident dread and apprehension.
>
> "Half-past three," muttered Mr. Squeers, turning from the window, and looking sulkily at the coffee-room clock. "There will be nobody here to-day."
>
> Much vexed by this reflection, Mr. Squeers looked at the little boy to see whether he was doing anything he could beat him for. As he happened not to be doing anything at all, he merely boxed his ears, and told him not to do it again.
>
> "At midsummer," muttered Mr. Squeers, resuming his complaint, "I took down ten boys; ten twentys is two hundred pound. I go back at eight o'clock to-morrow morning, and have got only three—three oughts is an ought—three twos is six—sixty pound. What's come of all the boys? what's parents got in their heads? what does it all mean?"
>
> Here the little boy on the top of the trunk gave a violent sneeze.
>
> "Halloa, sir!" growled the schoolmaster, turning round. "What's that, sir?"
>
> "Nothing, please, sir," said the little boy.
>
> "Nothing, sir?" exclaimed Mr. Squeers.
>
> "Please, sir, I sneezed," rejoined the boy, trembling till the little trunk shook under him.
>
> "Oh! sneezed, did you?" retorted Mr. Squeers. "Then what did you say 'nothing' for, sir?"
>
> In default of a better answer to this question, the little boy screwed a couple of knuckles into each of his eyes and began to

cry, wherefore Mr. Squeers knocked him off the trunk with a blow on one side of his face, and knocked him on again with a blow on the other.

"Wait till I get you down into Yorkshire, my young gentleman," said Mr. Squeers, "and then I'll give you the rest. Will you hold that noise, sir?"

"Ye—ye—yes," sobbed the little boy, rubbing his face very hard with the Beggar's Petition in printed calico.

"Then do so at once, sir," said Squeers. "Do you hear?"

The waiter at this juncture announced a gentleman who wished to interview Mr. Squeers, and the schoolmaster, in an undertone, said to the poor boy: "Put your handkerchief in your pocket, you little scoundrel, or I'll murder you when the gentleman goes."

Affecting not to see the gentleman when he entered, Mr. Squeers feigned to be mending a pen and trying to comfort the boy he had so grossly abused.

"My dear child," said Squeers, "all people have their trials. This early trial of yours, that is fit to make your little heart burst and your very eyes come out of your head with crying, what is it? Nothing—less than nothing. You are leaving your friends, but you will have a father in me, my dear, and a mother in Mrs. Squeers."

Our indignation is still further aroused when we hear the conversation between Mr. Squeers and his visitor, who is named Snawley, and who was "a sleek, flat-nosed man, bearing in his countenance an expression of much mortification and sanctity."

He had brought with him two little boys, whose stepfather he was. Their mother had a little money in her own right and he was afraid she might squander it on her boys, so he wished to dispose of them. Our blood runs cold as we hear the two scoundrels plotting against the unfortunate boys. They are to be kept by Squeers till grown up. No questions are to be asked "so long as the payments are regular." "They are to be supplied with razors when grown up, and never allowed home for holidays, and not permitted to write home, except a circular at Christmas to say they never were so happy and hope they may never be sent for, and no questions are to be asked in case anything happens to them."

We learn the unutterable selfishness of Squeers as he sits eating a sumptuous breakfast, while the five wretched and hungry little boys, who are to accompany him to Yorkshire to Dotheboys Hall, look at him. He had ordered bread and butter for three, which he cut into five portions, and "two-penn'orth of milk" for the five boys. While waiting for the bread to come he said, as he took a large mouthful of beef and toast, "Conquer your passions, boys, and don't be eager after vittles. Subdue your appetites, my dears, and you've conquered human natur."

Nicholas Nickleby had been engaged to teach under Squeers in Dotheboys Hall. He was shocked at many things he heard and saw the night he arrived in Yorkshire.

But the school itself and the appearance of the wretched pupils completed his discomfiture.

> The pupils—the young noblemen! How the last faint traces of hope, the remotest glimmering of any good to be derived from his efforts in this den, faded from the mind of Nicholas as he looked in dismay around! Pale and haggard faces, lank and bony figures, children with the countenances of old men, deformities with irons upon their limbs, boys of stunted growth, and others whose long meagre legs would hardly bear their stooping bodies, all crowded on the view together; there were the bleared eye, the harelip, the crooked foot, and every ugliness or distortion that told of unnatural aversion conceived by parents for their offspring, or of young lives which, from the earliest dawn of infancy, had been one horrible endurance of cruelty and neglect. There were little faces which should have been handsome, darkened with the scowl of sullen, dogged suffering; there was childhood with the light of its eye quenched, its beauty gone, and its helplessness alone remaining; there were vicious-faced boys, with leaden eyes, like malefactors in a jail; and there were young creatures on whom the sins of their frail parents had descended, weeping even for the mercenary nurses they had known, and lonesome even in their loneliness. With every kindly sympathy and affection blasted in its birth, with every young and healthy feeling flogged and starved down, with every revengeful passion that can fester in swollen hearts, eating its evil way to their core in silence, what an incipient hell was breeding here!

It was Mr. Squeers's custom on the first afternoon after his return from London to call the school together to make announcements, and read letters written by himself, which he pretended had been written by the relatives of the boys. Accordingly, the first afternoon after the arrival of Nicholas, Squeers entered the schoolroom "with a small bundle of papers in his hand, and Mrs. S. followed with a pair of canes."

"Let any boy speak a word without leave," said Mr. Squeers, "and I'll take the skin off his back."

Two letters will serve as samples of the rest:

"Graymarsh. Stand up, Graymarsh."

Graymarsh stood up, while Squeers read his letter:

> "Graymarsh's maternal aunt is very glad to hear he's so well and happy, and sends her respectful compliments to Mrs. Squeers, and thinks she must be an angel. She likewise thinks Mr. Squeers is too good for this world; but hopes he may long be spared to carry on the business. Would have sent the two pair of stockings as desired, but is short of money, so forwards a tract instead, and hopes Graymarsh will put his trust in Providence.

> Hopes, above all, that he will study in every thing to please Mr. and Mrs. Squeers, and look upon them as his only friends; and that he will love Master Squeers; and not object to sleeping five in a bed, which no Christian should. Ah!" said Squeers, folding it up, "a delightful letter. Very affecting indeed."

"Mobbs" was next called, and his letter was read to him:

> "Mobbs's stepmother," said Squeers, "took to her bed on hearing that he wouldn't eat fat, and has been very ill ever since. She wishes to know, by an early post, where he expects to go to, if he quarrels with his vittles; and with what feelings he could turn up his nose at the cow's-liver broth, after his good master had asked a blessing on it. This was told her in the London newspapers—not by Mr. Squeers, for he is too kind and too good to set anybody against anybody—and it has vexed her so much, Mobbs can't think. She is sorry to find he is discontented, which is sinful and horrid, and hopes Mr. Squeers will flog him into a happier state of mind; with this view, she has also stopped his halfpenny a week pocket-money, and given a double-bladed knife with a corkscrew in it to the missionaries, which she had bought on purpose for him."
>
> "A sulky state of feeling," said Squeers, after a terrible pause, during which he had moistened the palm of his right hand again, "won't do. Cheerfulness and contentment must be kept up. Mobbs, come to me!"
>
> Mobbs moved slowly toward the desk, rubbing his eyes in anticipation of good cause for doing so; and he soon afterward retired by the side door, with as good a cause as a boy need have.

There are still school tyrants who talk with philosophic air of flogging children to make them happier, and others who say with hard tones and clenched hands that "the one thing they will not allow in their schools is a sulky boy or girl," and they mean, when they say so, that if a boy is sulky they take no steps to find out the cause of his disease or the natural remedy for it, but they apply the universal remedy of the old-fashioned quack trainer and whip the poor boy, who is already suffering from some physical or nervous derangement. Squeers and such teachers are brother tyrants. They practise the Squeers's doctrine—"A sulky state of feeling won't do. Cheerfulness and contentment must be kept up. Mobbs, come to me"—to make children cheerful and contented.

One of the most heart-stirring cases in Dotheboys Hall was that of poor Smike. He had been sent to Squeers when an infant. He was a young man now, but he had been starved so that he wore still around his long neck the frill of the collar that loving hands had placed there when he was a little child. Ill treatment and lack of proper food had made him almost an imbecile, and he was the drudge of the institution. Nicholas was attracted by the anxious, longing looks of the boy, as his eyes followed Squeers from place to place on their arrival from London.

> He was lame; and as he feigned to be busy in arranging the table, glanced at the letters with a look so keen, and yet so dispirited and hopeless, that Nicholas could hardly bear to watch him.
>
> "What are you bothering about there, Smike?" cried Mrs. Squeers; "let the things alone, can't you."
>
> "Eh!" said Squeers, looking up. "Oh! it's you, is it?"
>
> "Yes, sir," replied the youth, pressing his hands together, as though to control, by force, the nervous wandering of his fingers; "is there— —"
>
> "Well!" said Squeers.
>
> "Have you—did anybody—has nothing been heard—about me?"
>
> "Devil a bit," replied Squeers testily.
>
> The lad withdrew his eyes, and, putting his hand to his face, moved toward the door.
>
> "Not a word," resumed Squeers, "and never will be."

This is one of the pathetic pictures that awoke the heart of humanity. Nicholas was the first person who had ever sympathized with Smike, so the poor fellow naturally gave to Nicholas the pent-up love of his dwarfed nature, and kept near him whenever it was possible to do so.

Dickens made Smike the centre of the terrible interest in Dotheboys Hall.

Poor Smike was so badly treated that he ran away, but, after a long chase, he was brought home in triumph by Mrs. Squeers, bound like an animal. Squeers, of course, determined to flog him before all the boys as an example, and this led to the first great step toward the overthrow of the power of Squeers in Dotheboys Hall.

> The news that Smike had been caught and brought back in triumph, ran like wildfire through the hungry community, and expectation was on tiptoe all the morning. On tiptoe it was destined to remain, however, until afternoon; when Squeers, having refreshed himself with his dinner, and further strengthened himself by an extra libation or so, made his appearance (accompanied by his amiable partner) with a countenance of portentous import, and a fearful instrument of flagellation, strong, supple, wax-ended, and new—in short, purchased that morning, expressly for the occasion.
>
> "Is every boy here?" asked Squeers, in a tremendous voice.
>
> Every boy was there, but every boy was afraid to speak; so Squeers glared along the lines to assure himself; and every eye drooped, and every head cowered down, as he did so.
>
> "Each boy keep his place," said Squeers, administering his fa-

vourite blow to the desk, and regarding with gloomy satisfaction the universal start which it never failed to occasion. "Nickleby! to your desk, sir."

It was remarked by more than one small observer that there was a very curious and unusual expression in the usher's face; but he took his seat, without opening his lips in reply. Squeers, casting a triumphant glance at his assistant, and a look of most comprehensive despotism on the boys, left the room, and shortly afterward returned, dragging Smike by the collar—or rather by that fragment of his jacket which was nearest the place where his collar would have been had he boasted such a decoration.

In any other place the appearance of the wretched, jaded, spiritless object would have occasioned a murmur of compassion and remonstrance. It had some effect, even there; for the lookers-on moved uneasily in their seats, and a few of the boldest ventured to steal looks at each other, expressive of indignation and pity.

They were lost on Squeers, however, whose gaze was fastened on the luckless Smike, as he inquired, according to custom in such cases, whether he had anything to say for himself.

"Nothing, I suppose?" said Squeers, with a diabolical grin.

Smike glanced round, and his eye rested for an instant on Nicholas, as if he had expected him to intercede; but his look was riveted on his desk.

"Have you anything to say?" demanded Squeers again; giving his right arm two or three flourishes to try its power and suppleness. "Stand a little out of the way, Mrs. Squeers, my dear; I've hardly got room enough."

"Spare me, sir!" cried Smike.

"Oh! that's all, is it?" said Squeers. "Yes, I'll flog you within an inch of your life, and spare you that."

"Ha, ha, ha," laughed Mrs. Squeers, "that's a good 'un!"

"I was driven to do it," said Smike faintly, and casting another imploring look on him.

"Driven to do it, were you?" said Squeers. "Oh! it wasn't your fault; it was mine, I suppose—eh?"

"A nasty, ungrateful, pig-headed, brutish, obstinate, sneaking dog," exclaimed Mrs. Squeers, taking Smike's head under her arm, and administering a cuff at every epithet; "what does he mean by that?"

"Stand aside, my dear," replied Squeers. "We'll try and find out."

Mrs. Squeers, being out of breath with her exertions, complied. Squeers caught the boy firmly in his grip; one desperate cut had fallen on his body—he was wincing from the lash, and uttering a scream of pain—it was raised again, and again about to fall—when Nicholas Nickleby suddenly starting up, cried: "Stop!" in a voice that made the rafters ring.

"Who cried stop?" said Squeers, turning savagely round.

"I," said Nicholas, stepping forward. "This must not go on."

"Must not go on!" cried Squeers, almost in a shriek.

"No!" thundered Nicholas.

Aghast and stupefied by the boldness of the interference, Squeers released his hold of Smike, and, falling back a pace or two, gazed upon Nicholas with looks that were positively frightful.

"I say must not," repeated Nicholas, nothing daunted; "shall not. I will prevent it."

Squeers continued to gaze upon him, with his eyes starting out of his head; but astonishment had actually, for the moment, bereft him of speech.

"You have disregarded all my quiet interference in the miserable lad's behalf," said Nicholas; "you have returned no answer to the letter in which I begged forgiveness for him, and offered to be responsible that he would remain quietly here. Don't blame me for this public interference. You have brought it upon yourself, not I."

"Sit down, beggar!" screamed Squeers, almost beside himself with rage, and seizing Smike as he spoke.

"Wretch!" rejoined Nicholas fiercely, "touch him at your peril! I will not stand by and see it done. My blood is up, and I have the strength of ten such men as you. Look to yourself, for, by Heaven, I will not spare you, if you drive me on!"

"Stand back!" cried Squeers, brandishing his weapon.

"I have a long series of insults to avenge," said Nicholas, flushed with passion; "and my indignation is aggravated by the dastardly cruelties practised on helpless infancy in this foul den. Have a care; for, if you do raise the devil within me, the consequences shall fall heavily upon your own head!"

He had scarcely spoken, when Squeers, in a violent outbreak of wrath, and with a cry like the howl of a wild beast, spit upon him, and struck him a blow across the face with his instrument of torture, which raised up a bar of livid flesh as it was inflicted.

Smarting with the agony of the blow, and concentrating into that one moment all his feelings of rage, scorn, and indignation, Nicholas sprang upon him, wrested the weapon from his hand, and pinning him by the throat, beat the ruffian till he roared for mercy.

The boys—with the exception of Master Squeers, who, coming to his father's assistance, harassed the enemy in the rear—moved not hand or foot; but Mrs. Squeers, with many shrieks for aid, hung on to the tail of her partner's coat, and endeavoured to drag him from his infuriated adversary; while Miss Squeers, who had been peeping through the keyhole in expectation of a very different scene, darted in at the very beginning of the attack, and after launching a shower of inkstands at the usher's head, beat Nicholas to her heart's content: animating herself at every blow with the recollection of his having refused her proffered love, and thus imparting additional strength to an arm which (as she took after her mother in this respect) was, at no time, one of the weakest.

Nicholas, in the full torrent of his violence, felt the blows no more than if they had been dealt with feathers; but, becoming tired of the noise and uproar, and feeling that his arm grew weak besides, he threw all his remaining strength into half a dozen finishing cuts and flung Squeers from him, with all the force he could muster. The violence of his fall precipitated Mrs. Squeers completely over an adjacent form; and Squeers, striking his head against it in his descent, lay at his full length on the ground, stunned and motionless.

Having brought affairs to this happy termination, and ascertained, to his thorough satisfaction, that Squeers was only stunned, and not dead (upon which point he had had some unpleasant doubts at first), Nicholas left his family to restore him and retired to consider what course he had better adopt. He looked anxiously round for Smike, as he left the room, but he was nowhere to be seen.

After a brief consideration, he packed up a few clothes in a small leathern valise, and, finding that nobody offered to oppose his progress, marched boldly out by the front door and started to walk to London.

Near the school he met John Browdie, the honest corn factor.

John saw that Nicholas had received a severe blow, and asked the reason.

"The fact is," said Nicholas, not very well knowing how to make the avowal, "the fact is, that I have been ill-treated."

"Noa!" interposed John Browdie, in a tone of compassion; for he was a giant in strength and stature, and Nicholas, very likely,

> in his eyes, seemed a mere dwarf; "dean't say thot."
>
> "Yes, I have," replied Nicholas, "by that man Squeers, and I have beaten him soundly, and am leaving this place in consequence."
>
> "What!" cried John Browdie, with such an ecstatic shout, that the horse quite shied at it. "Beatten the schoolmeasther! Ho! ho! ho! Beatten the schoolmeasther! who ever heard o' the loike o' that noo! Giv' us thee hond agean, yongster. Beatten the schoolmeasther! Dang it, I loove thee for't."

And the world agreed, and still agrees, with John Browdie.

Squeers and Smike began the real movement against cruelty and corporal punishment not only in schools, but in homes. Dickens described both characters so admirably that the world hated Squeers and pitied Smike to the limit of its power to hate and pity, and unconsciously the world associated cruelty and corporal punishment with Squeers. This was exactly what Dickens desired. The hatred of Squeers led to a strong disapproval of his practices. Corporal punishment was associated with an unpopular man, and it lost its respectable character and never regained it. The dislike for Squeers was accentuated by the long-continued sympathy and hopefulness felt for Smike as he gradually succumbed to the terrible disease, consumption, induced by poor food, neglect, and cruelty.

Squeers and Smike are doing their good work still, and doing it well. They could do it much better if men and women when they have become acquainted with Squeers would candidly ask themselves the question, "In what respects am I like Squeers?" instead of yielding to the feeling of self-satisfaction that they are so very unlike him.

Just before writing about the coercive tyranny of Squeers in his school, Dickens had written Oliver Twist, in which he had made a most vigorous attack upon two classes of characters for their tyrannical treatment of children, and especially on account of their frequent use of corporal punishment. Bumble represented the officials in institutions for children, and "the gentleman in the white waistcoat" was given as a type of the advanced Christian philanthropy of his time. He meant well, gave his time freely to attend the meetings of the board, and supposed he was doing right; but Dickens wished to let philanthropists see that they were terribly cruel to the helpless children, and that their good intentions could not condone their harshness, even though it resulted from ignorance and lack of reverence for childhood, and not from deliberate evil intentions.

Poor, friendless little Oliver! His beautiful face and gentle spirit might have touched the hardest heart, but the institutional heart becomes hard easily, even two generations after the time of Bumble and "the gentleman in the immaculate white waistcoat."

Dickens says:

> It must not be supposed that Oliver was denied the benefit of exercise, the pleasure of society, or the advantages of reli-

> gious consolation in the workhouse. As for exercise, it was nice cold weather, and he was allowed to perform his ablutions every morning under the pump, in a stone yard, in the presence of Mr. Bumble, who prevented his catching cold, and caused a tingling sensation to pervade his frame, by repeated applications of the cane. As for society, he was carried every other day into the hall, where the boys dined, and there sociably flogged as a public warning and example. And so far from being denied the advantage of religious consolation, he was kicked into the same apartment every evening at prayer time, and there permitted to listen to, and console his mind with, a general supplication of the boys, containing a special clause, therein inserted by authority of the board, in which they entreated to be made good, virtuous, contented, and obedient, and to be guarded from the sins and vices of Oliver Twist.

After Oliver had been sent to work for Mr. Sowerberry he was goaded to desperation one evening by the disrespectful remarks of Noah Claypole about his mother, and bravely gave the mean bully the personal chastisement he so richly deserved. Noah was sent to complain to the parish board, and the gentleman in the white waistcoat said:

> "Bumble, just step up to Sowerberry's with your cane, and see what's best to be done. Don't spare him, Bumble."
>
> "No, I will not, sir," replied the beadle, adjusting the wax end which was twisted round the bottom of his cane, for purposes of parochial flagellation.
>
> "Tell Sowerberry not to spare him either. They'll never do anything with him without stripes and bruises," said the gentleman in the white waistcoat.

The innocent, manly child was beaten unmercifully and abused cruelly by Sowerberry and Bumble, yet he bore all their taunts and floggings without a tear until he was alone. Then, "when there was none to see or hear him, he fell upon his knees on the floor, and, hiding his face in his hands, wept such tears as, God send for the credit of our nature, few so young may ever have cause to pour out before him!"

There are not many "gentlemen in white waistcoats" of the type described by Dickens now on charitable boards, and the enlightened sentiment of civilized countries turns the legal processes of nations upon officials who dare to treat children unkindly. Dickens made humane people everywhere sympathize with Mr. Meagles, who said: "Whenever I see a beadle in full fig coming down a street on a Sunday at the head of a charity school, I am obliged to turn and run away, or I should hit him."

Ten years after Squeers began his good work Dickens produced Squeers's associate, Mr. Creakle, the master of Salem House.

David Copperfield was sent to Salem House by his stepfather, Mr. Murdstone, because he bit his hand when he was punishing him unjustly. For this offence he was compelled to wear a placard on his back on which was written: "Take care of him. He bites." This dastardly practice of labelling youthful offenders persisted until very recent times. Children in schools are even yet in some places degraded by inconsiderate teachers by being compelled to wear some indication of their misconduct. Dickens vigorously condemned this outrage in 1849.

David was sent to school during the holidays, and was soon brought before Mr. Creakle by Tungay, his servant with the wooden leg.

> "So," said Mr. Creakle, "this is the young gentleman whose teeth are to be filed! Turn him round."
>
> Mr. Creakle's face was fiery, and his eyes were small and deep in his head; he had thick veins in his forehead, a little nose, and a large chin. He was bald on the top of his head; and had some thin, wet-looking hair that was just turning gray brushed across each temple, so that the two sides interlaced on his forehead.
>
> "Now," said Mr. Creakle. "What's the report of this boy?"
>
> "There's nothing against him yet," returned the man with the wooden leg. "There has been no opportunity."
>
> I thought Mr. Creakle was disappointed. I thought Mrs. and Miss Creakle (at whom I now glanced for the first time, and who were, both, thin and quiet) were not disappointed.
>
> "Come here, sir!" said Mr. Creakle, beckoning to me.
>
> "Come here!" said the man with the wooden leg, repeating the gesture.
>
> "I have the happiness of knowing your stepfather," whispered Mr. Creakle, taking me by the ear; "and a worthy man he is, and a man of strong character. He knows me, and I know him. Do *you* know me! Hey?" said Mr. Creakle, pinching my ear with ferocious playfulness.
>
> "Not yet, sir," I said, flinching with the pain.
>
> "Not yet! Hey?" repeated Mr. Creakle. "But you will soon. Hey?"
>
> "You will soon. Hey?" repeated the man with the wooden leg. I afterward found that he generally acted, with his strong voice, as Mr. Creakle's interpreter to the boys.
>
> I was very much frightened, and said, I hoped so, if he pleased. I felt all this while as if my ear were blazing; he pinched it so hard.
>
> "I'll tell you what I am," whispered Mr. Creakle, letting it go at last, with a screw at parting that brought the water to my eyes, "I'm a Tartar."

Mr. Creakle proved to be as good as his word. He was a Tartar.

On the first day of school he revealed himself. His opening address was very brief and to the point.

> "Now, boys, this is a new half. Take care what you're about in this new half. Come fresh up to the lessons, I advise you, for I come fresh up to the punishment. I won't flinch. It will be of no use your rubbing yourselves; you won't rub the marks out that I shall give you. Now get to work, every boy!"
>
> When this dreadful exordium was over, Mr. Creakle came to where I sat, and told me that if I were famous for biting, he was famous for biting, too. He then showed me the cane, and asked me what I thought of *that*, for a tooth? Was it a sharp tooth, hey? Was it a double tooth, hey? Had it a deep prong, hey? Did it bite, hey? Did it bite? At every question he gave me a fleshy cut with it that made me writhe.
>
> Not that I mean to say these were special marks of distinction, which only I received. On the contrary, a large majority of the boys (especially the smaller ones) were visited with similar instances of notice, as Mr. Creakle made the round of the schoolroom. Half the establishment was writhing and crying before the day's work began; and how much of it had writhed and cried before the day's work was over I am really afraid to recollect, lest I should seem to exaggerate.
>
> I should think there never can have been a man who enjoyed his profession more than Mr. Creakle did. He had a delight in cutting at the boys, which was like the satisfaction of a craving appetite. I am confident that he couldn't resist a chubby boy especially; that there was a fascination in such a subject which made him restless in his mind until he had scored and marked him for the day. I was chubby myself, and ought to know. I am sure when I think of the fellow now, my blood rises against him with the disinterested indignation I should feel if I could have known all about him without having ever been in his power; but it rises hotly, because I know him to have been an incapable brute, who had no more right to be possessed of the great trust he held than to be Lord High Admiral or Commander-in-chief: in either of which capacities it is probable that he would have done infinitely less mischief.
>
> Miserable little propitiators of a remorseless idol, how abject we were to him! what a launch in life I think it now, on looking-back, to be so mean and servile to a man of such parts and pretensions!

Twenty years after Dickens described Creakle a new teacher stood before a class in a large American city, and, holding a long rattan cane above his head, said in a fierce, threatening tone: "Do you see that cane? Would you like to feel it? Hey? Well, break any one of my forty-eight rules and you will feel it all right." The tyrant in adulthood dies hard. No wonder. Tyranny has been wrought into our natures by centuries of blind faith in corporal punishment as the supreme agency in saving the race from moral wreck and anarchy in childhood and youth. Men sought no agency for the development of the good in young lives. As they conceived it, their duty was done if they prevented their children from doing wrong, and the quickest, easiest, most effective way they knew to secure coercion was by corporal punishment. The most successful tyrant, he who could most thoroughly terrorize children and keep them down most completely, was regarded as the best disciplinarian. Squeers and Creakle were fair exponents of the almost universally recognised theory of their day, and they had many successors in the real schools of the generation that followed them. No man could remain a week in a school now if he began on the opening day in the way Creakle did.

Dickens was right in revealing the position of the teacher as one of "great trust," and he was right, too, in insisting that Creakle was no more fitted to be a teacher "than to be Lord High Admiral or Commander-in-chief, in either of which capacities it is probable he would have done infinitely less mischief." This was another plea for good normal schools and for state supervision.

Dickens makes a good point in his remark about the degradation of abject submission to a man of such parts and pretensions as Creakle. Subordination always dwarfs the human soul, but when the child is forced to a position of abject subordination to a coarse tyrant the degradation is more complete and more humiliating. It does not mend matters for the child when the tyrant is his father. The tyranny of parenthood is usually the hardest to escape from.

In the same book in which Creakle is described—David Copperfield—Dickens deals with the tyranny of the home. David's widowed mother married Mr. Murdstone, a hard, severe, austere, religious man, with an equally dreadful sister—Jane Murdstone.

> Firmness was the grand quality on which both Mr. and Miss Murdstone took their stand. However I might have expressed my comprehension of it at that time, if I had been called upon, I nevertheless did clearly comprehend in my own way that it was another name for tyranny, and for a certain gloomy, arrogant, devil's humour, that was in them both. The creed, as I should state it now, was this: Mr. Murdstone was firm; nobody in his world was to be so firm as Mr. Murdstone; nobody else in his world was to be firm at all, for everybody was to be bent to his firmness.

There was no more depressing tyranny in the time of Dickens than the tyranny exercised in the name of a rigid and repressive religion.

> The gloomy taint that was in the Murdstone blood darkened the Murdstone religion, which was austere and wrathful. I have thought, since, that its assuming that character was a necessary consequence of Mr. Murdstone's firmness, which wouldn't allow

> him to let anybody off from the utmost weight of the severest penalties he could find any excuse for. Be this as it may, I well remember the tremendous visages with which we used to go to church, and the changed air of the place. Again, the dreaded Sunday comes round, and I file into the old pew first, like a guarded captive brought to a condemned service. Again, Miss Murdstone, in a black-velvet gown, that looks as if it had been made out of a pall, follows close upon me; then my mother; then her husband. Again, I listen to Miss Murdstone mumbling the responses, and emphasizing all the dread words with a cruel relish. Again, I see her dark eyes roll round the church when she says "miserable sinners," as if she were calling all the congregation names. Again, I catch rare glimpses of my mother, moving her lips timidly between the two, with one of them muttering at each ear like low thunder. Again, I wonder with a sudden fear whether it is likely that our good old clergyman can be wrong, and Mr. and Miss Murdstone right, and that all the angels in heaven can be destroying angels. Again, if I move a finger or relax a muscle of my face, Miss Murdstone pokes me with her prayer book, and makes my side ache.

Mrs. Chillip said: "Mr. Murdstone sets up an image of himself and calls it the Divine Nature," and "what such people as the Murdstones call their religion is a vent for their bad humours and arrogance." Mild and cautious Mr. Chillip observed, "I don't find authority for Mr. and Miss Murdstone in the New Testament," and his good wife added, "The darker tyrant Mr. Murdstone becomes, the more ferocious is his religious doctrine."

When David first learned that Mr. Murdstone had married his mother he relieved the swelling in his little heart by crying in his bedroom. His mother naturally felt a sympathy for her boy. Mr. Murdstone reproved her for her lack of "firmness," ordered her out of the room, and gave David his first lesson in "obedience."

> "David," he said, making his lips thin, by pressing them together, "if I have an obstinate horse or dog to deal with, what do you think I do?"
>
> "I don't know."
>
> "I beat him."
>
> I had answered in a kind of breathless whisper, but I felt, in my silence, that my breath was shorter now.
>
> "I make him wince, and smart. I say to myself, 'I'll conquer that fellow;' and if it were to cost him all the blood he had, I should do it."

There are still a few schoolmaster tyrants who boast of their ability "to subdue children." They are barbarians, who understand neither the new education nor the new theology, who have not learned to recognise and reverence the individual selfhood of each child, who themselves fear God's power more than they feel his love.

When David was at home for the holidays he remained in his own room a considerable part of the time reading. This aroused the anger of Mr. Murdstone, and he charged David with being sullen.

> "I was sorry, David," said Mr. Murdstone, turning his head and his eyes stiffly toward me, "to observe that you are of a sullen disposition. This is not a character that I can suffer to develop itself beneath my eyes without an effort at improvement. You must endeavour, sir, to change it. We must endeavour to change it for you."
>
> "I beg your pardon, sir," I faltered. "I have never meant to be sullen since I came back."
>
> "Don't take refuge in a lie, sir!" he returned so fiercely, that I saw my mother involuntarily put out her trembling hand as if to interpose between us. "You have withdrawn yourself in your sullenness to your own room. You have kept your room when you ought to have been here. You know now, once for all, that I require you to be here, and not there. Further, that I require you to bring obedience here. You know me, David. I will have it done."
>
> Miss Murdstone gave a hoarse chuckle.
>
> "I will have a respectful, prompt, and ready bearing toward myself," he continued, "and toward Jane Murdstone, and toward your mother. I will not have this room shunned as if it were infected, at the pleasure of a child. Sit down."
>
> He ordered me like a dog, and I obeyed like a dog.

David's lessons, which had been "along a path of roses" when his mother was alone with him, became a path of thorns after the Murdstones came.

> The lessons were a grievous daily drudgery and misery. They were very long, very numerous, very hard—perfectly unintelligible.
>
> Let me remember how it used to be. I come into the parlour after breakfast with my books, an exercise book and a slate. My mother is ready for me, but not half so ready as Mr. Murdstone, or as Miss Murdstone, sitting near my mother stringing steel beads. The very sight of these two has such an influence over me, that I begin to feel the words I have been at infinite pains to get into my head all sliding away, and going I don't know where. I wonder where they *do* go, by the bye?
>
> I hand the first book to my mother. I take a last drowning look at the page as I give it into her hand, and start off aloud at a racing pace while I have got it fresh. I trip over a word. Mr. Murdstone looks up. I trip over another word. Miss Murdstone looks up. I

redden, tumble over half a dozen words, and stop. I think my mother would show me the book if she dared, but she does not dare, and she says softly:

"Oh, Davy, Davy!"

"Now, Clara," says Mr. Murdstone, "be firm with the boy. Don't say 'Oh, Davy, Davy!' That's childish. He knows his lesson, or he does not know it."

"He does *not* know it," Miss Murdstone interposed awfully.

"I am really afraid he does not," says my mother.

"Then you see, Clara," returns Miss Murdstone, "you should just give him the book back, and make him know it."

"Yes, certainly," says my mother; "that's what I intended to do, my dear Jane. Now, Davy, try once more, and don't be stupid."

I obey the first clause of the injunction by trying once more, but am not so successful with the second, for I am very stupid. I tumble down before I get to the old place, at a point where I was all right before, and stop to think. But I can't think about the lesson. I think of the number of yards of net in Miss Murdstone's cap, or of the price of Mr. Murdstone's dressing-gown, or any such ridiculous problem that I have no business with, and don't want to have anything at all to do with. Mr. Murdstone makes a movement of impatience which I have been expecting for a long time. Miss Murdstone does the same. My mother glances submissively at them, shuts the book, and lays it by as an arrear to be worked out when my other tasks are done.

There is a pile of these arrears very soon, and it swells like a rolling snowball. The bigger it gets the more stupid I get. The case is so hopeless, and I feel that I am wallowing in such a bog of nonsense, that I give up all idea of getting out, and abandon myself to my fate. The despairing way in which my mother and I look at each other, as I blunder on, is truly melancholy. But the greatest effect in these miserable lessons is when my mother (thinking nobody is observing her) tries to give me the cue by the motion of her lips. At that instant, Miss Murdstone, who has been lying in wait for nothing else all along, says in a deep warning voice:

"Clara!"

My mother starts, colours, and smiles faintly. Mr. Murdstone comes out of his chair, takes the book, throws it at me or boxes my ears with it, and turns me out of the room by the shoulders.

It seems to me, at this distance of time, as if my unfortunate studies generally took this course. I could have done very well if I had been without the Murdstones; but the influence of the Murdstones upon me was like the fascination of two snakes on a wretched young bird. Even when I did get through the morning with tolerable credit, there was not much gained but dinner; for Miss Murdstone never could endure to see me untasked, and if I rashly made any show of being unemployed, called her brother's attention to me by saying, "Clara, my dear, there's nothing like work—give your boy an exercise."

One morning when I went into the parlour with my books, I found my mother looking anxious, Miss Murdstone looking firm, and Mr. Murdstone binding something round the bottom of a cane—a lithe and limber cane, which he left off binding when I came in, and poised and switched in the air.

"I tell you, Clara," said Mr. Murdstone, "I have been often flogged myself."

"To be sure; of course," said Miss Murdstone.

"Certainly, my dear Jane," faltered my mother meekly. "But—but do you think it did Edward good?"

"Do you think it did Edward harm, Clara?" asked Mr. Murdstone, gravely.

"That's the point!" said his sister.

To this my mother returned "Certainly, my dear Jane," and said no more.

I felt apprehensive that I was personally interested in this dialogue, and sought Mr. Murdstone's eye as it lighted on mine.

"Now, David," he said—and I saw that cast again, as he said it—"you must be far more careful to-day than usual." He gave the cane another poise, and another switch; and having finished his preparation of it, laid it down beside him, with an expressive look, and took up his book.

This was a good freshener to my presence of mind, as a beginning. I felt the words of my lesson slipping off, not one by one, or line by line, but by the entire page. I tried to lay hold of them; but they seemed, if I may so express it, to have put skates on, and to skim away from me with a smoothness there was no checking.

We began badly, and went on worse. I had come in, with an idea of distinguishing myself rather, conceiving that I was very well prepared; but it turned out to be quite a mistake. Book after book was added to the heap of failures, Miss Murdstone being firmly watchful of us all the time. And when we came at last to the five thousand cheeses (canes he made it that day, I remember), my mother burst out crying.

> "Clara!" said Miss Murdstone, in her warning voice.
>
> "I am not quite well, my dear Jane, I think," said my mother.
>
> I saw him wink, solemnly, at his sister, as he rose and said, taking up the cane.
>
> "Why, Jane, we can hardly expect Clara to bear, with perfect firmness, the worry and torment that David has occasioned her to-day. That would be stoical. Clara is greatly strengthened and improved, but we can hardly expect so much from her. David, you and I will go upstairs, boy."

They went upstairs. David was beaten unmercifully, notwithstanding his piteous cries, and in his desperation he bit the hand of Murdstone. For this it seemed as if Murdstone would have beaten him to death but for the interference of the women. "Then he was gone, and the door locked outside; and I was lying, fevered and hot, and torn, and sore, and raging in my puny way, upon the floor."

Oh! Blind, self-satisfied "child-quellers," who so ignorantly boast of your ability to conquer children! Dickens described Murdstone for you. Think of that awful picture of the beautiful boy, created in the image of God, lying on the floor, "fevered and hot, and torn, and sore, and raging," with every element of sweetness and strength in his life turned to darkness and fury, and next time you propose to "conquer a child" who has been rendered partially insane, possibly by your treatment, and with whom you have unnecessarily forced a crisis, remember the Murdstone tragedy—a real tragedy, notwithstanding the fact that the boy's life was spared.

Remember, too, that your very presence and manner may blight the young lives that you are supposed to develop.

When Mr. Murdstone was sending David away to work he gave him his philosophy of coercion as his parting advice:

> "David," said Mr. Murdstone, "to the young, this is a world for action; not for moping and droning in."
>
> —"As you do," added his sister.
>
> "Jane Murdstone, leave it to me, if you please. I say, David, to the young, this is a world for action, and not for moping and droning in. It is especially so for a young boy of your disposition, which requires a great deal of correcting; and to which no greater service can be done than to force it to conform to the ways of the working world, and to bend it and break it."
>
> "For stubbornness won't do here," said his sister. "What it wants is to be crushed. And crushed it must be. Shall be, too!"

First he fills the boy as full as possible of self-depreciation, and then trains him to expect that his leading experiences in life will consist of being forced into submission, conforming to the plans of others, bending to authority, the breaking of his will, and the crushing of his interests and purposes. What a depressing outlook to give a child!

John Willet, in Barnaby Rudge, is used as a means of convincing parents that they should respect the feelings and opinions of children. No two maxims relating to child training are more utterly wrong in principle, more devoid of the simplest elements of child sympathy and child reverence, than the time-honoured nonsense that "children should be seen and not heard," and "children should speak only when they are spoken to."

Dickens exposes these maxims to deserved ridicule in John Willet's treatment of his son Joe. John kept the Maypole Inn. Joe was a fine, sturdy young man, but his father still ruled him with an unbending stubbornness that he believed to be a necessary exercise of authority. John was encouraged in his tyranny over his son by some of his old cronies, who were in the habit of sitting in the Maypole in the evenings and praising John for his firmness in training his son. One evening a stranger made a remark about a gentleman, to which Joe replied.

> "Silence, sir!" cried his father.
>
> "What a chap you are, Joe!" said Long Parkes.
>
> "Such a inconsiderate lad!" murmured Tom Cobb.
>
> "Putting himself forward and wringing the very nose off his own father's face!" exclaimed the parish clerk metaphorically.
>
> "What *have* I done?" reasoned poor Joe.
>
> "Silence, sir!" returned his father; "what do you mean by talking, when you see people that are more than two or three times your age sitting still and silent and not dreaming of saying a word?"
>
> "Why that's the proper time for me to talk, isn't it?" said Joe rebelliously.
>
> "The proper time, sir!" retorted his father, "the proper time's no time."
>
> "Ah, to be sure!" muttered Parkes, nodding gravely to the other two who nodded likewise, observing under their breaths that that was the point.
>
> "The proper time's no time, sir," repeated John Willet; "when I was your age I never talked, I never wanted to talk. I listened and improved myself, that's what I did."
>
> "It's all very fine talking," muttered Joe, who had been fidgeting in his chair with divers uneasy gestures. "But if you mean to tell me that I'm never to open my lips——"
>
> "Silence, sir!" roared his father. "No, you never are. When your opinion's wanted, you give it. When you're spoke to you speak. When your opinion's not wanted and you're not spoke to, don't give an opinion and don't you speak. The world's under-

gone a nice alteration since my time, certainly. My belief is that there an't any boys left—that there isn't such a thing as a boy—that there's nothing now between a male baby and a man—and that all the boys went out with his blessed majesty King George the Second."

On another occasion Joe had been hit with a whip by a stranger, and he expressed his opinion to Mr. Varden about the character of the man who hit him.

"Hold your tongue, sir," said his father.

"I won't, father. It's all along of you that he ventured to do what he did. Seeing me treated like a child, and put down like a fool, *he* plucks up a heart and has a fling at a fellow that he thinks—and may well think, too—hasn't a grain of spirit. But he's mistaken, as I'll show him, and as I'll show all of you before long."

"Does the boy know what he's saying of!" cried the astonished John Willet.

"Father," returned Joe, "I know what I say and mean, well—better than you do when you hear me. I can bear with you, but I can not bear the contempt that your treating me in the way you do brings upon me from others every day. Look at other young men of my age. Have they no liberty, no will, no right to speak? Are they obliged to sit mumchance, and to be ordered about till they are the laughingstock of young and old? I am a byword all over Chigwell, and I say—and it's fairer my saying so now, than waiting till you are dead, and I have got your money—I say, that before long I shall be driven to break such bounds, and that when I do, it won't be me that you'll have to blame, but your own self, and no other."

John never trusted his son, never entered into his plans, and treated even the most sacred things of Joe's life with contempt.

Joe was about to start to London on business for his father, and he was to ride a mare that was so slow that a young man could not enjoy the prospect of riding her.

"Don't you ride hard," said his father.

"I should be puzzled to do that, I think, father," Joe replied, casting a disconsolate look at the animal.

"None of your impudence, sir, if you please," retorted old John. "What would you ride, sir? A wild ass or zebra would be too tame for you, wouldn't he, eh, sir? You'd like to ride a roaring lion, wouldn't you, sir, eh, sir? Hold your tongue, sir." When Mr. Willet, in his differences with his son, had exhausted all the questions that occurred to him, and Joe had said nothing at all in answer, he generally wound up by bidding him hold his tongue.

"And what does the boy mean," added Mr. Willet, after he

> had stared at him for a little time, in a species of stupefaction, "by cocking his hat, to such an extent! Are you going to kill the wintner, sir?"
>
> "No," said Joe tartly; "I'm not. Now your mind's at ease, father."
>
> "With a military air, too!" said Mr. Willet, surveying him from top to toe; "with a swaggering, fire-eating, biling-water drinking sort of way with him! And what do you mean by pulling up the crocuses and snowdrops, eh, sir?"
>
> "It's only a little nosegay," said Joe, reddening. "There's no harm in that, I hope?"
>
> "You're a boy of business, you are, sir!" said Mr. Willet disdainfully, "to go supposing that wintners care for nosegays."
>
> "I don't suppose anything of the kind," returned Joe. "Let them keep their red noses for bottles and tankards. These are going to Mr. Varden's house."
>
> "And do you suppose *he* minds such things as crocuses?" demanded John.
>
> "I don't know, and to say the truth, I don't care," said Joe. "Come, father, give me the money, and in the name of patience let me go."
>
> "There it is, sir," replied John; "and take care of it; and mind you don't make too much haste back, but give the mare a long rest. Do you mind?"
>
> "Ay, I mind," returned Joe. "She'll need it, Heaven knows."
>
> "And don't you score up too much at the Black Lion," said John. "Mind that too."
>
> "Then why don't you let me have some money of my own?" retorted Joe sorrowfully; "why don't you, father? What do you send me into London for, giving me only the right to call for my dinner at the Black Lion, which you're to pay for next time you go, as if I was not to be trusted with a few shillings? Why do you use me like this? It's not right of you. You can't expect me to be quiet under it."

Dickens in this interview condemns several mistakes often made by parents in restraining instead of sympathizing with their children in the natural unfolding of their young manhood or womanhood. It was wrong for John Willet to ridicule Joe's desire to ride a smart horse. It was wrong to bid him "hold his tongue." It was wrong to criticise his method of dressing to look his very best. It was wrong to sneer at him because his consciousness of unfolding manhood and his hope of Dolly Varden's love made him carry himself with a "military air." What a difference it would make in the characters of young men if they all carried themselves with a military air, and walked with a consciousness of power and hope!

It was especially wrong to make fun of the nosegay Joe had pulled for Dolly Varden. What a pity it is that so few fathers or mothers can truly sympathize with their boys and girls during the period of courtship! Why should the most sacred feelings that ever stir the soul be made the subject of jest and levity by those whose hearts should most truly beat in unison with the young hearts that are aflame? If there is a time in the life of young men or women when father or mother may enter the hearts of their children as benedictions and form a blessed unity that can never be broken or undone it is surely when young hearts are hallowed by love. Yet there are few parents to whom their children can speak freely about the mysteries and the deep experiences of love that come into their lives.

It was wrong to treat Joe as if he was unworthy to be trusted with money.

Every wrong revealed by Dickens in this interview had its root in John's feeling that it was his duty to keep Joe down, to prevent the outflow of his inner life.

> Old John having long encroached a good standard inch, full measure, on the liberty of Joe, and having snipped off a Flemish ell in the matter of the parole, grew so despotic and so great, that his thirst for conquest knew no bounds. The more young Joe submitted, the more absolute old John became. The ell soon faded into nothing. Yards, furlongs, miles arose; and on went old John in the pleasantest manner possible, trimming off an exuberance in this place, shearing away some liberty of speech or action in that, and conducting himself in this small way with as much high mightiness and majesty as the most glorious tyrant that ever had his statue reared in the public ways, of ancient or of modern times.
>
> As great men are urged on to the abuse of power (when they need urging, which is not often) by their flatterers and dependents, so old John was impelled to these exercises of authority by the applause and admiration of his Maypole cronies, who, in the intervals of their nightly pipes and pots, would shake their heads and say that Mr. Willet was a father of the good old English sort; that there were no newfangled notions or modern ways in him; that he put them in mind of what their fathers were when they were boys; that there was no mistake about him; that it would be well for the country if there were more like him, and more was the pity that there were not; with many other original remarks of that nature. Then they would condescendingly give Joe to understand that it was all for his good, and he would be thankful for it one day; and in particular, Mr. Cobb would acquaint him, that when he was his age, his father thought no more of giving him a parental kick, or a box on the ears, or a cuff on the head, or some little admonition of that sort, than he did of any other ordinary duty of life; and he would further remark, with looks of great significance, that but for this judicious bringing up, he

> might have never been the man he was at that present speaking; which was probable enough, as he was, beyond all question, the dullest dog of the party. In short, between old John and old John's friends, there never was an unfortunate young fellow so bullied, badgered, worried, fretted, and browbeaten; so constantly beset, or made so tired of his life, as poor Joe Willet.

The end came at last. One evening Mr. Cobb was more aggravating than usual, and Joe's patience could hold out no longer. He knocked the offending Cobb into a corner among the spittoons, and ran away from the unbearable tyranny of home.

What a moral catastrophe occurs when a young man leaves home with a feeling of relief! Dickens develops this thought in the case of Tom Gradgrind. With the best of intentions, with a single desire of training his son in the best possible way, Mr. Gradgrind had repressed his natural tendencies and robbed him of the joys of childhood and youth to such an extent that when he was about to go to live with Mr. Bounderby, and his sister, Louisa, asked him "if he was pleased with his prospect?" he replied, "Well, it will be getting away from home." The boy is never to blame for such a catastrophe.

Dickens attacked another phase of the flogging mania in Barnaby Rudge, in a brief but suggestive scene. Barnaby and his mother were travelling, and were resting at the gate of a gentleman's grounds, when the proprietor himself came along and demanded to know who they were.

> "Vagrants," said the gentleman, "vagrants and vagabonds. Thee wish to be made acquainted with the cage, dost thee—the cage, the stocks, and the whipping post? Where dost come from?"

Learning that Barnaby was weak-minded, he asked how long he had been idiotic.

> "From his birth," said the widow.
>
> "I don't believe it," cried the gentleman, "not a bit of it. It's an excuse not to work. There's nothing like flogging to cure that disorder. I'd make a difference in him in ten minutes, I'll be bound."
>
> "Heaven has made none in more than twice ten years, sir," said the widow mildly.
>
> "Then why don't you shut him up? We pay enough for county institutions, damn 'em. But thou'd rather drag him about to excite charity—of course. Ay, I know thee."
>
> Now, this gentleman had various endearing appellations among his intimate friends. By some he was called "a country gentleman of the true school," by some "a fine old country gentleman," by some "a sporting gentleman," by some "a thoroughbred Englishman," by some "a genuine John Bull"; but they all agreed in one respect, and that was, that it was a pity that there were not more like him, and that because there were not, the country was going to rack and ruin every day.

Dickens always enjoyed ridiculing the people who long for the good old times and approve of the good old customs. There are some who even yet deplore the fact that children are not repressed and coerced as they used to be, and who prophesy untold evils unless the good old customs are re-established. They long for the recurrence of the days when "lickin' and larnin' went hand in hand," when "Wallop the boy, develop the man" was the popular motto, expressive of the general faith. Dickens pictured them in John Willet and this "country gentleman of the true school." He also criticised them severely in the Chimes.

The depressing influence of another form of coercion is shown in Our Mutual Friend by the effect of Mr. Podsnap's character on his daughter Georgiana. Mr. Podsnap was one of the absolutely positive people who know everything about everything, who never allow other people to express opinions without contradicting them, and who take every possible opportunity of expressing their own opinions in a loud, emphatic, dogmatic manner. Of course, no woman should hold opinions, according to Mr. Podsnap's way of thinking, although Mrs. Podsnap, in her own way, did credit to her more Podsnappery master. It was therefore not to be dreamt of for a moment that a "young person" like their daughter Georgiana could have any views of her own regarding life or any of its conditions, past, present, or future. She was a "young person" to be protected, and kept in the background, and guarded from evil, and sheltered, so that she should not even hear of anything improper, and shielded from temptation to do wrong, or to do anything, indeed, right or wrong. Her father was rich; why should she wish to do anything but listen to him, and go away when he told her to do so, if he wished to speak of subjects that he deemed it unwise to let a "young person" hear discussed?

> There was a Miss Podsnap. And this young rocking-horse was being trained in her mother's art of prancing in a stately manner without ever getting on. But the high parental action was not yet imparted to her, and in truth she was but an undersized damsel, with high shoulders, low spirits, chilled elbows, and a rasped surface of nose, who seemed to take occasional frosty peeps out of childhood into womanhood, and to shrink back again, overcome by her mother's headdress and her father from head to foot—crushed by the mere dead weight of Podsnappery.

Georgiana explained the reason of her shyness to Mrs. Lammle, for, strange as it may seem, considering her heredity, Georgiana was shy. Podsnappery as environment is always much stronger than Podsnappery as heredity.

> "What I mean is," pursued Georgiana, "that ma being so endowed with awfulness, and pa being so endowed with awfulness, and there being so much awfulness everywhere—I mean, at least, everywhere where I am—perhaps it makes me who am so deficient in awfulness, and frightened at it—I say it very badly—I don't know whether you can understand what I mean?"

Thoughtful people need no explanation regarding the influence of Podsnappery on children.

The time will come when in normal schools character analysis will be the supreme qualification of those who are to decide who may and who may not teach. When that time comes, as come it must, no Podsnaps will be allowed to teach.

It was no wonder that—

> Whenever Georgiana could escape from the thraldom of Podsnappery; could throw off the bedclothes of the custard-coloured phaeton, and get up; could shrink out of the range of her mother's rocking, and (so to speak) rescue her poor little frosty toes from being rocked over; she repaired to her friend, Mrs. Alfred Lammle.

Dickens fired another thunderbolt, in Our Mutual Friend, to set the world thinking about its method of teaching children, by his brief description of Pleasant Riderhood, the daughter of Rogue Riderhood.

> Show her a christening, and she saw a little heathen personage having a quite superfluous name bestowed upon it, inasmuch as it would be commonly addressed by some abusive epithet; which little personage was not in the least wanted by anybody, and would be shoved and banged out of everybody's way, until it should grow big enough to shove and bang. Show her a live father, and she saw but a duplicate of her own father, who from her infancy had been taken with fits and starts of discharging his duty to her, which duty was always incorporated in the form of a fist or a leather strap, and being discharged hurt her.

In Little Dorrit Dickens gives one of his most striking verbal descriptions of the effects of coercion in Arthur Clennam's account of his own early training. He said to Mr. Meagles, when the kind old gentleman spoke of working with a will:

> "I have no will. That is to say," he coloured a little, "next to none that I can put in action now. Trained by main force; broken, not bent; heavily ironed with an object on which I was never consulted and which was never mine; shipped away to the other end of the world before I was of age, and exiled there until my father's death there, a year ago; always grinding in a mill I always hated; what is to be expected from me in middle life? Will, purpose, hope? All those lights were extinguished before I could sound the words."
>
> "Light 'em up again!" said Mr. Meagles.
>
> "Ah! Easily said. I am the son, Mr. Meagles, of a hard father and mother. I am the only child of parents who weighed, measured, and priced everything; for whom what could not be weighed, measured, and priced had no existence. Strict people, as the phrase is, professors of a stern religion, their very religion was a gloomy sacrifice of tastes and sympathies that were never their own, offered up as a part of a bargain for the security of

> their possessions. Austere faces, inexorable discipline, penance in this world and terror in the next—nothing graceful or gentle anywhere, and the void in my cowed heart everywhere—this was my childhood, if I may so misuse the word as to apply it to such a beginning of life."

When he returned to the presence of his mother, after an absence of many years in China, "the old influence of her presence, and her stern, strong voice, so gathered about her son that he felt conscious of a renewal of the timid chill and reserve of his childhood."

It was a terrible indictment of all coercive, child-quelling, will-breaking training that Arthur made when he said to his stern mother:

> "I can not say that I have been able to conform myself, in heart and spirit, to your rules; I can not say that I believe my forty years have been profitable or pleasant to myself, or any one; but I have habitually submitted, and I only ask you to remember it."

Speaking of her own training, Mrs. Clennam said: "Mine were days of wholesome repression, punishment, and fear," and she frankly avowed her deliberate purpose of "bringing Arthur up in fear and trembling."

Those were the dreadful ideals that Dickens aimed to destroy. Repression, punishment, fear, and trembling are no longer the dominant ideals of the Christian world regarding child training. They are rapidly giving way to the new and true gospel of stimulation, happiness, freedom, and creative self-activity.

Great Expectations was a valuable contribution to the literature of child training. Mrs. Gargery was a type of repressive, coercive, unsympathetic women, who regard children as necessarily nuisances, and who are continually thankful for the fact that by the free use of "the tickler" they may be subdued and kept in a state of bearable subjection.

Mrs. Gargery had no children of her own, but she had a little brother, Pip, whom she "brought up by hand." Her husband, Joe Gargery, was an honest, affectionate, sympathetic man, who pitied poor Pip and tried to comfort him when his wife was not present. The dear old fellow said to Pip one evening, as they sat by the fire and he beat time to his kindly thoughts with the poker:

> "Your sister is given to government."
>
> "Given to government, Joe?" I was startled, for I had some shadowy idea (and I am afraid I must add hope) that Joe had divorced her in favour of the lords of the Admiralty, or Treasury.
>
> "Given to government," said Joe. "Which I meantersay the government of you and myself."
>
> "Oh!"
>
> "And she ain't over partial to having scholars on the premises," Joe continued, "and in particular would not be over partial to my being a scholar, for fear as I might rise. Like a sort of rebel,

don't you see?"

I was going to retort with an inquiry, and had got as far as "Why— —" when Joe stopped me.

"Stay a bit. I know what you're a-going to say, Pip? stay a bit! I don't deny that your sister comes the mo-gul over us, now and again. I don't deny that she do throw us back-falls, and that she do drop down upon us heavy. At such times as when your sister is on the ram-page, Pip," Joe sunk his voice to a whisper and glanced at the door, "candour compels fur to admit that she is a buster....

"I wish it was only me that got put out, Pip; I wish there warn't no tickler for you, old chap; I wish I could take it all on myself; but this is the up-and-down-and-straight on it, Pip, and I hope you'll overlook shortcomings."

Poor Joe! His father had been a blacksmith, but he took to drink, and, as Joe said, "Hammered at me with a wigour only to be equalled by the wigour with which he didn't hammer at his anwil."

Dickens gives an illustration of Mrs. Gargery's training which reveals not only her coercive and unsympathetic tendencies, but points to other errors in training children that are yet too common. Pip was warming himself before going to bed one night, when a cannon sounded from the Hulks, or prison ships, near the Gargery home.

"Ah!" said Joe; "there's another conwict off."

"What does that mean?" said I.

Mrs. Joe, who always took explanations upon herself, said snappishly: "Escaped. Escaped." Administering the definition like medicine.

"There was a conwict off last night," said Joe, aloud, "after sunset gun. And they fired warning of him. And now it appears they're firing warning of another."

"Who's firing?" said I.

"Drat that boy," interposed my sister, frowning at me over her work; "what a questioner he is! Ask no questions and you'll be told no lies."

It was not very polite to herself, I thought, to imply that I should be told lies by her, even if I did ask questions. But she never was polite, unless there was company.

"Mrs. Joe," said I, as a last resort, "I should like to know—if you wouldn't much mind—where the firing comes from?"

"Lord bless the boy!" exclaimed my sister, as if she didn't quite mean that, but rather the contrary. "From the hulks!"

"And please, what's hulks?" said I.

"That's the way with this boy!" exclaimed my sister, pointing me out with her needle and thread, and shaking her head at me. "Answer him one question, and he'll ask you a dozen directly. Hulks are prison ships, right 'cross th' country."

"I wonder who's put into prison ships, and why they're put there?" said I, in a general way, and with quiet desperation.

It was too much for Mrs. Joe, who immediately rose. "I tell you what, young fellow," said she, "I didn't bring you up by hand to badger people's lives out. It would be blame to me, and not praise, if I had. People are put in the hulks because they murder, and because they rob, and forge, and do all sorts of bad; and they always begin by asking questions. Now, you get along to bed!"

I was never allowed a candle to light me to bed, and, as I went upstairs in the dark, with my head tingling—from Mrs. Joe's thimble having played the tambourine upon it, to accompany her last words—I felt fearfully sensible of the great convenience that the hulks were handy for me. I was clearly on my way there.

Pip said later: "I suppose myself to be better acquainted than any living authority with the ridgy effect of a wedding ring passing unsympathetically over the human countenance."

My sister's bringing up had made me sensitive. In the little world in which children have their existence, whosoever brings them up, there is nothing so finely perceived and so finely felt as injustice. It may be only small injustice that the child can be exposed to; but the child is small, and its world is small, and its rocking-horse stands as many hands high, according to scale, as a big-boned Irish hunter. Within myself, I had sustained, from my babyhood, a perpetual conflict with injustice. I had known, from the time when I could speak, that my sister, in her capricious and violent coercion, was unjust to me. I had cherished a profound conviction that her bringing me up by the hand gave her no right to bring me up by jerks. Through all my punishments, disgraces, fasts and vigils, and other penitential performances, I had nursed this assurance; and to my communing so much with it, in a solitary and unprotected way, I in great part refer the fact that I was morally timid and very sensitive.

Mrs. Gargery's training was bad because she refused to answer the boy's questions, or abused him for asking them; and when she did condescend to answer she answered in a snappy, unsympathetic way. The cruelty of first scolding a child, then trying to terrify him from asking questions by telling him that "robbers, murderers, and all kinds of criminals began their downward career by asking questions," then rapping him on the head, and finally sending him to bed without a light, is admirably described. All these practices are terribly unjust to children.

Parents and teachers, in the picture of Mrs. Gargery, are warned against scolding, against threatening, against falsehood and misrepresentation in order to reduce children to submission, against corporal punishment with "the tickler," against the more dastardly and more exasperating corporal punishment by snapping and rapping the head, and against sending children to bed in the dark. He was especially careful to make the retiring hour in his own home a period of joyousness and freedom from all fear. He made the crime of sending children to bed without light and without sympathy one of the practices of that model of bad training—Mrs. Pipchin; and one of the most dreaded of little Oliver Twist's experiences was to be sent to sleep among the coffins in the dark at Sowerberry's.

The hour of retiring is the special time when children most need the affectionate spirit of motherhood, and wise mothers try to use this sacred hour to form their closest unity with the hearts of the little ones, and to sow in their young lives the apperceptive seeds of sweetness, and joy, and faith.

The wrong of making children sensitive, and then blaming them for being sensitive, is admirably shown in Pip's training.

The revelation of the child's consciousness of the sense of injustice in the treatment of those who train it is worthy of most careful study and thought by parents and teachers. There can be no doubt that infants have a clear sense of wrongs inflicted on them, even before they can speak.

The comparison of the child's rocking-horse with the big-boned Irish hunter reveals one of the most essential lessons for adulthood: that what may appear trifling to an adult may mean much to a child. Kind but thoughtless adulthood is often most grievously unjust to childhood, because it fails to consider how things appear to the child. However kind and good such adults are, they are utterly unsympathetic with the child. Many people are very considerate for childhood who are very unsympathetic with children. Consideration can never take the place of sympathy. An ounce of true sympathy is worth a ton of consideration to a child. Adulthood has measured a child's corn in the bushel of adulthood. Mr. Gradgrind, for instance, was a good man, and he meant to be kind and helpful to his children. He was most considerate for them, and spared no money to promote their welfare and happiness. But he did it in accordance with the tastes and opinions of adulthood, and totally ignored the fact that children have opinions and tastes, and he ruined the children whom he most loved. "The rocking-horse and the big-boned Irish hunter" suggest rich mines of child psychology.

The pernicious habit of so many adults who fill the imaginations of children with bogies and terrors of an abnormal kind in order to keep them in the path of rectitude by falsehood, is exposed in Mrs. Gargery's method of stopping Pip's questions by telling him that asking questions was the first step in a career of crime. This habit leads parents insensibly into a most dishonest attitude toward their children. It leads, too, in due time, to a lack of reverence for adulthood. Falseness is certain to lead to the disrespect it deserves. Parents who make untruthfulness a basis for terror should not be surprised at the irreverence or the scepticism of their children.

In The Schoolboy's Story, old Cheeseman was brought to school by a woman who was always taking snuff and shaking him.

There is a great deal of pedagogical thought in Dombey and Son. At the period of its issue (1846-48) Dickens appears to have devoted more attention to the study of wrong methods of teaching than at any other time, so in Dr. Blimber, Cornelia Blimber, and Mr. Feeder he gave his best illustrations of what in his opinion should be condemned in the popular methods of teaching. But while this was evidently his chief educational purpose in writing the book, he gave a good deal of attention to wrong methods of training, especially to the most awful doctrine of the ages—that children must be coerced, and repressed, and checked, and subdued. He evidently accepted as his supreme duty the responsibility for securing a free childhood for children. Mrs. Pipchin is an admirable delineation of the worst features of what was regarded as respectable child training. Her training is treated at length in Chapter XI. It is sufficient here to deal with her coerciveness, and recall the epithet "child-queller" which Dickens applied to her. No more expressive term was ever used to describe the wickedness of the coercionists. It means more than most volumes. It has new meaning every day as our reverence for the divinity in the child grows stronger, and the absolute need of the development of his selfhood by his own self-activity becomes clearer. It reveals a perfect charnel house full of dwarfed souls and blighted selfhood, and weak characters that should have been strong, and false characters that should have been true, and wailings that should have been music, and tears that should have been laughter, and darkness that should have been light, and wickedness that should have been a blessing. The one awful word "child-queller" means all of evil that can result from daring to stand between the child and God in our self-satisfied ignorance to check the free, natural output of its selfhood which God meant to be wrought out with increasing power throughout its life. Our work is to change the direction of the outflowing selfhood when it is wrong, to direct it to new and better interest centres, but never to stop it or turn it back upon itself.

There are thousands of child quellers teaching still. Would that they could see truly the dwarfed souls they have blighted, and the ghosts of the selfhood they have sacrificed on the altar of what they call discipline!

The term child-queller was the creation of genius.

Mrs. Pipchin disdained the idea of reasoning with children. "Hoity-toity!" exclaimed Mrs. Pipchin, shaking out her black bombazine skirts, and plucking up all the ogress within her. "If she don't like it, Mr. Dombey, she must be taught to lump it." She would "shake her head and frown down a legion of children," and "the wild ones went home tame enough after sojourning for a few months beneath her hospitable roof." She tamed them by robbing them of their power, as Froebel's boy tamed flies by tearing off their wings and legs, and then saying, "See how tame they are."

Teachers used to boast about their ability to tame children, when their ability really meant the power to destroy the tendency to put forth effort, to substitute negativeness for positiveness.

Susan Nipper, in her usual graphic style, expressed her views regarding the coercive practices of Mrs. Pipchin and the Blimbers.

> "Goodness knows," exclaimed Miss Nipper, "there's a-many we could spare instead, if numbers is a object; Mrs. Pipchin as a overseer would come cheap at her weight in gold, and if a knowledge of black slavery should be required, them Blimbers is the very people for the sitiwation."

One of Mrs. Pipchin's favourite methods of coercing, or taming, or child-quelling was to send children to bed.

> "The best thing you can do is to take off your things and go to bed this minute." This was the sagacious woman's remedy for all complaints, particularly lowness of spirits and inability to sleep; for which offence many young victims in the days of the Brighton Castle had been committed to bed at ten o'clock in the morning.

Another assault on coercion was made in Dombey and Son in the brief description of the Grinders' school.

> Biler's life had been rendered weary by the costume of the Charitable Grinders. The youth of the streets could not endure it. No young vagabond could be brought to bear its contemplation for a moment without throwing himself upon the unoffending wearer and doing him a mischief. His social existence had been more like that of an early Christian than an innocent child of the nineteenth century. He had been stoned in the streets. He had been overthrown into gutters; bespattered with mud; violently flattened against posts. Entire strangers to his person had lifted his yellow cap off his head and cast it to the winds. His legs had not only undergone verbal criticism and revilings, but had been handled and pinched. That very morning he had received a perfectly unsolicited black eye on his way to the Grinders' establishment, and had been punished for it by the master: a superannuated old Grinder of savage disposition, who had been appointed schoolmaster because he didn't know anything and wasn't fit for anything, and for whose cruel cane all chubby little boys had a perfect fascination.

Poor Biler went wrong, and when he was taken to task for it by Mr. Carker he gave his theory to account for the fact that he had not done better at school.

> "You're a nice young gentleman!" said Mr. Carker, shaking his head at him. "There's hemp-seed sown for *you*, my fine fellow!"
>
> "I'm sure, sir," returned the wretched Biler, blubbering again, and again having recourse to his coat cuff: "I shouldn't care, sometimes, if it was growed too. My misfortunes all began in wagging, sir, but what could I do, exceptin' wag?"

> "Excepting what?" said Mr. Carker.
>
> "Wag, sir. Wagging from school."
>
> "Do you mean pretending to go there, and not going?" said Mr. Carker.
>
> "Yes, sir, that's wagging, sir," returned the quondam Grinder, much affected. "I was chivied through the streets, sir, when I went there, and pounded when I got there. So I wagged and hid myself, and that began it."

When Mr. Dombey, by whose act of superior grace Biler had been sent to the Charitable Grinders' school, upbraided the boy's father for his failure to turn out well,

> the simple father said that he hoped his son, the quondam Grinder, huffed and cuffed, and flogged and badged, and taught, as parrots are, by a brute jobbed into his place of schoolmaster with as much fitness for it as a hound, might not have been educated on quite a right plan.

Sagacious teachers and parents often blame and punish children for being what they made them.

Still another illustration of the cruel coercion practised on children is found in Dombey and Son, in the training of Alice Marwood.

> "There was a child called Alice Marwood," said the daughter, with a laugh, and looking down at herself in terrible derision of herself, "born among poverty and neglect, and nursed in it. Nobody taught her, nobody stepped forward to help her, nobody cared for her."
>
> "Nobody!" echoed the mother, pointing to herself, and striking her breast.
>
> "The only care she knew," returned the daughter, "was to be beaten, and stinted, and abused sometimes; and she might have done better without that."

The picture of George Silverman's early life is one of the most touching of all the appeals of Dickens on behalf of childhood. He lived in a cellar, and when he was removed at length he knew only the sensations of "cold, hunger, thirst, and the pain of being beaten." The poor child used to speculate on his mother's feet having a good or ill temper as she descended the stairs to their cellar home, and he watched her knees, her waist, her face, as they came into view, to learn whether he was likely to be abused or not. Many mothers realized their own cruelty by reading such descriptions of cruelty toward little children.

The whole system of training of Mr. Gradgrind and his teacher, Mr. M'Choakumchild (the latter name contains volumes of coercion) was a scientific system of coerciveness and restraint, planned and carried out by a good man misguided by false ideas about child training and character building. Coercion was only one of several bad elements in his system, but he was terribly coercive. His children were lavishly supplied with almost everything they did not care for, and robbed of everything they should naturally be interested in.

The results were, as might be expected, disastrous. His son Tom became a monster of selfishness, sensuality, and criminality. Dickens uses the name "whelp" to describe him, and, in a satirical manner, accounts for his meanness and weaknesses in the following summary:

> It was very remarkable that a young gentleman who had been brought up under one continuous system of unnatural restraint should be a hypocrite; but it was certainly the case with Tom. It was very strange that a young gentleman who had never been left to his own guidance for five consecutive minutes should be incapable at last of governing himself; but so it was with Tom. It was altogether unaccountable that a young gentleman whose imagination had been strangled in his cradle should be still inconvenienced by its ghost in the form of grovelling sensualities; but such a monster, beyond all doubt, was Tom.

When Mr. Gradgrind became convinced that he had been altogether wrong in his educational ideals and was endeavouring to explain the matter to Mr. Bounderby, that gentleman gave expression to the views of many people of his time. Fortunately there are few Bounderbys now, but there are some even yet.

> "Well, well!" returned Mr. Gradgrind, with a patient, even a submissive air. And he sat for a little while pondering. "Bounderby, I see reason to doubt whether we have ever quite understood Louisa."
>
> "What do you mean by we?"
>
> "Let me say, I, then," he returned, in answer to the coarsely blurted question; "I doubt whether I have understood Louisa. I doubt whether I have been quite right in the manner of her education."
>
> "There you hit it," returned Bounderby. "There I agree with you. You have found it out at last, have you? Education! I'll tell you what education is—to be tumbled out of doors, neck and crop, and put upon the shortest allowance of everything except blows. That's what *I* call education."

In his last book—Edwin Drood—Dickens pictured Mr. Honeythunder as a type of coercive philanthropists, whom he regarded as intolerable as well as intolerant nuisances—people who would use force to compel everybody to think and act as they are told to think and act by the Honeythunders.

In speaking of Mr. Honeythunder and his class of philanthropists, Rev. Canon Crisparkle said:

> It is a most extraordinary thing that these philanthropists are so given to seizing their fellow-creatures by the scruff of the neck,

and (as one may say) bumping them into the paths of peace.

Neville Landless described his training to Canon Crisparkle in telling words:

> "And to finish with, sir: I have been brought up among abject and servile dependents of an inferior race, and I may easily have contracted some affinity with them. Sometimes I don't know but that it may be a drop of what is tigerish in their blood."

There is a profound philosophy of one phase of the evils of coercion in this statement. Coercion does not always destroy power by blighting it. Often the power that was intended to bless turns to poison when it is repressed, and makes men hypocritical and tigerish. It is true, too, that a child who is brought up with the idea of dominating a servile class, or even servile individuals, can never have a true conception of his own freedom.

Dickens was not satisfied with his numerous and sustained attacks on the more violent forms of coercion and repression. He began in Edwin Drood to draw a picture of Mrs. Crisparkle, the mother of the Canon, to show that the placid firmness of her strong will had a baleful influence on character. Her character was not completed, but the outlines given are most suggestive. What could surpass the absolute indifference she showed to the slightest consideration for the individuality or opinions of other people when she spoke of her wards, who were grown up, it should be remembered, to young manhood and womanhood.

> "I have spoken with my two wards, Neville and Helena Landless, on the subject of their defective education, and they give in to the plan proposed; as I should have taken good care they did, whether they liked it or not."

How exquisitely he reveals the character of the eminently dogmatic, though quiet, Christian lady by her remarking so definitely to her son, the Canon:

> "I have no objection to discuss it, Sept. I trust, my dear, I am always open to discussion." There was a vibration in the old lady's cap, as though she internally added, "And I should like to see the discussion that would change *my* mind!"

Dickens meant to show that whether the coercion partook of the nature of that exercised by Squeers or Mrs. Crisparkle, it resulted in forcing those compelled to submit to it to "give in," and that all children who are regularly made to "give in" acquire the habit of "giving in," and eventually become "give-iners" and hypocrites until circumstances make them rebels and anarchists. So he condemned every form of coercion, and taught the doctrine of true freedom for the child as a necessary element in his best development. When this doctrine is fully understood men will soon become truly free. All true education has been a movement toward freedom. All true national advancement has been toward more perfect freedom. The ideal of national, constitutional liberty has changed in harmony with the educational revelations of the broadening conception of freedom; and more progressive conceptions of national liberty have rendered it necessary for the educators to reveal truer, freer methods of training children in harmony with the higher national organization.

When the ideal of national organization was the divine right of kings to rule their subjects by absolute authority, the system of national organization required passive obedience on the part of the subject. To secure this coercive discipline the prompt submission of the child to the immediate authority over him was the ideal process. Passive submission was required as the full duty of the citizen, and passive obedience was the desired product of the school. But the new ideal of government is rule by the people through their representatives, and national citizenship means the intelligent co-operation of independent individuals; so the true educational ideal is a free selfhood, and a free selfhood in maturity demands a free selfhood in childhood. To secure this it is essential that schools shall become "free republics of childhood."

"But a free selfhood in childhood must lead to anarchy," say those who cling to the coercive ideal. Anarchy never springs from freedom. Anarchy is the foul son of coercion. True freedom does not include liberty to do wrong. The "perfect law of liberty" is the only basis for perfect happiness, because it is not freedom beyond law, but freedom within law, freedom because of law. Law should never be coercive to the child. When it becomes so the law is wrong and it makes the child wrong, and produces the apperceptive centres of anarchy in feeling and thought out of the very elements that should have produced joyous co-operation. Law should give the child consciousness of power, and not of restraint. Undirected selfhood, uncontrolled selfhood, is not true freedom. The exercise of power without limitations leads to confusion, indecision, and anarchy in everything except its spirit of rebellion. The guidance and control of adulthood and the limitations of law are necessary to the accomplishment of the best results in the immediate product of effort put forth by the child, in the effect on his character, and in the development of a true consciousness of freedom in his life.

The terrible blunder of the past in child training has been to make law coercive instead of directive. Law has been prohibitive, not stimulative. Law has defined barriers to prevent effort, instead of outlining the direction effort should take. The limitations of law have been used to define the course the child should not take; they should have defined the course he ought to take, and within the range of which course he should use his selfhood in the freest possible way. Law has said "thou shalt not" when it should have said "thou shalt"; it has said "don't" when it should have said "do"; it has said "quit" when it should have said "go on"; it has said "be still" when it should have said "work"; it has stood in the way to check when it should have moved on to lead to victory and progress along the most direct lines; it has given a consciousness of weakness instead of a consciousness of power; it has developed moroseness instead of joyousness, self-depreciation instead of self-reverence; and children for these reasons have been led to dislike law, and the apperceptive centres of anarchy have been laid by a coercive instead of a stimulative use of law.

By false ideals of coercive law adulthood has been made repressive instead of suggestive, depressive instead of helpful, dogmatic instead of reasonable, tyrannical instead of free, "child-quellers" instead of sympathetic friends of childhood, executors of penalties instead of wise guides, agents to keep children under instead of helping them up; and so children have learned to dislike school, and work, and teachers, and often home and parents. And the children have not been to blame for their dislike of law and their distrust of adulthood.

And the children themselves by coercion have been made don'ters instead of doers, quitters instead of workers, give-iners instead of persevering winners, yielders to opposition instead of achievers of victory, negative instead of positive, apathetic instead of energetic, passive instead of active, imitative instead of original, followers instead of leaders, dependent instead of independent, servile instead of free, conscious of weakness instead of power, defect shunners instead of triumphant creative representatives of the God in whose image man was created.

Every agency that robs a child of his originality and freedom and prevents the spontaneous output of his creative self-activity destroys the image of God in him. Man is most like God when he is freely working out the plans of his own creative selfhood for good purposes. Coercion has been the greatest destroyer of the image of God in the child, and anarchy is the product of the perversion of the very powers that should have made man hopefully constructive. The seeds of anarchy are sown in the child's life, when his selfhood is blighted and checked. The fountain that finds free outlet for its waters forms a pure stream that remains always a blessing, but the fountain that is obstructed forms a noisome marsh, wasting the good land it should have watered and destroying the plant life it should have nourished.

The great salt seas and lakes and marshes of the world have been formed by the checking of beautiful fresh-water streams and rivers and the prevention of their outflow to the ocean they should have reached. So when the outflow of the soul of the child is checked the powers that should have ennobled his own life and enriched the lives of others turn to evil instead of good, and make a dangerous instead of a helpful character. So far as coercion can influence selfhood it destroys its power for good and makes it a menace to civilization, instead of a beneficent agency in the accomplishment of high purposes. The reason that coercion does not more effectively blight and dwarf the child is that childhood is not under the direct influence of adulthood all the time. The blessed hours of freedom in play and work have saved the race.

The absurd idea that "anarchy will result from giving true freedom to the child" persists in the minds of so many people, partly through the strength of the race conception of the need of coercion, from which we have not yet been able fully to free ourselves; partly from a terrible misconception regarding the true function of law; partly through gross ignorance of the child and lack of reverence for him; and partly from failure to understand our own higher powers for guiding the child properly, or the vital relationships of adulthood to childhood.

The child should recognise law as a beneficent guide in the accomplishment of his own plans. In Froebel's wonderful kindergarten system the child is always guided by law, but he is always perfectly free to work out his own designs, and in doing so he is aided by law, not kept back or down by law. Law is, to the truly trained child, a revealer of right outlets for power, and the supreme duties of adulthood in training childhood are to change the centre of its interest when from lack of wisdom its interest centre is wrong, and to reveal to it in logical sequence the laws of nature, of beauty, of harmony, and of life. With such training life and law will always be in harmony, and the seeds of anarchy will find no soil in human hearts or minds in which to take root.

Dickens uses the French Revolution, in A Tale of Two Cities, to show that anarchy results from coercion, from the unreasoning subordination of a lower to a higher or ruling class. Against the reasoning of wisdom the Marquis said: "Repression is the only lasting philosophy. The dark deference of fear and slavery, my friend, will keep the dogs obedient to the whip as long as this roof shuts out the sky." The roof came off one wild night—burned off by an infuriated mob of the dogs who had been repressed and whipped into anarchy. Yet the aristocracy of France claimed, as coercionist educators claim, that the anarchy was the result of insufficient coercion, instead of the natural harvest of the seed they had sown.

> It was too much the way of monseigneur under his reverses as a refugee, and it was much too much the way of native British orthodoxy, to talk of this terrible revolution as if it were the one only harvest ever known under the skies that had not been sown—as if nothing had ever been done that had led to it—as if the observers of the wretched millions in France, and of the misused and perverted resources that should have made them prosperous, had not seen it inevitably coming, years before, and had not in plain words recorded what they saw.

When the Revolution was at its fearful height, and the repressed dogs were having their wild carnival of revenge, Dickens says:

> Along the Paris streets the death-carts rumble, hollow and harsh. Six tumbrels carry the day's wine to la guillotine. All the devouring and insatiate monsters imagined since imagination could record itself, are fused in the one realization, guillotine. And yet there is not in France, with its rich variety of soil and climate, a blade, a leaf, a root, a sprig, a peppercorn, which will grow to maturity under conditions more certain than those that have produced this horror. Crush humanity out of shape once more, under similar hammers, and it will twist itself into the same tortured forms. Sow the same seed of rapacious license and oppression over again, and it will surely yield the same fruit according to its kind.
>
> Six tumbrels roll along the streets. Change these back again to what they were, thou powerful enchanter, Time, and they shall be seen to be the carriages of absolute monarchs, the equipages of feudal nobles, the toilets of flaring Jezebels, the churches that are not My Father's house but dens of thieves, and huts of millions of starving peasants!

This is the most profound and most ably written exposition of the philosophy of anarchy.

"But by coercion I can make the child do right, and in this way I can form habits of doing right that will control the child when he grows up."

The habit that is really formed by coercion is the habit of submission, of passive yielding to authority, of subordination, and, in the last analysis, this means the degradation and enslavement of the soul. Two habits are thus wrought into the child's nature by coercion: the habit of doing things because ordered to do them, which is slavery; and the habit of doing things he does not like or wish to do, which is the basis of hypocrisy. The meanest products that can be made from beings created in God's image are slaves and hypocrites. One of the remarkable facts regarding coercionists is that they blame God for creating the monstrosities they have themselves produced by false methods of training.

"We should break the child's will, if it is wrong, to set it right, just as we should break a crooked leg to make it straight."

This is a statement that betrays a lack of modern surgical knowledge, and a carelessness of psychological thought. Modern treatment for the cure of deformity of body avoids harsh treatment whenever it is possible to do so. It has been found that many deformities of body may be cured by proper exercise of the undeveloped part or parts, and with wider knowledge of Nature's laws will come a wiser use of the law of self-transformation, and a smaller and smaller use of the severer methods of treatment. But no good child psychologist now doubts that a child's will possesses the power of self-development and self-adjustment under proper guidance, nor should any one be ignorant of the fact that all true will development comes from within outward.

It is only necessary that man should study the child more thoroughly, and learn how to change his interest centres from wrong to right, and how to surround him with an environment suitable to his progressive stages of development, in order to keep his own will in operation along productive lines of self-reformation and self-regulation by creative self-activity. Thus the will can be set to work truly with undiminished power. When a will is broken, however, it can never regain its full power; the breaking process blights it forever. More rational processes retain its tendency to act and its energy of action while changing the purpose and direction of its action.

One of the interesting anomalies of our language is the marvellous fact that the term "self-willed" should ever have been considered a term of reproach or a description of a defect in character. The child with strongest self-will may become the greatest champion for righteousness if properly trained. He needs a wise and sympathetic trainer, who will be reverently grateful for his strong self-will, and whose reverence will prevent him from doing anything that would weaken the strength or selfhood of the will. The attempt to break his will may make him a destroying force instead of a leader for truth and progress. If a strangled will ever regains vitality it rarely acts truly. There is perhaps no other relic of the theories of barbaric ignorance concerning child training still left that is so baneful and so illogical as the theory that justifies will breaking.

"But God punishes the child. The child who touches the fire gets burned, and therefore it is right that coercive punishment should be used by adulthood in dealing with the child."

The punishments referred to are the revelation of natural laws. There is no personal element of the punishing agency manifest to the child. God does not appear to the child as a punisher, and it is an astounding error in training to reveal such a consciousness of God to the child. Responsibility for the consequences of their acts is a law of which all children approve. This appeals to their sense of justice, and there is no other sense to which we can appeal with success so universally in children as the sense of justice. "Squareness" is the highest quality named in the lexicon of childhood. A boy would rather be deemed "square" than receive praise for any other characteristic or accomplishment. So he recognises the justice of being held accountable for the directly resulting consequences of his acts quite as readily as he accepts the fact, without blaming any one else, that he will be burned if he touches fire. There is no element of coercion in the law of consequences. It is a just and universal law in harmony with his moral responsibility; therefore he will respect it. Coercion is directly contrary to the fundamental laws of his happiness and his true growth, and therefore he naturally and properly dislikes and disapproves of it, and of the individual who outrages justice by using it.

The wonderful stories of Dickens set the world thinking by first arousing the strongest feelings of sympathy for the child and then developing sentiment and thought against every form of coercion, more especially coercion by corporal punishment. The awakening has been most satisfactory in its results. When Dickens began his writing against corporal punishment the rod was the almost universal remedy for all defects in animals or human beings. Whatever the defect, the superior in the eyes of the law used the one agency to overcome it. Mothers used the rod to subdue their children. Husbands used the rod to keep their children and wives in order. Men whipped their horses with impunity, as they did their children or wives. They owned them, and their right to punish them as they chose was unquestioned. Men trained animals to perform tricks in menageries by beating them, and they trained dancing, or performing, or learning girls and boys quite as inhumanly. Ownership or subordination justified unspeakable cruelty. The weakness of the child, the helplessness of the animal, appealed to the hardness of human nature, and not to its chivalry or sympathy. Even the poor feeble-minded and idiotic, who were confined in asylums, were terribly flogged by the most advanced philanthropists of the highest Christian civilization. They were weak. It was the duty of the authorities to control them, and "stripes and bruises" were regarded as the only true agencies for securing obedience. The rod was the highest controlling and directing force in the world.

What a change has been wrought! Horses and children and wives are protected from brutal treatment now by law. The insane are not flogged to make them sane in any well-conducted institutions. More than half the children in the schools of the civilized world are free from the terror and degradation of corporal punishment by law, or by the higher consciousness of more intelligent teachers. Parenthood everywhere is studying the child and trying to become conscious of its own higher powers of guiding character so that it may be able to train the children in truer and more productive and less dangerous ways than formerly. And Charles Dickens was the great apostle of these grand reforms.

We shudder now as we read of the outrages practised on helpless children and on the insane half a century ago not by the heathen, but by earnest, conscientious Christians. The men who live half a century hence will shudder when they read that in some schools at the close of the nineteenth century children who were partially or temporarily insane from hereditary taint, or imperfect nutrition, or cruel treatment, or anger, or from some other removable or remediable cause were whipped, and that men, some of whom occupied respectable positions, advocated the breaking of children's wills! If these "will-breaking" educators were in charge of asylums they would resurrect the straitjacket and the whipping post for the insane.

The few who advocate corporal punishment openly claim that they have the authority of the Bible for their faith in the rod. They should remember that good men have stood with Bibles in their hands misrepresenting God and attempting to stop the progress of every great movement toward freedom and reform. Galileo was imprisoned by the Church because he taught that the earth turns round. Men had no difficulty in showing that the Bible approved of slavery, or that it prohibited woman from the exercise of the right or the performance of the duties of responsible individuality. So men still quote Solomon to show that corporal punishment is approved by God, though such a conclusion would be rejected by the highest interpreters.

"Whipping makes strong characters." No, it makes hard characters, and hardness is but one element of strength, and not the best element of strength. The strength of the English character has not been developed, as is claimed by some, by the whipping done in English schools and homes. It comes partly by race heredity from the sturdiness of the Saxon and Norman founders of the race, partly from the general practice of working hard from youth up, and largely from the fact that the English playgrounds are so universally used, and are the scenes of the severest struggles for supremacy in skill and power that are witnessed in any part of the world. The winning half inch or half length, the valorous struggle for leadership on track or river—these are the things that have preserved and developed English force and bravery, in spite of the fact that England in her schools and homes has done fully her share of whipping. A boy or girl who spends as much time in free strong play as the English boy, works out the effects of a great many evils from his or her life. When men see the futility of dependence on flogging for developing energetic strength of character they will study the influence of play to the great advantage of racial vigour, and courage, and moral energy.

Corporal punishment, like all other forms of coercion, robs the child of joyousness, and joyousness is one of the most essential elements in the true growth of a child. Corporal punishment affects the nervous systems of children injuriously, and when applied to certain parts of the body it stimulates prematurely the action of the sexual nature, and leads to one of the worst forms of depravity.

Corporal punishment is ineffective as a disciplinary agency. In one American city during the generation after Dickens began his great crusade against corporal punishment it was the practice to whip with a rawhide all children who came late, but the lateness steadily increased in defiance of the rawhide. It was reduced to less than one one-hundredth part of its former proportion when whipping for lateness was entirely abolished and more rational means adopted.

The order and co-operation of pupils is best in those schools in which no corporal punishment is used. If in any school only one teacher relies on the rod as a stimulator to work and a restrainer of evil, her class is sure to be the most disorderly, the least co-operative, and the most defective in original power in the school. As the children throughout the school come from the same homes, play with the same companions, attend the same churches, and are subject to the same general influences, it is perfectly clear that the whipping is the distinctive feature of character training that deforms the children. They will become normal, reasonable children when they reach the next room. This illustration assumes that all the teachers are possessed of good natural ability to direct the child properly. The one who uses corporal punishment fails because she has been dwarfed by her faith in corporal punishment. She has believed in it so fully that she has not sought to understand higher and better means. She has studied neither the child nor her own powers of child guidance.

Dickens taught the inefficiency of coercion to accomplish what men hoped to accomplish by it in his criticism of the revolting use of capital punishment in former times. In A Tale of Two Cities he says:

> Accordingly, the forger was put to Death; the utterer of a bad note was put to Death; the unlawful opener of a letter was put to Death; the purloiner of forty shillings and sixpence was put to Death; the holder of a horse at Tellson's door, who made off with it, was put to Death; the coiner of a bad shilling was put to Death; the sounders of three fourths of the notes in the whole gamut of crime were put to Death. Not that it did the least good in the way of prevention—it might always have been worth remarking that the fact was *exactly the reverse*.

The great prophets of modern education—Pestalozzi, Froebel, Barnard, and Mann—strongly condemned corporal punishment. These were men of clear insight and correct judgment. The opinion of one such man is worth more than the views of ten thousand ordinary men in regard to the subject of their special study. They were prophet souls who saw the higher truth toward which the race had been slowly growing, and revealed it.

Their revelations have been appreciated and adopted more and more fully as they have been understood more and more clearly. In the case of corporal punishment and all forms of coercion Dickens has been the John the Baptist and the Paul of the revelation of the gospel of sympathy for the child.

Not one blow in a thousand is given to a child now as compared with the time of Dickens's childhood. Corporal punishment is prohibited in the schools of France, Italy, Switzerland, Finland, Brazil, New Jersey, and in the following cities: New York, Chicago, Cleveland, Albany, Syracuse, Toledo, and Savannah. In Washington and Philadelphia teachers voluntarily gave up the practice of whipping. This is true of the majority of individual teachers in the cities of America, and the number of those who do without all forms of coercive discipline is rapidly increasing.

The whipping of girls is prohibited in Saxony, Hessen, Oldenburg, and in many cities. Few girls are now whipped in schools anywhere. Corporal punishment has been abolished for the higher grades in Norway and in the lower grades in Saxony, Hessen, Bremen, and Hamburg. In the last-named city the cane is kept under lock and key. In some places the consent of parents must be obtained before children may be whipped, in some places the number of strokes is limited; in other places a record is kept of every case of corporal punishment and reports made monthly to the school boards. Everywhere action has been taken to prohibit or restrict the use of the once universally respected and universally dominant rod.

All wise trainers of children recognise the value of obedience, but truly wise trainers no longer aim to make children merely submissively obedient, nor even willingly responsive in their obedience. They try to make them independently, co-operatively, and reverently obedient; independent in free development of will, co-operative in unity of effort with their fellows and their adult guides, and reverent in their attitude to law. The substitution of independence for subserviency, of co-operation for formal, responsive obedience, and of reverence for law for fear of law are the most important development in child training.

In Dickens's ideal school, Doctor Strong's, there was "plenty of liberty."

Gladstone's criticism, when over seventy, of his own teachers was that they were afraid of freedom. He said: "I did not learn to set a due value on the imperishable and inestimable principles of human liberty. The temper which I think prevailed among them was that liberty was regarded with jealousy, and fear could not be wholly dispensed with." The true teacher is not afraid of freedom, but makes it the dominant element in his training and in his educational theory.

May the profounder truth in regard to child training spread to the ends of the earth! May the time soon come when there shall be no disciples of Susan Nipper's doctrine, "that childhood, like money, must be shaken and rattled and jostled about a good deal to keep it bright"! May Christian civilization soon be free from such memories as the remembrance of Mr. Obenreizer, in No Thoroughfare, had of his parents: "I was a famished naked little wretch of two or three years when they were men and women with hard hands to beat me"! May Christ's teaching soon be so fully understood that there will be no child anywhere like the shivering little boy in The Haunted Man, who was "used already to be worried and hunted like a beast, who crouched down as he was looked at, and looked back again, and interposed his arm to ward off the expected blow, and threatened to bite if he was hit"! May teachers and all trainers of children learn the underlying philosophy of the statement made by Dickens, in connection with the schools of the Stepney Union, in The Uncommercial Traveller: "In the moral health of these schools—where corporal punishment is unknown—truthfulness stands high"!

CHAPTER IV.

THE DOCTRINE OF CHILD DEPRAVITY.

Dickens heartily accepted Froebel's view of the doctrine of child depravity. They did not teach that the child is totally divine, but neither did they believe that a being created in God's image is entirely depraved.

They recognised very clearly that the doctrine of child depravity was the logical (or illogical) basis of the theory of corporal punishment and all forms of coercion. What more natural or more logical than the practice of checking the outflow of a child's inner life if we believe his inner life to be depraved? The firm belief in the doctrine of child depravity compelled conscientious men to be repressive and coercive in their discipline. Dickens understood this fully, and therefore he gave the doctrine no place in his philosophy.

Mrs. Pipchin's training was based squarely on the doctrine of child depravity, for "the secret of her management of children was to give them everything that they didn't like, and nothing that they did." If the training of children under the "good old *régime*," for which some reactionary philosophers are still pleading, is carefully analyzed, it will be found that Mrs. Pipchin's plan was the commonly approved plan, and it was the perfectly logical outcome of the doctrine that the child, being wholly depraved, desired everything it should not have and objected to everything it should have.

That was a touching question addressed by a little boy to his father: "Say, papa, did mamma stop you from doing everything you wished to do when *you* were a little boy?"

How Dickens despised the awful theology of the Murdstones, who would not let David play with other children, because they believed "all children to be a swarm of little vipers [though there *was* a child once set in the midst of the Disciples], and held that they contaminated one another"!

How he laughed at Mrs. Varden and Miggs, her maid!

> "If you hadn't the sweetness of an angel in you, mim, I don't think you could abear it, I raly don't."
>
> "Miggs," said Mrs. Varden, "you're profane."
>
> "Begging your pardon, mim," returned Miggs with shrill rapidity, "such was not my intentions, and such I hope is not my character, though I am but a servant."

> "Answering me, Miggs, and providing yourself," retorted her mistress, looking round with dignity, "is one and the same thing. How dare you speak of angels in connection with your sinful fellow-beings—mere"—said Mrs. Varden, glancing at herself in a neighbouring mirror, and arranging the ribbon of her cap in a more becoming fashion—"mere worms and grovellers as we are!"
>
> "I do not intend, mim, if you please, to give offence," said Miggs, confident in the strength of her compliment, and developing strongly in the throat as usual, "and I did not expect it would be took as such. I hope I know my own unworthiness, and that I hate and despise myself and all my fellow-creatures as every practicable Christian should."

Oliver Twist was described by the philanthropists who cared for him as "under the exclusive patronage and protection of the powers of wickedness, and an article direct from the manufactory of the very devil himself."

Mr. Grimwig had no faith in boys, and he tried hard to shake Mr. Brownlow's faith in Oliver.

> "He is a nice-looking boy, is he not?" inquired Mr. Brownlow.
>
> "I don't know," replied Mr. Grimwig pettishly.
>
> "Don't know?"
>
> "No. I don't know. I never see any difference in boys. I only know two sorts of boys: mealy boys and beef-faced boys."
>
> "And which is Oliver?"
>
> "Mealy. I know a friend who has a beef-faced boy—a fine boy, they call him; with a round head, and red cheeks, and glaring eyes; a horrid boy; with a body and limbs that appear to be swelling out of the seams of his blue clothes; with the voice of a pilot, and the appetite of a wolf. I know him! The wretch!"
>
> "Come," said Mr. Brownlow, "these are not the characteristics of young Oliver Twist; so he needn't excite your wrath."
>
> "They are not," replied Mr. Grimwig. "He may have worse. He is deceiving you, my good friend."
>
> "I'll swear he is not," replied Mr. Brownlow warmly.
>
> "If he is not," said Mr. Grimwig, "I'll——" and down went the stick.
>
> "I'll answer for that boy's truth with my life!" said Mr. Brownlow, knocking the table.
>
> "And I for his falsehood with my head!" rejoined Mr. Grimwig, knocking the table also.
>
> "We shall see," said Mr. Brownlow, checking his rising anger.

> "We will," replied Mr. Grimwig, with a provoking smile; "we will."

Dickens always pleaded for more faith in children.

In Great Expectations poor Pip was continually reminded of the fact that he was "naterally wicious," and at the great Christmas dinner party Mr. Pumblechook took him as the illustration of his theological discourse on "swine" and Mrs. Hubble commiserated Mrs. Gargery about the trouble he had caused her by all his waywardness.

> "Trouble?" echoed my sister, "trouble?" And then entered on a fearful catalogue of all the illnesses I had been guilty of, and all the acts of sleeplessness I had committed, and all the high places I had tumbled from, and all the low places I had tumbled into, and all the injuries I had done myself, and all the times she had wished me in my grave, and I had contumaciously refused to go there.

Again, when Pip was just beginning his life away from home his guardian, Mr. Jaggers, said to him at their first interview: "I shall by this means be able to check your bills, and to pull you up if I find you outrunning the constable. Of course you'll go wrong somehow, but that's no fault of mine."

"Of course you'll go wrong somehow," was an inspiring start in life for a young gentleman.

Abel Magwitch, Pip's friend, told him near the close of his career how he came to lead such a dissipated and criminal life. He evidently had ability and possessed a deep sense of gratitude, and might have developed the other virtues if he had been treated properly. Dickens used him as an illustration of the fact that society fails often to do the best for a boy and make the most out of him through sheer lack of faith in childhood, and that this lack of faith results from the belief that a boy is so depraved that he would rather do wrong than right, and that when he starts to do wrong there is no hope of his reform.

> "Dear boy and Pip's comrade. I am not a-going fur to tell you my life, like a song or a story-book. But to give it you short and handy, I'll put it at once into a mouthful of English. In jail and out of jail, in jail and out of jail, in jail and out of jail. There, you've got it. That's *my* life pretty much, down to such times as I got shipped off, arter Pip stood my friend.
>
> "I've been done everything to, pretty well—except hanged. I've been locked up, as much as a silver teakittle. I've been carted here and carted there, and put out of this town and put out of that town, and stuck in the stocks, and whipped and worried and drove. I've no more notion where I was born, than you have—if so much. I first become aware of myself, down in Essex, a-thieving turnips for my living. Summun had run away from me—a man—a tinker—and he'd took the fire with him, and left me wery cold.

> "I know'd my name to be Magwitch, chrisen'd Abel. How did I know it? Much as I know'd the birds' names in the hedges to be chaffinch, sparrer, thrush. I might have thought it was all lies altogether, only as the birds' names come out true, I supposed mine did.
>
> "So fur as I could find, there warn't a soul that see young Abel Magwitch, with as little on him as in him, but wot caught fright at him, and either drove him off or took him up. I was took up, took up, took up, to that extent that I reg'larly grow'd up took up.
>
> "This is the way it was, that when I was a ragged little cree-tur as much to be pitied as ever I see (not that I looked in the glass, for there warn't many insides of furnished houses known to me), I got the name being hardened. 'This is a terrible hardened one,' they says to prison wisitors, picking out me. 'May be said to live in jails, this boy.' Then they looked at me, and I looked at them, and they measured my head, some on 'em—they had better a-measured my stomach—and others on 'em giv' me tracts what I couldn't read, and made me speeches what I couldn't understand. They always went on agen me about the devil."

Poor old Toby Veck, in The Chimes, reflected the theories that Dickens wished to overthrow.

> "It seems as if we can't go right, or do right, or be righted," said Toby. "I hadn't much schooling, myself, when I was young; and I can't make out whether we have any business on the face of the earth, or not. Sometimes I think we must have—a little; and sometimes I think we must be intruding. I get so puzzled some-times that I am not even able to make up my mind whether there is any good at all in us, or whether we are born bad. We seem to be dreadful things; we seem to give a deal of trouble; we are always being complained of and guarded against."

The most realistic picture of the influence of the child-depravity ideal on the training of childhood is given in Mrs. Clennam, in Little Dorrit. She was a hard, malignant, dishonest, unsympathetic woman, who had deliberately driven Arthur's mother to madness and blighted his father's life in the name of her false religion, and blasphemously claimed that she was doing it in God's stead, as his devoted servant. Yet she was sure she was truly religious, and had a pious vanity in the fact that she was "filled with an abhorrence of evil doers." She was filled with gladness, too, at the prospect of marrying a man of like training with herself. Speaking of the training of herself and her husband she said:

> "You do not know what it is to be brought up strictly and straitly. I was so brought up. Mine was no light youth of sinful gaiety and pleasure. Mine were days of wholesome repression, punishment, and fear. The corruption of our hearts, the evil of our ways, the curse that is upon us, the terrors that surround us—

> these were the themes of my childhood. They formed my character, and filled me with an abhorrence of evil doers. When old Mr. Gilbert Clennam proposed his orphan nephew to my father for my husband, my father impressed upon me that his bringing-up had been, like mine, one of severe restraint. He told me, that besides the discipline his spirit had undergone, he had lived in a starved house, where rioting and gaiety were unknown, and where every day was a day of toil and trial like the last. He told me that he had been a man in years long before his uncle had acknowledged him as one; and that from his school days to that hour, his uncle's roof had been a sanctuary to him from the contagion of the irreligious and dissolute."

Speaking of her training of Arthur, she said:

> "I devoted myself to reclaim the otherwise predestined and lost boy; to bring him up in fear and trembling, and in a life of practical contrition for the sins that were heavy on his head before his entrance into this condemned world."

Dickens describes her religious character as such as might naturally be expected to develop in a woman whose childhood revealed to her only the self-abnegation and terrors of religion and the utter contempt for humanity shrouded in the doctrine of child depravity. She had seen God as an awful character of sleepless watchfulness to see her evil doing and record it, of wrathfulness, and of vengeance, but never of loving sympathy and forgiveness. So she fitted her religion to the character that such training had formed in her.

> Great need had the rigid woman of her mystical religion, veiled in gloom and darkness, with lightnings of cursing, vengeance, and destruction, flashing through the sable clouds. Forgive us our debts as we forgive our debtors, was a prayer too poor in spirit for her. Smite Thou my debtors, Lord, wither them, crush them; do Thou as I would do, and Thou shalt have my worship: this was the impious tower of stone she built up to scale heaven.

The old discipline and the old training were based on the belief that children like to do wrong better than to do right. There could be no greater error, or one more certain to lead to false principles of training, and prevent the recognition of the true methods of developing character in childhood.

Children do not like to do wrong better than to do right. They like to do. They like to do the things they themselves plan to do. They like to do the things that are interesting to themselves. Their lack of wisdom leaves them at the mercy of their interests, and without guidance their constructiveness may turn to destructiveness. When it does so, it is because of the neglect of their adult guides to surround them with plenty of suitable material for construction or transformation adapted to their stage of development. With a sufficient variety of material for constructive plays the child will rarely exhibit destructive tendencies, and when he does so, the wisdom of his adult guide should find little trouble in changing his interest centre from the wrong to the right. The skilful trainer changes the interest centre without making the child conscious of adult interference.

It costs little to supply the child with sand and blocks, and soft clay, and colors, and colored paper, and blunt scissors and gum, and other similar materials—much less than is usually spent for toys; yet such materials would save parents from much worry, and help them to get rid of the wrong ideals, and they would preserve the natural tendency of children to constructiveness, and afford them an opportunity for the comfort and the development of real self-activity.

The child's most dominant tendency is activity in using the material things of his environment to transform them into new forms or relationships in harmony with his own plans. This tendency is intended to accomplish four great purposes in the child's development. It reveals the child's own powers to himself, it develops his originality, it trains him to use his constructive powers, and it gives him the habit of transforming his environment to suit his own plans. If he is not supplied with suitable material to play with he will appropriate the material he finds most available. In this way, through the absolute neglect of his adult guides, he has acquired a bad reputation.

The instinct that leads the child to transform his material environment should lead to the conscious desire and determination to improve the physical, intellectual, and spiritual conditions around him at maturity. It is therefore a very essential element in his training, and to check or neglect it may weaken and warp his character as much as it was intended to strengthen and direct it.

Thus the children have been coerced because men believed them to be depraved, and the coercion has developed the apparent depravity.

The darkest clouds have been lifted from the vision of adults and from the lives of the little ones by the breaking of the power of the doctrine of child depravity. The teacher especially has a more hopeful field opened to him. His great work of training is no longer restricted to putting blinders on the eyes of children to prevent their seeing evil, and bits in their mouths to keep them from going wrong. He believes that every child has an element of divinity, however small and enfeebled by heredity or encrusted by evil environment, and that his chief duty is to arouse this divinity (his selfhood or individuality) to consciousness and start it on its conscious growth toward the divine. The revelation of this new and grander ideal has led to all intelligent child study for the purpose of discovering what adulthood can do, and especially what childhood itself can do, in accomplishing its most perfect training for its highest destiny.

Dickens expressed his general faith in childhood in Mrs. Lirriper's remark to the Major about Jemmy:

> "Ah, Major," I says, drying my eyes, "we needn't have been afraid. We might have known it. Treachery don't come natural to beaming youth; but trust and pity, love and constancy—they do, thank God!"

He taught his philosophy of the origin of many of the evils that are attributed to child depravity in Nobody's Story. "Nobody" means the workingman. He says to the Master:

> "The evil consequences of imperfect instruction, the evil consequences of pernicious neglect, the evil consequences of unnatural restraint and the denial of humanizing enjoyments, will all come from us, and none of them will stop with us. They will spread far and wide. They always do; they always have done—just like the pestilence. I understand so much, I think, at last."

There is profoundness in these doctrines.

CHAPTER V.

CRAMMING.

Although Dickens paid much more attention in his writings to the methods of training than to the methods of teaching, he studied the methods of teaching sufficiently to recognise some of their gravest defects. Dombey and Son is unquestionably the greatest book ever written to expose the evils of cramming. Doctor Blimber, Cornelia, and Mr. Feeder, when closely studied, represent in the varied phases of their work all the worst forms of cramming.

> Whenever a young gentleman was taken in hand by Doctor Blimber, he might consider himself sure of a pretty tight squeeze. The doctor only undertook the charge of ten young gentlemen, but he had always ready a supply of learning for a hundred, on the lowest estimate; it was at once the business and delight of his life to gorge the unhappy ten with it.
>
> In fact, Doctor Blimber's establishment was a great hothouse, in which there was a forcing apparatus incessantly at work. All the boys blew before their time. Mental green peas were produced at Christmas, and intellectual asparagus all the year round. Mathematical gooseberries (very sour ones too) were common at untimely seasons, and from mere sprouts of bushes, under Doctor Blimber's cultivation. Every description of Greek and Latin vegetable was got off the dryest twigs of boys, under the frostiest circumstances. Nature was of no consequence at all. No matter what a young gentleman was intended to bear, Doctor Blimber made him bear to pattern, somehow or other. This was all very pleasant and ingenious, but the system of forcing was attended with its usual disadvantages. There was not the right taste about the premature productions, and they didn't keep well. Moreover, one young gentleman, with a swollen nose and an excessively large head (the oldest of the ten who had "gone through" everything) suddenly left off blowing one day, and remained in the establishment a mere stalk. And people did say that the doctor had rather overdone it with young Toots, and that when he began to have whiskers he left off having brains.
>
> The doctor was a portly gentleman in a suit of black, with strings at his knees, and stockings below them. He had a bald

head, highly polished; a deep voice, and a chin so very double that it was a wonder how he ever managed to shave into the creases. He had likewise a pair of little eyes that were always half shut up and a mouth that was always half expanded into a grin, as if he had, that moment, posed a boy, and were waiting to convict him from his own lips. Insomuch that when the doctor put his right hand into the breast of his coat, and, with his other hand behind him and a scarcely perceptible wag of his head, made the commonest observation to a nervous stranger, it was like a sentiment from the sphinx, and settled his business.

Miss Blimber, too, although a slim and graceful maid, did no soft violence to the gravity of the house. There was no light nonsense about Miss Blimber. She kept her hair short and crisp, and wore spectacles. She was dry and sandy with working in the graves of deceased languages. None of your live languages for Miss Blimber. They must be dead—stone dead—and then Miss Blimber dug them up like a ghoul.

As to Mr. Feeder, B. A., Dr. Blimber's assistant, he was a kind of human barrel organ, with a little list of tunes at which he was continually working, over and over again, without any variation. He might have been fitted up with a change of barrels, perhaps, in early life, if his destiny had been favourable; but it had not been; and he had only one, with which, in a monotonous round, it was his occupation to bewilder the young ideas of Dr. Blimber's young gentlemen. The young gentlemen were prematurely full of carking anxieties. They knew no rest from the pursuit of stony-hearted verbs, savage noun-substantives, inflexible syntactic passages, and ghosts of exercises that appeared to them in their dreams. Under the forcing system, a young gentleman usually took leave of his spirits in three weeks. He had all the care of the world on his head in three months. He conceived bitter sentiments against his parents or guardians in four; he was an old misanthrope in five; envied Curtius that blessed refuge in the earth in six; and at the end of the first twelvemonth had arrived at the conclusion, from which he never afterward departed, that all the fancies of the poets, and lessons of the sages, were a mere collection of words and grammar, and had no other meaning in the world.

But he went on blow, blow, blowing, in the doctor's hothouse all the time; and the doctor's glory and reputation were great when he took his wintry growth home to his relations and friends.

Upon the doctor's doorsteps one day, Paul stood with a fluttering heart, and with his small right hand in his father's. His other hand was locked in that of Florence. How tight the tiny pressure of that one; and how loose and cool the other!

> The doctor was sitting in his portentous study, with a globe at each knee, books all round him, Homer over the door, and Minerva on the mantelshelf. "And how do you do, sir?" he said to Mr. Dombey; "and how is my little friend?"
>
> "Very well I thank you, sir," returned Paul, answering the clock quite as much as the doctor.
>
> "Ha!" said Dr. Blimber. "Shall we make a man of him?"
>
> "Do you hear, Paul?" added Mr. Dombey; Paul being silent.
>
> "Shall we make a man of him?" repeated the doctor.
>
> "I had rather be a child," replied Paul.

Paul's reply is one of the most touchingly beautiful of even Dickens's wonderful expressions—wonderful in their exquisite simplicity and their profound philosophy. When this book was written Dickens was beginning to get the conception of the great truth, which he illustrated at length in Hard Times and other works, that it is a crime against a child to rob it of its childhood.

When Doctor Blimber in his cold, formal manner asked Paul "why he preferred to be a child," the little fellow was unable to answer, and as they stared at him, he at length put his hand on the neck of Florence and burst into tears.

> "Mrs. Pipchin," said his father in a querulous manner, "I am really very sorry to see this."
>
> "Never mind," said the doctor blandly, nodding his head to keep Mrs. Pipchin back. "Nev-er mind; we shall substitute new cares and new impressions, Mr. Dombey, very shortly. You would still wish my little friend to acquire— —"
>
> "Everything, if you please, doctor," returned Mr. Dombey firmly.
>
> "Yes," said the doctor, who, with his half-shut eyes and his usual smile, seemed to survey Paul with the sort of interest that might attach to some choice little animal he was going to stuff. "Yes, exactly. Ha! We shall impart a great variety of information to our little friend, and bring him quickly forward, I dare say. I dare say. Quite a virgin soil, I believe you said, Mr. Dombey?"

On leaving, Mr. Dombey said to Paul:

> "You'll try and learn a great deal here, and be a clever man, won't you?"
>
> "I'll try," returned the child wearily.
>
> "And you'll soon be grown up now?" said Mr. Dombey.
>
> "Oh! very soon!" replied the child. Once more the old, old look passed rapidly across his features like a strange light.

After his father and Florence had left him the doctor said to Cornelia:

> "Cornelia, Dombey will be your charge at first. Bring him on, Cornelia, bring him on. Take him round the house, Cornelia, and familiarize him with his new sphere. Go with that young lady, Dombey."
>
> Cornelia took him first to the schoolroom. Here there were eight young gentlemen in various stages of mental prostration, all very hard at work, and very grave indeed.
>
> Mr. Feeder, B. A., had his Virgil stop on, and was slowly grinding that tune to four young gentlemen. Of the remaining four, two, who grasped their foreheads convulsively, were engaged in solving mathematical problems; one, with his face like a dirty window from much crying, was endeavouring to flounder through a hopeless number of lines before dinner; and one sat looking at his task in stony stupefaction and despair—which, it seemed, had been his condition ever since breakfast time.

After being shown through the dormitories, Cornelia told him dinner would be ready in fifteen minutes, and that in the meantime he had better go into the schoolroom among his "friends."

> His friends were all dispersed about the room except the stony friend, who remained immovable. Mr. Feeder was stretching himself in his gray gown, as if, regardless of expense, he were resolved to pull the sleeves off.
>
> "Heigh-ho-hum!" cried Mr. Feeder, shaking himself like a cart horse "oh dear me, dear me! Ya-a-a-ah!"
>
> "You sleep in my room, don't you?" asked a solemn young gentleman, whose shirt collar curled up the lobes of his ears.
>
> "Master Briggs?" inquired Paul.
>
> "Tozer," said the young gentleman.
>
> Paul answered yes; and Tozer, pointing out the stony pupil, said that it was Briggs. Paul had already felt certain that it must be either Briggs or Tozer, though he didn't know why.
>
> "Is yours a strong constitution?" inquired Tozer.
>
> Paul said he thought not. Tozer replied that *he* thought not also, judging from Paul's looks, and that it was a pity, for it need be. He then asked Paul if he were going to begin with Cornelia; and on Paul saying "Yes," all the young gentlemen (Briggs excepted) gave a low groan.

At dinner no boy was allowed to speak; every one was compelled to listen to the tedious discourse of Doctor Blimber on the customs of the Romans. The cramming of youth was continued with great dignity even during meals. One boy, Johnson, was unfortunate enough to choke himself by too suddenly swallowing his water in order to catch Doctor Blimber's eye when he began an account of the dinners of Vitellius; and to punish him for his breach of manners, Doctor Blimber said before the boys were dismissed from the table:

> "Johnson will repeat to-morrow morning before breakfast, without book, and from the Greek Testament, the first chapter of the Epistle of Saint Paul to the Ephesians. We will resume our studies, Mr. Feeder, in half an hour."

It used to be a common practice to cultivate a loving reverence for God by using the Bible as a means of punishment. This was in harmony with the old educational and the old theological ideal of punishment, as the supreme means available for guiding children properly. It was considered a perfectly appropriate use of the best book to use it for this best of purposes.

> The young gentlemen bowed and withdrew; Mr. Feeder did likewise. During the half hour the young gentlemen, broken into pairs, loitered arm in arm up and down a small piece of ground behind the house. But nothing happened so vulgar as play. Punctually at the appointed time the gong was sounded, and the studies, under the joint auspices of Doctor Blimber and Mr. Feeder, were resumed.
>
> Tea was served in a style no less polite than dinner; and after tea the young gentlemen, rising and bowing as before, withdrew to fetch up the unfinished tasks of that day or to get up the already looming tasks of to-morrow. After prayers and light refreshments at eight o'clock or so, the "young gentlemen" were sent to bed by the doctor rising and solemnly saying, "We will resume our studies at seven to-morrow"; the pupils bowed again, and went to bed.
>
> In the confidence of their own room upstairs, Briggs said his head ached ready to split, and that he should wish himself dead if it wasn't for his mother and a blackbird he had at home. Tozer didn't say much, but he sighed a good deal, and told Paul to look out, for his turn would come to-morrow. After uttering those prophetic words, he undressed himself moodily and got into bed. Briggs was in his bed too, and Paul in his bed too, before the weak-eyed young man appeared to take away the candle, when he wished them good-night and pleasant dreams. But his benevolent wishes were in vain as far as Briggs and Tozer were concerned; for Paul, who lay awake for a long while, and often woke afterward, found that Briggs was ridden by his lesson as a nightmare; and that Tozer, whose mind was affected in his sleep by similar causes, in a minor degree, talked unknown tongues, or scraps of Greek and Latin—it was all one to Paul—which, in the silence of night, had an inexpressibly wicked and guilty effect.

As Paul was going downstairs in the morning Miss Blimber called him into her room, and, pointing to a pile of new books on her table, said:

"These are yours, Dombey."

"All of 'em, ma'am?" said Paul.

"Yes," returned Miss Blimber; "and Mr. Feeder will look you out some more very soon, if you are as studious as I expect you will be, Dombey."

"Thank you, ma'am," said Paul.

"I am going out for a constitutional," resumed Miss Blimber; "and while I am gone—that is to say, in the interval between this and breakfast, Dombey—I wish you to read over what I have marked in these books, and to tell me if you quite understand what you have got to learn. Don't lose time, Dombey, for you have none to spare, but take them downstairs, and begin directly."

"Yes, ma'am," answered Paul.

There were so many of them, that although Paul put one hand under the bottom book and his other hand and his chin on the top book, and hugged them all closely, the middle book slipped out before he reached the door, and then they all tumbled down on the floor. Having at last amassed the whole library and climbed into his place, he fell to work, encouraged by a remark from Tozer to the effect that he "was in for it now"; which was the only interruption he received till breakfast time. At that meal, for which he had no appetite, everything was quite as solemn and genteel as at the others; and when it was finished, he followed Miss Blimber upstairs.

"Now, Dombey," said Miss Blimber, "how have you got on with those books?"

They comprised a little English, and a deal of Latin—names of things, declensions of articles and substantives, exercises thereon, and preliminary rules—a trifle of orthography, a glance at ancient history, a wink or two at modern ditto, a few tables, two or three weights and measures, and a little general information. When poor Paul had spelled out number two, he found he had no idea of number one; fragments whereof afterward obtruded themselves into number three, which slided into number four, which, grafted itself on to number two. So that whether twenty Romuluses made a Remus, or hic hæc hoc was troy weight, or a verb always agreed with an ancient Briton, or three times four was Taurus a bull, were open questions with him.

"Oh, Dombey, Dombey!" said Miss Blimber, "this is very shocking."

So Paul's cramming went on day by day. The delicate little boy, who should not have been sent to school at all, was forced to memorize confused masses of words that had no meaning to him, but he learned to repeat the words, and so got the credit of doing well, and because he learned easily was driven harder and harder. The more easily he carried his burden the higher it was piled on his back.

It was not that Miss Blimber meant to be too hard upon him, or that Doctor Blimber meant to bear too heavily on the young gentlemen in general. Cornelia merely held the faith in which she had been bred; and the doctor, in some partial confusion of his ideas, regarded the young gentlemen as if they were all doctors, and were born grown up. Comforted by the applause of the young gentlemen's nearest relations, and urged on by their blind vanity and ill-considered haste, it would have been strange if Doctor Blimber had discovered his mistake, or trimmed his swelling sails to any other tack.

Thus in the case of Paul. When Doctor Blimber said he made great progress, and was naturally clever, Mr. Dombey was more bent than ever on his being forced and crammed. In the case of Briggs, when Doctor Blimber reported that he did not make great progress yet, and was not naturally clever, Briggs senior was inexorable in the same purpose. In short, however high and false the temperature at which the doctor kept his hothouse, the owners of the plants were always ready to lend a helping hand at the bellows and to stir the fire.

When the midsummer vacation approached, no indecent manifestations of joy were exhibited by the leaden-eyed young gentlemen assembled at Doctor Blimber's. Any such violent expression as "breaking up" would have been quite inapplicable to that polite establishment. The young gentlemen oozed away, semi-annually, to their own homes; but they never broke up. They would have scorned the action.

Tozer, who was constantly galled and tormented by a starched white cambric neckerchief, which he wore at the express desire of Mrs. Tozer, his parent, who, designing him for the Church, was of opinion that he couldn't be in that forward state of preparation too soon—Tozer said, indeed, that choosing between two evils, he thought he would rather stay where he was, than go home. However inconsistent this declaration might appear with that passage in Tozer's essay on the subject, wherein he had observed "that the thoughts of home and all its recollections awakened in his mind the most pleasing emotions of anticipation and delight," and had also likened himself to a Roman general, flushed with a recent victory over the Iceni, or laden with Carthaginian spoil, advancing within a few hours' march of the Capitol, presupposed, for the purposes of the simile, to be the dwelling place of Mrs. Tozer, still it was very sincerely made. For it seemed that Tozer had a dreadful uncle, who not only volunteered examinations of him, in the holidays, on abstruse points, but twisted innocent events and

> things, and wrenched them to the same fell purpose. So that if this uncle took him to the play, or, on a similar pretence of kindness, carried him to see a giant, or a dwarf, or a conjurer, or anything, Tozer knew he had read up some classical allusion to the subject beforehand, and was thrown into a state of mortal apprehension; not foreseeing where he might break out, or what authority he might not quote against him.
>
> As to Briggs, *his* father made no show of artifice about it. He never would leave him alone. So numerous and severe were the mental trials of that unfortunate youth in vacation time, that the friends of the family (then resident near Bayswater, London) seldom approached the ornamental piece of water in Kensington Gardens without a vague expectation of seeing Master Briggs's hat floating on the surface and an unfinished exercise lying on the bank. Briggs, therefore, was not at all sanguine on the subject of holidays; and these two sharers of little Paul's bedroom were so fair a sample of the young gentlemen in general, that the most elastic among them contemplated the arrival of those festive periods with genteel resignation.

Dickens did not wish to lay all the blame for the stupid process of cramming on the teachers. He properly revealed to parents that they were even more to blame than the teachers, because they got what they demanded. Doctor Blimber summed up the whole philosophy of the adulthood of his time in regard to a child's education when he said to his daughter, "Bring him on, Cornelia! Bring him on!"

The standard of knowledge cramming fixed by parents and school boards is changing very slowly. Even yet a teacher's success is measured and his chances of re-engagement decided in most places by the answer to the question, "How does he bring the children on?"

When asked by Doctor Blimber what he wished his little sickly son to learn, Mr. Dombey answered, "Oh, everything."

When Paul learned easily, his father pressed for more studies; and because Briggs was dull, his father demanded that he be driven harder at school, and made the poor boy's life miserable at home by tedious lessons during the holidays.

The uncle who made Tozer wretched by asking him unexpected questions on all occasions is a type of an ogre who sometimes blights the lives of children still.

Dickens had a beautiful sympathy with childhood in its sufferings not merely on account of deliberate cruelty and neglect, but because of the burdens placed upon it by adults who, with the best intentions, robbed it of its natural rights of joyousness and freedom.

Whenever Doctor Blimber was informed that Paul was "old-fashioned" or "peculiar," he said, as he had said when Paul first came, that study would do much; and he also said, as he said on that occasion, "Bring him on, Cornelia! Bring him on!"

Just before the close of the term Paul fainted and had to be carried to his room, and after an examination the physician advised Doctor Blimber to "release the young gentleman from his books just now, the vacation being so near at hand."

It was so very considerate to release him from study, when he was utterly unable to study any longer.

At the close of the school party when he was leaving—

> Cornelia, taking both Paul's hands in hers, said, "Dombey, Dombey, you have always been my favourite pupil. God bless you!" And it showed, Paul thought, how easily one might do injustice to a person; for Miss Blimber meant it—though she *was* a Forcer.

Paul never returned to school. His life was sacrificed to his father's desire to have him "learn everything."

In a brief look at the results of Doctor Blimber's teaching, Dickens tersely outlines three common results of cramming:

> Mr. Tozer, now a young man of lofty stature, in Wellington boots, was so extremely full of antiquity as to be nearly on a par with a genuine ancient Roman in his knowledge of English; a triumph that affected his good parents with the tenderest emotions, and caused the father and mother of Mr. Briggs (whose learning, like an ill-arranged luggage, was so tightly packed that he couldn't get at anything he wanted) to hide their diminished heads. The fruit laboriously gathered from the tree of knowledge by this latter young gentleman, in fact, had been subjected to so much pressure, that it had become a kind of intellectual Norfolk Biffin, and had nothing of its original form or flavour remaining. Master Bitherstone now, on whom the forcing system had the happier and not uncommon effect of leaving no impression whatever, when the forcing apparatus ceased to work was in a much more comfortable plight; and being then on shipboard, bound for Bengal, found himself forgetting with such admirable rapidity, that it was doubtful whether his declensions of noun-substantives would hold out to the end of the voyage.

Dickens, in his very able description of Doctor Blimber's school, directs attention to nearly every phase of the evils of cramming. Toots is an illustration of the destruction of mental power by the "hard mathematics" and other subjects, when they are taught improperly. It is a serious result of an educational system, when the brightest young men "cease to have brains when they begin to have whiskers."

Paul's experience is used to show the terrible physical evils of cramming in any life, especially in the life of a delicate child. Paul was killed by his father and Doctor Blimber. He should have lived.

Cornelia's aversion to live languages and her delight in "digging up the dead languages like a ghoul," and the address presented to Doctor Blimber "which contained very little of the mother tongue, but fifteen quotations from the Latin and seven from the Greek," were intended as a protest against paying too much attention to the classics to the neglect of other studies. He returned to this subject again in Bleak House. Richard Carstone "could make Latin verses," but although his powers were naturally excellent he was a complete failure in life. He was not educated properly, notwithstanding his ability to make Latin verses.

Mr. Feeder is the perfect type of a mechanical crammer, "a sort of barrel organ with a little list of tunes at which he was continually working, over and over again, without any variation." What suggestiveness there is in the sentence "Mr. Feeder had his Virgil stop on, and was grinding that tune to four young gentlemen"!

"Bewilder the young ideas of Doctor Blimber's young gentlemen," used to be considered too strong a criticism, but modern psychology fully sustains Dickens in his view. "Arrested development" is well understood now to result from too much grinding at any one subject or department of a subject, from the monotonous drill of the crammer, or from directing the child's attention too much to any one study.

The influence of uninteresting study on the spirits was clear to Dickens. There is inspiration and physical advantage of a decided character in the successful study of an interesting subject—interesting to the child, of course—if the process of study includes the true self-activity of the child. There is blight, and nervous irritation, and "carking anxiety," if the child works under compulsion at the dead matter of study. No wonder the young gentlemen at Doctor Blimber's took leave of their spirits in three weeks, and passed through the subsequent stages of deeper gloom described by Dickens. They had none of the joy of living interest in their study, none of the vital enthusiasm connected with independent thought, none of the health that comes from pleasant occupation, none of the happiness that is found in self-activity alone.

One of the best criticisms of wrong methods of teaching done by Mr. Feeder is the criticism of the method of teaching literature. "At the end of the first twelvemonth the boys had arrived at the conclusion, from which they never afterward departed, that all the fancies of the poets, and the lessons of the sages, were a mere collection of words and grammar, and had no other meaning in the world." There are high schools yet in which more attention is paid to the "words and grammar" than to the sacred and inspiring thought of the author.

A professor in one of the leading educational institutions of America travelled in Scotland with his daughters. They were graduates of a high school. He observed with deep regret that they visited the mountains, and valleys, and rivers, and islands, and battlefields, and cathedrals of the land, that to him had been filled with sacred interests by the writings of Scott, and saw them all without emotion. One day he said to them: "Why are you not interested here? To me every foot of ground here is full of living memories. Scott describes it in The Lady of the Lake." One of them explained the reason. "Oh!" she said, "we're sick of Scott; we had enough of him in the high school."

There are Feeders yet who profane the temple of literature; who never connect the souls of their pupils with the soul life of the authors they study. Very few of the graduates of high schools have learned the high art of loving literature for its beauty and ennobling thought, fewer still have learned how to dig successfully in the rich mines of wealth that literature contains, and even a smaller number have learned to transmute the revelations of literature into character and new revelations in life or richer literature for the happiness and culture of coming generations. We may yet learn from Dickens.

Tozer became an antique pedant, learned but not educated.

Briggs grew to be dull and heavy-witted, and had his "knowledge so tightly packed that he couldn't get at anything he wanted."

Bitherstone was one of the few fortunate fellows who are gifted with natural power to pass through the cramming system without being affected seriously in any way. They get little, if any, good, and they speedily forget the wrongs inflicted upon them and the learning with which their teachers attempted to cram them.

Briggs showed the evil effects of cramming in the destruction of individuality. "His fruit had nothing of its original flavour remaining." This is one of the general charges made against Doctor Blimber's forcing establishment, or hothouse. "Nature was of no consequence at all. No matter what a young gentleman was intended to bear, Doctor Blimber made him bear to pattern somehow or other." The destruction of selfhood was the great evil of the old system of teaching.

Another important criticism made by Dickens of the hothouse system is worthy of special attention by educators. He recognised the evil effects of giving any study or work to children, that is naturally adapted to a later stage of their development. The development of children is always arrested when the work of a higher stage is forced into a lower stage of their growth. The true evolution of the child consists in a growth through a series of progressive and interdependent stages. This was not recognised in the educational system Dickens desired to improve. It is not yet recognised to a very large extent in practice. "All the boys blew before their time," in Doctor Blimber's school. "The doctor, in some partial confusion of ideas, regarded the young gentlemen as if they were all doctors, and were born grown up."

Dickens was so careful to make his names and terms express volumes of meaning that he probably meant the phrase "mathematical gooseberries" to be especially significant. The fact that they were grown on "mere sprouts of bushes," and as a consequence were "very sour ones, too," reveals the philosophy since made so clear by Doctor Harris, that early "drilling" in arithmetic has been one of the prolific causes of arrested development in children. The appeal against the common practice of growing "every description of Greek and Latin vegetable" *from "dry twigs of boys"* was comprehensive and timely. They were not merely twigs, but dry twigs in whom the sap had not begun to circulate freely. No expressions, no volumes, could state the evil of untimely cramming more clearly than this group of phrases used by Dickens in describing Doctor Blimber's school.

"The frostiest circumstances" is another of the thought-laden phrases, which was evidently intended to warn teachers against the mistake of trying to produce any intellectual fruit at untimely periods of the child's development. "Wintry growth" means unseasonable or untimely development.

The condemnation of the feeling shown by Paul in parting from Florence, and the Doctor's cold-blooded observation, "Never mind; we shall substitute new cares and new impressions, Mr. Dombey, very shortly," were intended to show how utterly the knowledge cramming ideal had prevented the recognition of the fundamental fact that feeling is the basis and the battery power of intellectual force and energy. The same principle is taught by Cornelia's shock at Paul's affection for old Glubb, and her father's summary settlement of the case, when he realized that the little child was intensely affectionate and sympathetic. "Ha!" said the Doctor, shaking his head, "this—is—bad, but study will do much."

Dickens deals in a most thorough manner with the absolute wickedness of neglecting, or attempting to smother feeling in the training and education of children in Hard Times. He undoubtedly received his clear conceptions relating to the intellectual value of feeling from Froebel's writings.

The bad effects of cramming on the physical constitution of children are pointed out in "the convulsive grasping of their foreheads" by the two boys engaged in solving mathematical problems. Nervous exhaustion is here plainly indicated. They were "very feverish," too, and poor Briggs was in even a worse condition, for "he was in a state of stupefaction and was flabby and quite cold." Both Briggs and Tozer frightened Paul the first night he tried to sleep in their room by talking Latin and Greek in their dreams. Paul thought they were swearing. Education should never interfere with a child's sleep, either with its soundness or its duration. Even the boys told Paul on the first day of his school life that he would need a good constitution to withstand the strain at Doctor Blimber's.

The exhaustive and exasperating practice of piling up arrears of work, so naturally connected with cramming—in fact, so essential a part of the unnatural process—comes in for its share of condemnation, too. One of the boys, "whose face was like a dirty window, from much crying, was endeavouring to flounder through a hopeless number of lines." The friends of Briggs were constantly in terror "lest they should find his hat floating on a pond and an unfinished exercise on the bank."

The same practice of charging up arrears of work is condemned in David Copperfield by associating it with the hateful Murdstones.

The crammer's absolute indifference and contempt for any semblance of correlation in studies is revealed by Cornelia's action in giving him a collection of books on his first morning before school with instructions to study them at the places she had marked for him. No wonder that "when poor Paul had spelled out number two he found he had no idea of number one; fragments whereof afterward obtruded themselves into number three, which sidled into number four, which grafted itself on to number two—so that whether twenty Romuluses made a Remus, or hic hæc hoc was troy weight, or a verb always agreed with an ancient Briton, or three times four was Taurus, a bull, were open questions with him."

Whenever words are given before thought, or as a substitute for thought, and without definite relationship to the thought already in the mind, they lie in the mind as unrelated, and therefore unavailable knowledge.

A boy in London had received considerable historical teaching, and his mind had made a certain kind of unity out of the confused mass. When asked at his final examination "What he knew about Cromwell," he answered: "Cromwell interfered with the Irish, and he was put in prison. When he was in prison he wrote the Pilgrim's Progress, and he afterward married Mrs. O'Shea."

This was equalled by the other boy who wrote at an examination: "Wolsey was a famous general who fought in the Crimean War, and who, after being decapitated several times, said to Cromwell: 'If I had served you as you have served me I would not have been deserted in my old age.'"

Paul's studies were always dark and crooked to him till Florence bought copies of his books and studied them, and by patient sympathy made all that had been dark light, and all that had been crooked straight.

The habit of giving definitions of abstractions to children, and expecting the definitions alone to be comprehended by children, is held up to deserved ridicule in the explanation of the word "analysis" to Paul, when Cornelia proposed to read the analysis of his character.

"If my recollection serves me, the word analysis, as opposed to synthesis, is thus defined by Walker: 'The resolution of an object, whether of the senses or of the intellect, into its first elements.' As opposed to synthesis, you observe. *Now* you know what analysis is, Dombey."

How perfectly simple and clear and expanding this would be to a child's mind! Dickens says: "Dombey didn't seem absolutely blinded by the light let in upon his intellect, but he made Miss Blimber a little bow."

What loose habits of thought, and how much hypocrisy and mental vagueness are caused by using words instead of realities in the early teaching of children, and then asking them if they understand what we have been telling them! The "little bow" has usually a demoralizing effect.

It is a mere farce to call the committing to memory of definitions "education."

Whatever the subjects, it is a dwarfing process, whether the definitions are memorized at home or at school, silently, by oral repetition, or by singing them. All definition learning as the origin of thought is certain to destroy interest and arrest development and lead to inaccuracy of thought. Miss Le Row's collection of blunders made by children could never have been made if the children had been taught properly.

Such mistakes as "The body is mostly composed of water, and about one half of avaricious tissue" or "Parasite, a kind of umbrella," or "Emphasis, putting more distress on one word than on another," should suggest to teachers the absurdity of committing definitions to memory. It is one of the weakest forms of cramming, and is most ridiculous and least useful when the memorizing is done by simultaneous oral repetition.

Hard Times exposes the evils of cramming in the teaching practised in the normal school in which Mr. M'Choakumchild was trained, and in the definition repetition as given by Bitzer, and so highly praised by Mr. Gradgrind:

> "Bitzer, your definition of a horse:"
>
> "Quadruped, graminivorous. Forty teeth, namely, twenty-four grinders, four eyeteeth, and twelve incisors. Sheds coat in the spring; in marshy countries sheds hoofs, too. Hoofs hard, but requiring to be shod with iron. Age known by marks in mouth."

How clear this would make the conception of a horse to a man who had never seen one! Sissy Jupe, too, is used to show the failure of cramming to educate a girl of quick intellect and strong emotions. She could not be crammed.

> M'Choakumchild reported that she had a very dense head for figures; that, once possessed with a general idea of the globe, she took the smallest conceivable interest in its exact measurements; that she was extremely slow in the acquisition of dates, unless some pitiful incident happened to be connected therewith; that she would burst into tears on being required (by the mental process) immediately to name the cost of two hundred and forty-seven muslin caps at fourteenpence half-penny; that she was as low down in the school as low as could be; that after eight weeks of induction into the elements of political economy, she had only yesterday been set right by a prattler three feet high, for returning to the question, "What is the first principle of this science?" the absurd answer, "To do unto others as I would that they should do unto me."
>
> Mr. Gradgrind observed, shaking his head, that all this was very bad; that it showed the necessity of infinite grinding at the mill of knowledge as per system, schedule, blue book, report, and tabular statements A to Z; and that Jupe "must be kept to it." So Jupe was kept to it, and became low-spirited, but no wiser.

Dickens makes the artist in Somebody's Luggage say:

> "Who are you passing every day at your competitive excruciations? The fortunate candidates whose heads and livers you have turned upside down for life? Not you, you are really passing the crammers and coaches."

And Jemmy Lirriper, in describing his teacher, said: "Oh, he was a Tartar! Keeping the boys up to the mark, holding examinations once a month, lecturing upon all sorts of subjects at all sorts of times, and knowing everything in the world out of a book."

Dickens saw the evils of competitive examinations more clearly than many educators do two generations after him.

When educators in schools, colleges, and universities learn a better way to promote pupils, to classify men and women and to rank them at graduation, than by holding promotion and graduation examinations cramming will be of no use, and there shall be no more cramming.

Dickens was right as usual. The crammers and coaches are those who are tested by "competitive excruciations"; and how those who force through most students boast and strut and lord it over the less successful crammers and coaches on commencement days and other public occasions! What a misleading mockery examinations are as tests of power and character!

Few even of Dickens's phrases contain such a condensation of fact and philosophy as the phrase "whose heads and livers you have turned upside down for life." Few phrases deserve more careful consideration from educators.

Dickens makes the effect on the head still more startling by the description of Miss Wozenham's brother in Mrs. Lirriper's Legacy. "Miss Wozenham out of her small income had to support a brother that had had the misfortune to soften his brain against the hard mathematics."

In the same story he laughs at the practical results of language cramming usually done in the schools:

> And the way in which Jemmy spoke his French was a real charm. It was often wanted of him, for whenever anybody spoke a syllable to me I says "Noncomprenny, you're very kind but it's no use—Now Jemmy!" and then Jemmy he fires away at 'em lovely, the only thing wanting in Jemmy's French being as it appeared to me that he hardly ever understood a word of what they said to him, which made it scarcely of the use it might have been.

Dickens attempted to picture the feelings of a boy toward his teachers in the days when cramming was almost universally practised in the story of Lieutenant-Colonel Robin Redforth, aged nine. When the Latin master was captured, he was saved by Captain Boldheart from the punishment of death to which he was condemned by the crew of The Beauty. Captain Boldheart had been one of his pupils, and he said: "Without taking your life, I must yet forever deprive you of the power of spiting other boys. I shall turn you adrift in this boat. You will find in her two oars, a compass, a bottle of rum, a small cask of water, a piece of pork, a bag of biscuit, and my Latin grammar. Go! and spite the natives if you can find any."

When he afterward released him from the savages who were about to eat him, he granted him his life for the second time on condition:

"1. That he should never under any circumstances presume to teach any boy anything any more.

"2. That, if taken back to England, he should pass his life in travelling to find out boys who wanted their exercises done, and should do their exercises for nothing, and never say a word about it."

When it finally became necessary to hang the Latin master, Boldheart "impressively pointed out to him that this is what spiters come to."

There are many kinds of cram that yet pass as fairly respectable in schools and universities. When the teachers or the professors give notes to be copied by the pupils and memorized, they are cramming. When teachers are storing the memories of children with facts, tables, dates, etc., to be used at some future time, they are cramming. All memorizing by repetition of words, even if they are understood, is cram, if the pupil can work the thought into his life by repetition of process or of operation. Words can never take the place of self-activity, nor even of activity.

So long as knowledge storing is placed above character development, examinations by "examiners" will retain their power for evil, and so long as such examinations are held cramming will continue.

All processes that attempt to educate from without inward, instead of from within outward, are in the last analysis cram. The selfhood must be active in going out for the new knowledge. The child must himself be originative, directive, and executive in the learning process if cram is to be avoided completely. This is the only sure way to secure perfect apperception, and without apperception the new knowledge lies dormant, if not dead, and unrelated in the memory until it disappears, as did Bitherstone's. His declensions, according to Dickens, were not likely to last out his journey from England to India.

CHAPTER VI.

FREE CHILDHOOD.

Adulthood can never be truly free till childhood is free. Perfect freedom can not be developed in a soul filled with the apperceptive experiences of tyranny. No man is fully free in the freest country in the world who wishes to dominate even his child. The practice of tyranny develops the tyrant. Guiding control is entirely different from domination.

Dickens taught the doctrine of a rich, full, free childhood from the time he wrote Nicholas Nickleby in 1839.

> Even the sunburned faces of gipsy children, half naked though they be, suggest a drop of comfort. It is a pleasant thing to see that the sun has been there; to know that the air and light are on them every day; to feel that they *are* children, and lead children's lives; that if their pillows be damp, it is with the dews of heaven, and not with tears; that the limbs of their girls are free, and that they are not crippled by distortions, imposing an unnatural and horrible penance upon their sex; that their lives are spent, from day to day, at least among the waving trees, and not in the midst of dreadful engines which make young children old before they know what childhood is, and give them the exhaustion and infirmity of age, without, like age, the privilege to die. God send that old nursery tales were true, and that gipsies stole such children by the score!

If he had written nothing but this exquisite quotation from Nicholas Nickleby he would have deserved recognition as an educator. It shows a clear insight into the great principles of physical freedom, intellectual freedom, and spiritual freedom.

In The Old Curiosity Shop he made the world sympathize with a child who lived with an old man. He gives the keynote to this fundamental thought of the book in the opening chapter:

> It always grieves me to contemplate the initiation of children into the ways of life when they are scarcely more than infants. It checks their confidence and simplicity—two of the best qualities that Heaven gives them—and demands that they share our sorrows before they are capable of entering into our enjoyments.

Little Nell had the sadness of a lonely childhood, though her grandfather lived with but the one aim of making her happy.

In Martin Chuzzlewit—

> Tom Pinch's sister was governess in a family, a lofty family; perhaps the wealthiest brass and copper founder's family known to mankind. They lived at Camberwell; in a house so big and fierce that its mere outside, like the outside of a giant's castle, struck terror into vulgar minds and made bold persons quail.

When Mr. Pecksniff and his daughters went to visit Miss Pinch she

> was at that moment instructing her eldest pupil; to wit, a premature little woman of thirteen years old, who had already arrived at such a pitch of whalebone and education that she had nothing girlish about her, which was a source of great rejoicing to all her relations and friends.

One of the unsolved mysteries is the fact that such a large proportion of parents are so anxious to have their children grow up. The desire may be understood when poverty longs for the time when the little hands may help to win bread, but that wealthy parents should hasten the premature state of adulthood in their children is incomprehensible.

A great deal of attention is paid to the blunder of robbing children of real childhood in Dombey and Son, which is so rich in several departments of educational philosophy. Doctor Blimber regarded the young gentlemen "as if they were born grown up."

Paul's life and death were intended as warnings to ambitious parents. Florence was robbed of a true childhood by her mother's death and her father's lack of sympathy. Briggs and Tozer had no childhood; they were persecuted by the ingenious and ignorantly learned adults at home during vacations, as well as by Doctor Blimber during school time; so that "Tozer said, indeed, that choosing between two evils, he would rather stay at school than go home."

Poor Bitherstone had no childhood. He was shipped away from his parents in India to the respectable hell conducted by that widely known and highly reputed child trainer Mrs. Pipchin.

Poor little Miss Pankey spent a great deal of her time in Mrs. Pipchin's "correctional dungeon." What a mercy it would be if all such unfortunate children could be stolen by the gipsies!

Mrs. Pipchin's theory taught "that it was wrong to encourage a child's mind to develop and expand itself like a young flower, but to open it by force like an oyster."

When Doctor Blimber asked Paul, six-year-old Paul, "if he would like them to make a man of him," the child replied:

"I had rather be a child."

One of Dickens's most successful hits at the common philosophy, that the desired adult characteristics must be developed in childhood in their adult forms, was made in describing Mrs. Tozer's effort to qualify Tozer for the position of a clergyman by making him wear a stiff, starched necktie while he was a boy.

When Edith upbraided her mother for practically compelling her to marry Mr. Dombey, her mother asked angrily:

> "What do you mean? Haven't you from a child— —"
>
> "A child!" said Edith, looking at her; "when was I a child? What childhood did you ever leave to me? I was a woman—artful, designing, mercenary, laying snares for men—before I knew myself or you, or even understood the base and wretched aim of every new display I learned. You gave birth to a woman. Look upon her. She is in her pride to-night."
>
> "You talk strangely to-night, Edith, to your own mother."
>
> "It seems so to me; stranger to me than to you," said Edith. "But my education was completed long ago. I am too old now and have fallen too low, by degrees, to take a new course, and to stop yours, and to help myself. The germ of all that purifies a woman's breast, and makes it true and good, has never stirred in mine, and I have nothing else to sustain me when I despise myself."

Later, on the night before she was to marry Mr. Dombey, she said:

> "Oh, mother, mother, if you had but left me to my natural heart when I too was a girl—a younger girl than Florence—how different I might have been!"

Bleak House gives Dickens's most striking picture of the deterioration resulting from giving no real childhood to children for a series of generations.

> During the whole time consumed in the slow growth of this family tree, the house of Smallweed, always early to go to business and late to marry, has strengthened itself in its practical character, has discarded all amusements, discountenanced all storybooks, fairy tales, fictions, and fables, and banished all levities whatsoever. Hence the gratifying fact that it has had no child born to it, and that the complete little men and women whom it has produced have been observed to bear a likeness to old monkeys with something depressing on their minds.
>
> There has been only one child in the Smallweed family for several generations. Little old men and women there have been, but no child, until Mr. Smallweed's grandmother, now living, became weak in her intellect, and fell (for the first time) into a childish state. With such infantine graces as a total want of observation, memory, understanding, and interest, and an eternal disposition to fall asleep over the fire and into it, Mr. Smallweed's grandmother has undoubtedly brightened the family.

There could be no more awful picture than that of a family in which for a series of generations the children had been, through heredity and training, made "little old men and women," who were never permitted to indulge in any childish plays, or to enjoy any stories, or in any way have a genuine childhood, so that they not only came to look like monkeys, but "like monkeys with something depressing on their minds"; and in which the only child for several generations had been Mr. Smallweed's grandmother, when she became weak in intellect and "fell (for the first time) into a childish state."

In The Haunted House the wretched child who came to Mr. Redlaw's room is described as "a baby savage, a young monster, a child who had never been a child."

Dickens made his greatest plea for a free childhood in Hard Times. The whole of the educational part of the book condemns the training of Mr. Gradgrind, although he was an earnest, high-minded gentleman, whose supreme purpose was to train his family in the best possible way. Indeed Mr. Gradgrind was so sure he was right in his views regarding child training that he founded a school to teach the children of Coketown in accordance with what he believed to be correct principles.

Mr. Gradgrind is described as

> a kind cannon loaded to the muzzle with facts, and prepared to blow children clean out of the regions of childhood at one discharge. He seemed a galvanizing apparatus, too, charged with a grim mechanical substitute for the tender young imaginations that were to be stormed away.
>
> There were five young Gradgrinds, and they were models every one. They had been lectured at from their tenderest years; coursed, like little hares. Almost as soon as they could run alone they had been made to run to the lecture room. The first object with which they had an association or of which they had a remembrance was a large blackboard with a dry ogre chalking ghastly white figures on it.
>
> Not that they knew, by name or nature, anything about an ogre. Fact forbid! I only use the word to express a monster in a lecturing castle, with heaven knows how many heads manipulated into one, taking childhood captive, and dragging it into gloomy statistical dens by the hair.
>
> No little Gradgrind had ever seen a face in the moon; it was up in the moon before it could speak distinctly. No little Gradgrind had ever learned the silly jingle, "Twinkle, twinkle, little star; how I wonder what you are"; it had never known wonder on the subject, having at five years old dissected the Great Bear like a Professor Owen and driven Charles's Wain like a locomotive engine driver. No little Gradgrind had ever associated a cow in a field with that famous cow with the crumpled horn who tossed the dog

> who worried the cat who killed the rat who ate the malt, or with that yet more famous cow who swallowed Tom Thumb; it had never heard of those celebrities, and had only been introduced to a cow as a graminivorous ruminating quadruped with several stomachs.

The effect of preventing all kinds of enjoyment for his children in their own home was that they naturally sought for enjoyment surreptitiously in a way of which their father disapproved. But when a man disapproves of legitimate amusements in his family his condemnation of what is improper will have little weight with his children.

When Mr. Gradgrind was going home from the school examination he had to pass near the circus, and he was amazed to find his daughter Louisa and his son Thomas stealing a view of the performance.

> Phenomenon almost incredible though distinctly seen, what did he then behold but his own metallurgical Louisa peeping with all her might through a hole in a deal board, and his own mathematical Thomas abasing himself on the ground to catch but a hoof of the graceful equestrian Tyrolean flower act!
>
> Dumb with amazement, Mr. Gradgrind crossed to the spot where his family was thus disgraced, laid his hand upon each erring child, and said:
>
> "Louisa! Thomas!"
>
> Both rose, red and disconcerted. But Louisa looked at her father with more boldness than Thomas did. Indeed, Thomas did not look at him, but gave himself up to be taken home like a machine.
>
> "In the name of wonder, idleness, and folly!" said Mr. Gradgrind, leading each away by a hand; "what do you do here?"
>
> "Wanted to see what it was like," returned Louisa shortly.
>
> "What it was like?"
>
> "Yes, father."
>
> There was an air of jaded sullenness in them both, and particularly in the girl; yet, struggling through the dissatisfaction of her face, there was a light with nothing to rest upon, a fire with nothing to burn, a starved imagination keeping life in itself somehow, which brightened its expression. Not with the brightness natural to cheerful youth, but with uncertain, eager, doubtful flashes, which had something painful in them, analogous to the changes on a blind face groping its way.
>
> "You! Thomas and you, to whom the circle of the sciences is open, Thomas and you, who may be said to be replete with facts, Thomas and you, who have been trained to mathematical exact-

ness, Thomas and you, here!" cried Mr. Gradgrind. "In this degraded position! I am amazed."

"I was tired, father. I have been tired a long time," said Louisa.

"Tired? Of what?" asked the astonished father.

"I don't know of what—of everything, I think."

When they reached home, Mr. Gradgrind in an injured tone said to Mrs. Gradgrind, after telling her where he had found the children:

"I should as soon have expected to find my children reading poetry."

"Dear me," whimpered Mrs. Gradgrind. "How can you, Louisa and Thomas! I wonder at you. As if, with my head in its present throbbing state, you couldn't go and look at the shells and minerals and things provided for you, instead of circuses!" said Mrs. Gradgrind. "You know as well as I do, no young people have circus masters, or keep circuses in cabinets, or attend lectures about circuses. What can you possibly want to know of circuses then? I am sure you have enough to do, if that's what you want. With my head in its present state, I couldn't remember the mere names of half the facts you have got to attend to."

"That's the reason!" pouted Louisa.

"Don't tell me that's the reason, because it can be nothing of the sort," said Mrs. Gradgrind. "Go and be something-ological directly."

After Louisa had married Mr. Bounderby, Tom and Mr. Harthouse were discussing her one evening, and Tom said she thought a great deal when she was alone:

"Ay, ay? Has resources of her own," said Harthouse.

"Not so much of that as you may suppose," returned Tom; "for our governor had her crammed with all sorts of dry bones and sawdust. It's his system."

"Formed his daughter on his own model?" suggested Harthouse.

"His daughter? Ah! and everybody else. Why, he formed me that way," said Tom.

"Impossible!"

"He did though," said Tom, shaking his head. "I mean to say, Mr. Harthouse, that when I first left home and went to old Bounderby's, I was as flat as a warming-pan, and knew no more about life than any oyster does."

Dickens describes a visit Louisa made to her father's house, and shows how little of the true home feeling was stirred in her heart, as she approached the place, where she should have had a happy childhood.

> Neither, as she approached her old home now, did any of the best influences of old home descend upon her. Her remembrances of home and childhood were remembrances of the drying up of every spring and fountain in her young heart as it gushed out. The golden waters were not there. They were flowing for the fertilization of the land where grapes are gathered from thorns, and figs from thistles.

When her father proposed to Louisa that she should marry Mr. Bounderby, she said:

> "The baby preference that even I have heard of as common among children has never had its innocent resting place in my breast. You have been so careful of me, that I never had a child's heart. You have trained me so well, that I never dreamed a child's dream. You have dealt so wisely with me, father, from my cradle to this hour, that I never had a child's belief or a child's fear."

Mr. Gradgrind was delighted at his apparent success. He could not see, he was so practical and so self-opinionated, that her heart was breaking while she was yielding with external calmness.

But the reaping time came soon. Mr. Harthouse, young, attractive, and unscrupulous, made love to Louisa, and finally persuaded her to run away with him. Unable to resist the temptation in her own strength, she fled to her father's house through an awful storm.

> The thunder was rolling into distance, and the rain was pouring down like a deluge, when the door of his room opened. He looked round the lamp upon his table, and saw with amazement his eldest daughter.
>
> "Louisa!"
>
> "Father, I want to speak to you."
>
> "What is the matter? What is it? I conjure you, Louisa, tell me what is the matter."
>
> She dropped into a chair before him, and put her cold hand on his arm.
>
> "Father, you have trained me from my cradle."
>
> "Yes, Louisa."
>
> "I curse the hour in which I was born to such a destiny."
>
> He looked at her in doubt and dread, vacantly repeating, "Curse the hour! Curse the hour!"
>
> "How could you give me life, and take from me all the inap-

> preciable things that raise it from the state of conscious death? Where are the graces of my soul? Where are the sentiments of my heart? What have you done, O father, what have you done, with the garden that should have bloomed once, in this great wilderness here?"
>
> She struck herself with both her hands upon her bosom.
>
> "If it had ever been here, its ashes alone would save me from the void in which my whole life sinks."
>
> He tightened his hold in time to prevent her sinking on the floor, but she cried out in a terrible voice, "I shall die if you hold me! Let me fall upon the ground!" And he laid her down there, and saw the pride of his heart and the triumph of his system lying, an insensible heap, at his feet.

In the Schoolboy's Story, the boy who was to have no holiday at home was invited to spend his holidays with "Old Cheeseman" and Mrs. Cheeseman.

> So I went to their delightful house, and was as happy as I could possibly be. They understand how to conduct themselves toward boys, *they* do. When they take a boy to the play, for instance, they *do* take him. They don't go in after it's begun, or come out before it's over. They know how to bring a boy up, too. Look at their own! Though he is very little as yet, what a capital boy he is! Why, my next favourite to Mrs. Cheeseman and Old Cheeseman is young Cheeseman.

When Dickens came to his last book his heart was still full of sympathy with the child.

Edwin Drood said to Mr. Jasper: "Life for you is a plum with the natural bloom on. It hasn't been over-carefully wiped off for *you*."

In the same book Mr. Grewgious is described:

> He was an arid, sandy man, who, if he had been put into a grinding mill, looked as if he would have ground immediately into high-dried snuff. He had a scanty flat crop of hair, in colour and consistency like some very mangy yellow fur tippet; it was so unlike hair, that it must have been a wig, but for the stupendous improbability of anybody's voluntarily sporting such a head. The little play of feature that his face presented was cut deep into it, in a few hard curves that made it more like work; and he had certain notches in his forehead, which looked as though Nature had been about to touch them into sensibility or refinement, when she had impatiently thrown away the chisel, and said, "I really can not be worried to finish off this man; let him go as he is."

He tried to explain the reason for his peculiarities to Rosa:

> "I mean," he explained, "that young ways were never my

> ways. I was the only offspring of parents far advanced in life, and I half believe I was born advanced in life myself. No personality is intended toward the name you will so soon change, when I remark that while the general growth of people seem to have come into existence buds, I seem to have come into existence a chip. I was a chip—and a very dry one—when I first became aware of myself."

Dickens takes a front rank among the educators who have tried to save the child from "child-quellers," and preserve for them the right to a free, rich, real childhood. The saddest sight in the world to him was a child such as he pictured in A Tale of Two Cities: "The children of St. Antoine had ancient faces and grave voices."

In Barbox Brothers Mr. Jackson said of himself: "I am, to myself, an unintelligible book, with the earlier chapters all torn out and thrown away. My childhood had no grace of childhood, my youth had no charm of youth, and what can be expected from such a lost beginning?"

Dickens tried to save all children from such a beginning.

CHAPTER VII.

INDIVIDUALITY.

Dickens began to write definitely about individuality in Martin Chuzzlewit in 1844. Martin described a company he met in America "who were so strangely devoid of individual traits of character that any one of them might have changed minds with the other and nobody would have found it out."

In David Copperfield he makes Traddles, who was trained by Mr. Creakle, say: "I have no invention at all, not a particle. I suppose there never was a young man with less originality than I have."

David himself said sagely: "I have encountered some fine ladies and gentlemen who might as well have been born caterpillars."

David emphasizes the phase of individuality that teaches the power of each individual to do some special good, when he said to Martha when she spoke of the river as the end of her useless life:

"In the name of the great Judge, before whom you and all of us must stand at his dread time, dismiss that terrible idea! We can all do some good, if we will."

In Bleak House Sir Leicester Dedlock is represented as of opinion that he should at least think for every one in connection with his estate.

> The present representative of the Dedlocks is an excellent master. He supposes all his dependents to be utterly bereft of individual characters, intentions, or opinions, and is persuaded that he was born to supersede the necessity of their having any. If he were to make a discovery to the contrary, he would be simply stunned—would never recover himself, most likely, except to gasp and die.

The same absolute contempt for the individuality of the poor is ridiculed in The Chimes. Sir Joseph Bowley is a type of the English squire who used to act on the assumption that he had to care for the workmen on his estate, and the poor of his neighbourhood, as he did for his horses and other animals.

> "I do my duty as the Poor Man's Friend and Father; and I endeavour to educate his mind by inculcating on all occasions the one great moral lesson which that class requires—that is, entire Dependence on myself. They have no business whatever with—with themselves. If wicked and designing persons tell them otherwise, and they become impatient and discontented, and are guilty of insubordinate conduct and black-hearted ingratitude—which

> is undoubtedly the case—I am their Friend and Father still. It is so ordained. It is in the nature of things. They needn't trouble themselves to think about anything. I will think for them; I know what is good for them; I am their perpetual parent. Such is the dispensation of an all-wise Providence."

It is strange that men so commonly ascribe to Providence the dreadful conditions which have resulted from man's ignorance and selfishness, and which Providence intended man to reform.

Esther, in Bleak House, speaking of the influence of the chancery suit on Richard Carstone, said:

> "The character of much older and steadier people may be even changed by the circumstances surrounding them. It would be too much to expect that a boy's, in its formation, should be the subject of such influences, and escape them."
>
> I felt this to be true; though, if I may venture to mention what I thought besides, I thought it much to be regretted that Richard's education had not counteracted those influences or directed his character. He had been eight years at a public school, and had learned, I understood, to make Latin verses of several sorts, in the most admirable manner. But I never heard that it had been anybody's business to find out what his natural bent was, or where his failings lay, or to adapt any kind of knowledge to *him*. *He* had been adapted to the verses, and had learned the art of making them to such perfection, that if he had remained at school until he was of age I suppose he could only have gone on making them over and over again, unless he had enlarged his education by forgetting how to do it. Still, although I had no doubt that they were very beautiful, and very improving, and very sufficient for a great many purposes of life, and always remembered all through life, I did doubt whether Richard would not have profited by some one studying him a little, instead of his studying them quite so much.

Richard was one of those unstable men who have good abilities, but who do not use them persistently in the accomplishment of any one purpose, and who never seem to find the sphere for which they are best fitted. They are man-products, not God-products. When Richard, after several attempts to work at other things with high enthusiasm for a few weeks, decided to be a physician, Esther said:

> Mistrusting that he only came to this conclusion because, having never had much chance of finding out for himself what he was fitted for, and having never been guided to the discovery, he was taken with the newest idea, and was glad to get rid of the trouble of consideration, I wondered whether the Latin verses often ended in this, or whether Richard's was a solitary case.
>
> Richard very often came to see us while we remained in Lon-

> don (though he soon failed in his letter writing), and with his quick abilities, his good spirits, his good temper, his gaiety and freshness, was always delightful. But though I liked him more and more the better I knew him, I still felt more and more how much it was to be regretted that he had been educated in no habits of application and concentration. The system which had addressed him in exactly the same manner as it had addressed hundreds of other boys, all varying in character and capacity, had enabled him to dash through his tasks, always with fair credit, and often with distinction; but in a fitful, dazzling way that had confirmed his reliance on those very qualities in himself which it had been most desirable to direct and train. They were great qualities, without which no high place can be meritoriously won; but, like fire and water, though excellent servants, they were very bad masters. If they had been under Richard's direction, they would have been his friends; but Richard being under their direction, they became his enemies.

Any educational system that "addresses hundreds of boys exactly in the same manner" must destroy their individuality.

In Hard Times Tom Gradgrind became a low, degraded, sensual, dissipated criminal, and Dickens accounts for his failure by the unnatural restraint, constant oversight, and the strangling of his imagination in his cradle and afterward. In other words, the boy's selfhood never had a chance to develop, and every power he had naturally to make him strong, true, and independent had helped to work his ruin.

In Little Dorrit Mrs. General is herself a model to be avoided, and her system of training is ridiculed because she paid no attention whatever to the selfhood of her pupils except to conceal it artfully and prevent the recognition of any of the evils by which it was surrounded and which it should help to overcome.

> Mrs. General had no opinions. Her way of forming a mind was to prevent it from forming opinions. She had a little circular set of mental grooves or rails, on which she started little trains of other people's opinions, which never overtook one another and never got anywhere. Even her propriety could not dispute that there was impropriety in the world; but Mrs. General's way of getting rid of it was to put it out of sight, and make believe that there was no such thing. This was another of her ways of forming a mind—to cram all articles of difficulty into cupboards, lock them up, and say they had no existence. It was the easiest way and, beyond all comparison, the properest.
>
> Mrs. General was not to be told of anything shocking. Accidents, miseries, and offences were never to be mentioned before her. Passion was to go to sleep in the presence of Mrs. General, and blood was to change to milk and water. The little that was left

> in the world, when all these deductions were made, it was Mrs. General's province to varnish. In that formation process of hers, she dipped the smallest of brushes into the largest of pots, and varnished the surface of every object that came under consideration. The more cracked it was, the more Mrs. General varnished it.
>
> There was varnish in Mrs. General's voice, varnish in Mrs. General's touch, an atmosphere of varnish round Mrs. General's figure.

Dickens wished the training of the real inner selfhood, not the varnishing of the surface merely. Not what George Macdonald describes as "sandpapering a boy into a saint," but genuine character development by the working out of the selfhood in the improvement of its environment, physically, intellectually, and spiritually.

Briggs's education, in Dombey and Son, had been of such a character that "his intellectual fruit had nothing of its original flavour remaining." The character of his real selfhood had been destroyed, not developed, by his "education."

In Our Mutual Friend Mr. Podsnap is used as a type of the men who not only see no need for any person else forming opinions, but who take pains to prevent others forming opinions, so far as possible.

> As Mr. Podsnap stood with his back to the drawing-room fire, pulling up his shirt collar, like a veritable cock of the walk literally pluming himself in the midst of his possessions, nothing would have astonished him more than an intimation that Miss Podsnap, or any young person properly born and bred, could not be exactly put away like the plate, brought out like the plate, polished like the plate, counted, weighed, and valued like the plate. That such a young person could possibly have a morbid vacancy in the heart for anything younger than the plate, or less monotonous than the plate, or that such a young person's thoughts could try to scale the region bounded on the north, south, east, and west by the plate, was a monstrous imagination which he would on the spot have flourished into space.

Eugene Wrayburn's criticism of his father's habit of choosing professions for his sons almost as soon as they were born, or even before, without the slightest possible consideration for their natural aptitudes for the work to which they were assigned, is a severe attack on a condition which exists even yet through the failure of the schools or the homes to discover and reveal to boys and girls their highest powers, so that they may reach their best growth in school or college and choose the profession in which they can do most good and attain their most complete evolution. There is no better field for co-ordinate work by the home and the school than the joint study of the children to find their sphere of greatest power. Every child should be helped to find the sphere in which he can most successfully achieve the highest destiny for himself and for humanity.

Eugene Wrayburn's father extended his paternal care and forethought for his children not only by choosing their professions without regard for their selfhood, but by considerately selecting partners for his sons without regard for their individual tastes.

Eugene, speaking to Mortimer Lightwood, said:

> "My respected father has found, down in the parental neighbourhood, a wife for his not-generally-respected son."
>
> "With some money, of course?"
>
> "With some money, of course, or he would not have found her. My respected father—let me shorten the dutiful tautology by substituting in future M. R. F., which sounds military, and rather like the Duke of Wellington."
>
> "What an absurd fellow you are, Eugene!"
>
> "Not at all. I assure you. M. R. F. having always in the clearest manner provided (as he calls it) for his children by prearranging from the hour of the birth of each, and sometimes from an earlier period, what the devoted little victim's calling and course in life should be, M. R. F. prearranged for myself that I was to be the barrister I am (with the slight addition of an enormous practice, which has not accrued), and also the married man I am not."
>
> "The first you have often told me."
>
> "The first I have often told you. Considering myself sufficiently incongruous on my legal eminence, I have until now suppressed my domestic destiny. You know M. R. F., but not as well as I do. If you knew him as well as I do, he would amuse you."
>
> "Filially spoken, Eugene!"
>
> "Perfectly so, believe me; and with every sentiment of affectionate deference toward M. R. F. But if he amuses me, I can't help it. When my eldest brother was born, of course the rest of us knew (I mean the rest of us would have known, if we had been in existence) that he was heir to the family embarrassments—we call it before company the family estate. But when my second brother was going to be born by and by, 'This,' says M. R. F., 'is a little pillar of the church.' *Was* born, and became a pillar of the church—a very shaky one. My third brother appeared considerably in advance of his engagement to my mother; but M. R. F., not at all put out by surprise, instantly declared him a circumnavigator. Was pitchforked into the navy, but has not circumnavigated. I announced myself, and was disposed of with the highly satisfactory results embodied before you. When my younger brother was half an hour old, it was settled by M. R. F. that he should have a mechanical genius, and so on. Therefore I say M. R. F. amuses me."

In the same book Bradley Headstone's school is described as one of a system of schools in which "school buildings, school-teachers, and school pupils are all according to pattern, and all engendered in the light of the latest Gospel according to Monotony."

Bradley Headstone himself was a mechanical product of a mechanical system of uniformity that destroyed independence and individuality of character.

> Bradley Headstone, in his decent black coat and waistcoat, and decent white shirt, and decent formal black tie, and decent pantaloons of pepper and salt, with his decent silver watch in his pocket and its decent hair guard round his neck, looked a thoroughly decent young man of six-and-twenty. He was never seen in any other dress, and yet there was a certain stiffness in his manner of wearing this, as if there were a want of adaptation between him and it, recalling some mechanics in their holiday clothes. He had acquired mechanically a great store of teacher's knowledge. He could do mental arithmetic mechanically, sing at sight mechanically, blow various wind instruments mechanically, even play the great church organ mechanically. From his early childhood up, his mind had been a place of mechanical stowage. The arrangement of his wholesale warehouse, so that it might be always ready to meet the demands of retail dealers—history here, geography there, astronomy to the right, political economy to the left—natural history, the physical sciences, figures, music, the lower mathematics, and what not, all in their several places—this care had imparted to his countenance a look of care.
>
> Suppression of so much to make room for so much had given him a constrained manner over and above.

The most remarkable description of a system of training that totally ignored individuality and chipped and battered and moulded and squeezed all students into the same pattern or mould is the description of the normal school in which Mr. Gradgrind's teacher, Mr. M'Choakumchild, was trained. "Mr. M'Choakumchild and one hundred and forty other schoolmasters had been lately *turned* at the same time, in the same factory, on the same principles, like so many piano legs."

Volumes could not make the sacrifice of individuality clearer than this sentence does.

At "the grinders' school boys were taught as parrots are."

Doctor Blimber was condemned because in his system "Nature was of no consequence at all; no matter what a boy was intended to bear, Doctor Blimber made him bear to pattern somehow or other."

In Doctor Strong's school "we had plenty of liberty." The boys had also "noble games out of doors" in this model school of Dickens. Liberty and noble outdoor sports are the best agencies yet revealed to man for the development of full selfhood in harmony with the fundamental law of education, self-activity.

CHAPTER VIII.

THE CULTURE OF THE IMAGINATION.

In the preface to the first number of Household Words Dickens said that one of the objects he had in view in publishing the magazine was to aid in the development of the imagination of children.

From the time of Barnaby Rudge his unconscious recognition of the right of the child to have his imagination made freer and stronger can be felt in his writings. His conscious recognition of the absolute necessity of child freedom included the ideal of the culture of the imagination.

He reached his educational meridian in Hard Times, and the pedagogy of this book was devoted almost entirely to child freedom and the imagination; to revealing the fatal error of Mr. Gradgrind's philosophy, which taught that fact storing was the true way to form a child's mind and character, entirely ignoring the fact that feeling and imagination are the strongest elements of intellectual power and clearness.

In Bleak House, which immediately preceded Hard Times, he gave a very able description of the effects of the neglect of the development of the imagination for several generations in the characteristics of the Smallweed family.

> The Smallweeds had strengthened themselves in their practical character, discarded all amusements, discountenanced all storybooks, fairy tales, fictions, and fables, and banished all levities whatsoever. Hence the gratifying fact that it has had no child born to it, and that the complete little men and women it has produced have been observed to bear a likeness to old monkeys with something depressing on their minds.
>
> Mr. Smallweed's grandfather is in a helpless condition as to his lower, and nearly so as to his upper limbs; but his mind is unimpaired. It holds, as well as it ever held, the first four rules of arithmetic, and a certain small collection of the hardest facts. In respect of ideality, reverence, wonder, and other such phrenological attributes, it is no worse off than it used to be. Everything that Mr. Smallweed's grandfather ever put away in his mind was a grub at first, and is a grub at last. In all his life he has never bred a single butterfly.

This alone is a treatise of great suggestiveness on the need of the development of the imagination and the means by which it should be developed.

Hard Times was evidently intended to show the weakness of the Herbartian psychology. Dickens believed in the distinctive soul as the real selfhood of each child, and as the only true reality in his nature, the dominating influence in his life and character. He did not believe that knowledge formed the soul, but that the soul transformed knowledge. He did not believe that knowledge gave form, colour, and tone to the soul, but that the soul gave new form, colour, and tone to knowledge. He ridiculed the idea that the educator by using great care in the selection of his knowledge could produce a man of such a character as he desired; that ten pounds of yellow knowledge and ten pounds of blue knowledge judiciously mixed in a boy would certainly produce twenty pounds of green manhood.

He believed that in every child there is an element "defying all the calculations ever made by man, and no more known to his arithmetic than his Creator is." He did not agree with the psychology of which Mr. Gradgrind was the impersonation. Mr. Gradgrind believed that he could reduce human nature in all its complexities to statistics, and that "with his rule, and a pair of scales, and the multiplication table, he could weigh and measure any parcel of human nature, and tell you exactly what it comes to."

Mr. Gradgrind had established a school for the training of the children of Coketown, and had engaged Mr. M'Choakumchild to teach it. Dickens criticised the normal school training of his time in his description of Mr. M'Choakumchild's preparation for the work of stimulating young life to larger, richer growth.

> He and some one hundred and forty other schoolmasters had been lately turned at the same time, in the same factory, on the same principles, like so many pianoforte legs. He had been put through an immense variety of paces, and had answered volumes of head-breaking questions. Orthography, etymology, syntax, and prosody, biography, astronomy, geography as general cosmography, the sciences of compound proportion, algebra, land surveying and levelling, vocal music, and drawing from models, were all at the ends of his ten chilled fingers. He had worked his stony way through her Majesty's Most Honourable Privy Council's Schedule B, and had taken the bloom off the higher branches of mathematics and physical science, French, German, Latin, and Greek. He knew all about all the watersheds of all the world (whatever they are), and all the histories of all the peoples, and all the names of all the rivers and mountains, and all the productions, manners, and customs of all the countries, and all their boundaries and bearings on the two-and-thirty points of the compass.
>
> Ah! Mr. M'Choakumchild, rather overdone. If he had only learned a little less, how infinitely better he might have taught much more!

Dickens criticised the lack of professional training, and the fact-storing process which subordinated feeling and imagination.

Mr. Gradgrind's school was to be opened. The government officer was present to examine it. Mr. Gradgrind made a short opening address:

> "Now, what I want is facts. Teach these boys and girls nothing but facts. Facts alone are wanted in life. Plant nothing else, and root out everything else. You can only form the minds of reasoning animals upon facts; nothing else will ever be of any service to them. This is the principle on which I bring up my own children, and this is the principle on which I bring up these children. Stick to facts, sir!"
>
> The scene was a plain, bare, monotonous vault of a schoolroom, and the speaker's square forefinger emphasized his observations by underscoring every sentence with a line on the schoolmaster's sleeve. The emphasis was helped by the speaker's square wall of a forehead, which had his eyebrows for its base, while his eyes found commodious cellarage in two dark caves, overshadowed by the wall. The emphasis was helped by the speaker's mouth, which was wide, thin, and hard set. The emphasis was helped by the speaker's voice, which was inflexible, dry, and dictatorial.
>
> "In this life we want nothing but facts, sir; nothing but facts."
>
> The speaker, and the schoolmaster, and the third grown person present, all backed a little, and swept with their eyes the inclined plane of little vessels then and there arranged in order, ready to have imperial gallons of facts poured into them until they were full to the brim.

Most of the schoolrooms of the world are yet "plain, bare, monotonous vaults," although nearly fifty years after Dickens pointed out the need of artistic form and artistic decoration in schools we are beginning to awake to the idea that the architecture, the colouring, and the art on the walls and in the cabinets of schools may influence the characters of children more even than the teaching.

Mr. Gradgrind proceeded to ask a few questions of the pupils, who in this new school were to be known by numbers—so much more statistical and mathematical—and not by their names.

As he stood before the pupils, who were seated in rows on a gallery, "he seemed a kind of cannon loaded to the muzzle with facts, and prepared to blow them clean out of the regions of childhood at one discharge. He seemed a galvanizing apparatus, too, charged with a grim mechanical substitute for the tender young imaginations that were to be stormed away."

In the last sentence Dickens reveals the true philosophy of sustaining and developing natural and therefore productive interest, and explains how, after destroying it, teachers try to galvanize it into spasmodic activity.

> "Girl number twenty," said Mr. Gradgrind, squarely pointing with his square forefinger. "I don't know that girl. Who is that

girl?"

"Sissy Jupe, sir," explained number twenty, blushing, standing up, and courtesying.

"Sissy is not a name," said Mr. Gradgrind. "Don't call yourself Sissy. Call yourself Cecilia."

"It's father as calls me Sissy, sir," returned the young girl in a trembling voice, and with another courtesy.

"Then he has no business to do it," said Mr. Gradgrind. "Tell him he mustn't. Cecilia Jupe. Let me see. What is your father?"

"He belongs to the horse riding, if you please, sir."

Mr. Gradgrind frowned and waved off the objectionable calling with his hand.

"We don't want to know anything about that here. You mustn't tell us about that here. Your father breaks horses, don't he?"

"If you please, sir, when they can get any to break, they do break horses in the ring, sir."

"You mustn't tell us about the ring, here. Very well, then, describe your father as a horsebreaker. He doctors sick horses, I dare say?"

"Oh, yes, sir."

"Very well, then. He is a veterinary surgeon, a farrier, and horsebreaker. Give me your definition of a horse."

(Sissy Jupe thrown into the greatest alarm by this demand.)

"Girl number twenty unable to define a horse!" said Mr. Gradgrind for the general behoof of all the little pitchers. "Girl number twenty possessed of no facts in reference to one of the commonest of animals! Some boy's definition of a horse. Bitzer, yours."

Bitzer: "Quadruped. Graminivorous. Forty teeth, namely, twenty-four grinders, four eyeteeth, and twelve incisors. Sheds coat in the spring; in marshy countries sheds hoofs too. Hoofs hard, but requiring to be shod with iron. Age known by marks in mouth——" Thus (and much more) Bitzer.

"Now, girl number twenty," said Mr. Gradgrind, "you know what a horse is."

The keen edge of Dickens's sarcasm will be felt when it is remembered that Sissy Jupe was born among horses, had lived with them, played with them, and ridden them all her life, but was "ignorant of the commonest facts regarding a horse." She could not define a horse.

The government examiner then stepped forward:

"Very well," said this gentleman, briskly smiling, and folding his arms. "That's a horse. Now let me ask you girls and boys, would you paper a room with representations of horses?"

After a pause, one half the children cried in chorus, "Yes, sir!" Upon which the other half, seeing in the gentleman's face that "Yes" was wrong, cried out in chorus, "No, sir!"—as the custom is in these examinations.

"Of course, no. Why wouldn't you?"

A pause. One corpulent slow boy, with a wheezy manner of breathing, ventured the answer, because he wouldn't paper a room at all, but would paint it.

"You *must* paper it," said the gentleman rather warmly.

"You must paper it," said Thomas Gradgrind, "whether you like it or not. Don't tell *us* you wouldn't paper it. What do you mean, boy?"

"I'll explain to you, then," said the gentleman, after another and a dismal pause, "why you wouldn't paper a room with representations of horses. Do you ever see horses walking up and down the sides of rooms in reality—in fact? Do you?"

"Yes, sir!" from one half, "No, sir!" from the other.

"Of course, no," said the gentleman, with an indignant look at the wrong half. "Why, then, you are not to see anywhere what you don't see in fact; you are not to have anywhere what you don't have in fact. What is called taste is only another name for fact."

Thomas Gradgrind nodded his approbation.

"This is a new principle, a discovery, a great discovery," said the gentleman. "Now, I'll try you again. Suppose you were going to carpet a room. Would you use a carpet having a representation of flowers upon it?"

There being a general conviction by this time that "No, sir!" was always the right answer to this gentleman, the chorus of "No" was very strong. Only a few feeble stragglers said "Yes," among them Sissy Jupe.

"Girl number twenty," said the gentleman, smiling in the calm strength of knowledge.

Sissy blushed, and stood up.

"So you would carpet your room—or your husband's room, if you were a grown woman and had a husband—with representations of flowers, would you? Why would you?"

> "If you please, sir, I am very fond of flowers," said the girl.
>
> "And is that why you would put tables and chairs upon them, and have people walking over them with heavy boots?"
>
> "It wouldn't hurt them, sir. They wouldn't crush and wither, if you please, sir. They would be the pictures of what was very pretty, and pleasant, and I would fancy— —"
>
> "Ay, ay, ay! But you mustn't fancy," cried the gentleman, quite elated by coming so happily to this point. "That's it! You are never to fancy."
>
> "Fact, fact, fact," said the gentleman.
>
> "Fact, fact, fact," repeated Mr. Gradgrind.
>
> "You are to be in all things regulated and governed," said the gentleman, "by fact. We hope to have, before long, a board of fact, composed of commissioners of fact, who will force the people to be a people of fact, and of nothing but fact. You must discard the word Fancy altogether. You have nothing to do with it. You are not to have, in any object of use or ornament, what would be a contradiction in fact. You don't walk upon flowers in fact; you can not be allowed to walk upon flowers in carpets. You don't find that foreign birds and butterflies come and perch upon your crockery; you can not be permitted to paint foreign birds and butterflies upon your crockery. You must use for all these purposes combinations and modifications (in primary colours) of mathematical figures, which are susceptible of proof and demonstration. This is the new discovery. This is fact. This is taste."

Then Mr. M'Choakumchild was asked to teach his first lesson.

> He went to work in this preparatory lesson not unlike Morgiana in the Forty Thieves: looking into all the vessels ranged before him, one after another, to see what they contained. Say, good M'Choakumchild, when from thy boiling store thou shalt fill each jar brim full by and by, dost thou think that thou wilt always kill outright the robber Fancy lurking within—or sometimes only maim him and distort him?

The "maiming and distorting" of the imagination filled Dickens with alarm. He recognised with great clearness the law that all evil springs from misused good, and he knew that if the imagination is not cultivated properly the child not only loses the many intellectual and spiritual advantages that would result from its true culture, but that it is exposed to the terrible danger of a distorted imagination. Tom Gradgrind is used as a type of the degradation that results from "the strangling of the imagination." Its ghost lived on to drag him down "in the form of grovelling sensualities." That which, truly used, has most power to ennoble, has also, when warped or dwarfed, most power to degrade.

As Mr. Varden told his wife, "All good things perverted to evil purposes are worse than those which are naturally bad."

The five young Gradgrinds had little opportunity to develop their imaginations. They were watched too closely to have any imaginative plays; they were not allowed to read poetry or fiction; they heard no stories; they had no fairies or genii in their lives; they heard nothing of giants or such false things; no little Boy Blue ever blew his horn for them; no Jack Horner took a plum out of any pie in their experience; no such ridiculous person as Santa Claus ever put anything in their stockings; no cow ever performed the impossible feat of jumping over the moon, so far as they knew; they had never even heard of the cow with the crumpled horn that tossed the dog that worried the cat that killed the rat that ate the malt that lay in the house that Jack built. They knew, or they could say, that a cow was "a graminivorous ruminating quadruped," and that was enough, in the philosophy of Mr. Gradgrind.

Sissy Jupe's father got into difficulties in Coketown, and he became discouraged and ran away. Mr. Gradgrind was a good man, and meant to do right, so he adopted Sissy.

He told her his intentions rather bluntly:

> "Jupe, I have made up my mind to take you into my house, and, when you are not in attendance at the school, to employ you about Mrs. Gradgrind, who is rather an invalid. I have explained to Miss Louisa—this is Miss Louisa—the miserable but natural end of your late career; and you are to expressly understand that the whole of that subject is past, and is not to be referred to any more. From this time you begin your history. You are, at present, ignorant, I know."
>
> "Yes, sir, very," she answered, courtesying.
>
> "I shall have the satisfaction of causing you to be strictly educated; and you will be a living proof to all who come into communication with you, of the advantages of the training you will receive. You will be reclaimed and formed. You have been in the habit of reading to your father and those people I found you among, I dare say?" said Mr. Gradgrind, beckoning her nearer to him before he said so, and dropping his voice.
>
> "Only to father and Merrylegs, sir. At least, I mean to father, when Merrylegs was always there."
>
> "Never mind Merrylegs, Jupe," said Mr. Gradgrind with a passing frown. "I don't ask about him. I understand you to have been in the habit of reading to your father?"
>
> "Oh, yes, sir, thousands of times. They were the happiest—oh, of all the happy times we had together, sir!"
>
> It was only now, when her grief broke out, that Louisa looked at her.

> "And what," asked Mr. Gradgrind in a still lower voice, "did you read to your father, Jupe?"
>
> "About the Fairies, sir, and the Dwarf, and the Hunchback, and the Genies," she sobbed out.
>
> "There," said Mr. Gradgrind, "that is enough. Never breathe a word of such destructive nonsense any more."

One night, in their study den,

> Louisa had been overheard to begin a conversation with her brother by saying, "Tom, I wonder—" upon which Mr. Gradgrind, who was the person overhearing, stepped forth into the light, and said, "Louisa, never wonder!"
>
> Herein lay the spring of the mechanical art and mystery of educating the reason without stooping to the cultivation of the sentiments and affections. Never wonder. By means of addition, subtraction, multiplication, and division settle everything somehow, and never wonder. "Bring to me," says Mr. M'Choakumchild, "yonder baby just able to walk, and I will engage that it will never wonder."

Mr. Gradgrind and Mr. M'Choakumchild deliberately planned, as a result of a false psychology, to destroy all foolish dreamings and imaginings and wonderings by the children. This same wonder power is the mightiest stimulus to mental and spiritual effort, the source of all true interest, man's leader in his work of productive investigation.

Wonder power should increase throughout the life of the child. Unfortunately, the Gradgrind philosophy is practised by many educators. The child's natural wonder power is dwarfed, and an unnatural interest is substituted for it. Teachers kill the natural interest, and then try to galvanize its dead body into temporary activity. The child who was made a wonderer and a problem finder by God is made a problem solver by teachers. His dreamings and fancies have been stopped, and he has been stored with facts and made "practical."

Mr. Gradgrind was much exercised by the fact that the people of Coketown did not read the scientific and mathematical books in the library so much as poetry and fiction. It was a melancholy fact that after working for fifteen hours a day "they sat down to read mere fables about men and women more or less like themselves, and about children more or less like their own. They took De Foe to their bosoms instead of Euclid, and seemed to be, on the whole, more comforted by Goldsmith than by Cocker." This was very discouraging to Mr. Gradgrind.

One night Louisa and Tom were sitting alone conversing about themselves and the way they were being trained by their father. In the course of their conversation Tom said:

> "I am sick of my life, Loo; I hate it altogether, and I hate everybody except you. As to me, I am a donkey, that's what I am. I am as obstinate as one, I am more stupid than one, I get as much

pleasure as one, and I should like to kick like one."

"Not me, I hope, Tom."

"No, Loo, I wouldn't hurt *you*. I made an exception of you at first. I don't know what this—jolly old—jaundiced jail"—Tom had paused to find a sufficiently complimentary and expressive name for the parental roof, and seemed to relieve his mind for a moment by the strong alliteration of this one—"would be without you."

"Tom," said his sister, after silently watching the sparks a while, "as I get older, and nearly growing up, I often sit wondering here, and think how unfortunate it is for me that I can't reconcile you to home better than I am able to do. I don't know what other girls know. I can't play to you, or sing to you. I can't talk to you so as to lighten your mind, for I never see any amusing sights or read any amusing books that it would be a pleasure or a relief to you to talk about, when you are tired."

"Well, no more do I. I am as bad as you in that respect; and I am a mule too, which you're not. If father was determined to make me either a prig or a mule, and I am not a prig, why, it stands to reason, I must be a mule. And so I am."

"I wish I could collect all the Facts we hear so much about," said Tom, spitefully setting his teeth, "and all the Figures, and all the people who found them out; and I wish I could put a thousand barrels of gunpowder under them and blow them all up together."

Louisa sat looking at the fire so long that Tom asked, "Have you gone to sleep, Loo?"

"No, Tom, I am looking at the fire."

"What do you see in it?"

"I don't see anything in it, Tom, particularly, but since I have been looking at it I have been wondering about you and me, grown up."

"Wondering again?" said Tom.

"I have such unmanageable thoughts," returned his sister, "that they *will* wonder."

"Then I beg of you, Louisa," said Mrs. Gradgrind, who had opened the door without being heard, "to do nothing of that description, for goodness' sake, you inconsiderate girl, or I shall never hear the last of it from your father. And, Thomas, it is really shameful, with my poor head continually wearing me out, that a boy brought up as you have been, and whose education has cost what yours has, should be found encouraging his sister to won-

> der, when he knows his father has expressly said that she was not to do it."
>
> Louisa denied Tom's participation in the offence; but her mother stopped her with the conclusive answer, "Louisa, don't tell me, in my state of health; for unless you had been encouraged, it is morally and physically impossible that you could have done it."
>
> "I was encouraged by nothing, mother, but by looking at the red sparks dropping out of the fire, and whitening and dying. It made me think, after all, how short my life would be, and how little I could hope to do in it."
>
> "Nonsense!" said Mrs. Gradgrind, rendered almost energetic. "Nonsense! Don't stand there and tell me such stuff, Louisa, to my face, when you know very well that if it was ever to reach your father's ears I should never hear the last of it. After all the trouble that has been taken with you! After the lectures you have attended, and the experiments you have seen! After I have heard you myself, when the whole of my right side has been benumbed, going on with your master about combustion, and calcination, and calorification, and I may say every kind of ation that could drive a poor invalid distracted, to hear you talking in this absurd way about sparks and ashes!"

When a boy hates home, and a girl in her teens is rejoicing at the prospect of a short life, there has been some serious blunder in their training.

When her father was proposing to her that she should marry old Bounderby, Louisa said:

> "What do *I* know, father, of tastes and fancies; of aspirations and affections; of all that part of my nature in which such light things might have been nourished? What escape have I had from problems that could be demonstrated, and realities that could be grasped?" As she said it, she unconsciously closed her hand, as if upon a solid object, and slowly opened it as though she were releasing dust or ash.

After her marriage to Bounderby Louisa rarely came home, and Dickens gives in detail a sequence of thought that passed through her mind on her approach to the old home after a long absence. None of the true feelings were stirred in her heart.

The dreams of childhood—its airy fables, its graceful, beautiful, humane, impossible adornments of the world beyond, so good to be believed in once, so good to be remembered when outgrown, for then the least among them rises to the stature of a great charity in the heart, suffering little children to come into the midst of it, and to keep with their pure hands a garden in the stony ways of this world, wherein it were better for all the children of Adam that they should oftener sun themselves, simple and trustful, and not worldly-wise—what had she to do with these? Remembrances of how she had journeyed to the little that she knew by the enchanted roads of what she and millions of innocent creatures had hoped and imagined; of how, first coming upon reason through the tender light of fancy, she had seen it a beneficent god, deferring to gods as great as itself; not a grim idol, cruel and cold, with its victims bound hand to foot, and its big dumb shape set up with a sightless stare, never to be moved by anything but so many calculated tons of leverage—what had she to do with these?

This quotation shows how clearly Dickens saw the relationship between the imagination and the reason. Her imagination had been dwarfed and perverted; and her power to feel, and to think, and to appreciate beauty, and to love, and to see God and understand him, was dwarfed and perverted as a consequence.

Her poor mother, who had always felt that there was something wrong with her husband's training, but dared not oppose him, and fully supported him for the sake of peace which never really came, was worn out, and had almost become a mental wreck. Her mind was struggling with the one great question. She tried and tried vainly to find what the great defect of her husband's system was, but she was very sure it had a great weakness somewhere. She tried to explain the matter to Louisa when she came to see her.

> "You learned a great deal, Louisa, and so did your brother. Ologies of all kinds, from morning to night. If there is any ology left, of any description, that has not been worn to rags in this house, all I can say is, I hope I shall never hear its name."
>
> "I can hear you, mother, when you have strength to go on." This, to keep her from floating away.
>
> "But there's something—not an ology at all—that your father has missed, or forgotten, Louisa. I don't know what it is. I have often sat with Sissy near me, and thought about it. I shall never get its name now. But your father may. It makes me restless. I want to write to him, to find out, for God's sake, what it is. Give me a pen, give me a pen."

When Louisa, unable to resist alone the temptation to go with Mr. Harthouse, fled to her father and told him in such earnest words that she cursed the hour she had been born to submit to his training, she said:

> "I don't reproach you, father. What you have never nurtured in me, you have never nurtured in yourself; but oh! if you had only done so long ago, or if you had only neglected me, what a much better and much happier creature I should have been this day!"
>
> On hearing this, after all his care, he bowed his head upon his hand and groaned aloud.
>
> "Father, if you had known, when we were last together here, what even I feared while I strove against it—as it has been my

> task from infancy to strive against every natural prompting that has arisen in my heart; if you had known that there lingered in my breast sensibilities, affections, weakness capable of being cherished into strength, defying all the calculations ever made by man, and no more known to his arithmetic than his Creator is—would you have given me to the husband whom I am now sure that I hate?"
>
> He said, "No, no, my poor child."
>
> "Would you have doomed me, at any time, to the frost and blight that have hardened and spoiled me? Would you have robbed me—for no one's enrichment—only for the greater desolation of this world—of the immaterial part of my life, the spring and summer of my belief, my refuge from what is sordid and bad in the real things around me, my school in which I should have learned to be more humble, and more trusting with them, and to hope in my little sphere to make them better?"
>
> "Oh, no, no! No, Louisa."
>
> "Yet, father, if I had been stone blind; if I had groped my way by my sense of touch, and had been free, while I knew the shapes and surfaces of things, to exercise my fancy somewhat in regard to them, I should have been a million times wiser, happier, more loving, more contented, more innocent and human in all good respects, than I am with the eyes I have. Now, hear what I have come to say. With a hunger and thirst upon me, father, which have never been for a moment appeased; with an ardent impulse toward some region where rules, and figures, and definitions were not quite absolute, I have grown up, battling every inch of my way.
>
> "In this strife I have almost repulsed and crushed my better angel into a demon. What I have learned has left me doubting, misbelieving, despising, regretting what I have not learned; and my dismal resource has been to think that life would soon go by, and that nothing in it could be worth the pain and trouble of a contest."

When she had finished the story of her acquaintance with Mr. Harthouse and his influence over her, she said: "All that I know is, your philosophy and your teaching will not save me. Now, father, you have brought me to this. Save me by some other means."

Dickens pictured Mr. Gradgrind as a good, earnest man, who desired to do only good for his family.

> In gauging fathomless deeps with his little mean excise rod, and in staggering over the universe with his rusty stiff-legged compasses, he had meant to do great things. Within the limits of

> his short tether he had tumbled about, annihilating the flowers of existence with greater singleness of purpose than many of the blatant personages whose company he kept.

A careful study of what Louisa said to her father will show that Dickens had made a profound study of Froebel's philosophy of the feelings and the imagination which is now the dominating theory of psychology, and that he clearly understood what Wordsworth meant when he wrote:

> "Whose heart the holy forms of young imagination had kept pure."

Sissy Jupe failed utterly to satisfy Mr. M'Choakumchild at school. She could not remember facts and dates. She could not be crammed successfully, and she had a very dense head for figures. "She actually burst into tears when required (by the mental process) to name immediately the cost of two hundred and forty-seven muslin caps at fourteen pence halfpenny," so Mr. Gradgrind told her she would have to leave school.

> "I can not disguise from you, Jupe," said Mr. Gradgrind, knitting his brow, "that the result of your probation there has disappointed me—has greatly disappointed me. You have not acquired, under Mr. and Mrs. M'Choakumchild, anything like that amount of exact knowledge which I look for. You are extremely deficient in your facts. Your acquaintance with figures is very limited. You are altogether backward, and below the mark."
>
> "I am sorry, sir," she returned; "but I know it is quite true. Yet I have tried hard, sir."
>
> "Yes," said Mr. Gradgrind, "yes, I believe you have tried hard; I have observed you, and I can find no fault in that respect."
>
> "Thank you, sir. I have thought sometimes"—Sissy very timid here—"that perhaps I tried to learn too much, and that if I had asked to be allowed to try a little less, I might have——"
>
> "No, Jupe, no," said Mr. Gradgrind, shaking his head in his profoundest and most eminently practical way. "No. The course you pursued, you pursued according to the system—the system—and there is no more to be said about it. I can only suppose that the circumstances of your early life were too unfavourable to the development of your reasoning powers, and that we began too late. Still, as I have said already, I am disappointed."
>
> "I wish I could have made a better acknowledgment, sir, of your kindness to a poor forlorn girl who had no claim upon you, and of your protection of her."
>
> "Don't shed tears," said Mr. Gradgrind. "Don't shed tears. I don't complain of you. You are an affectionate, earnest, good young woman, and—and we must make that do."

How blind a man must become when his faith in a system or a philosophy can make him estimate fact storing so much and character forming so little! Sissy could not learn facts, therefore Mr. Gradgrind mourned. The fact that she was "affectionate, earnest, good," was only a trifling matter—a very poor substitute for brilliant acquirements in dates and facts and mental arithmetic.

Sissy became, however, the good angel of the Gradgrind household. She helped Louisa back to a partial hope and sweetness; she gave the younger children, with Mr. Gradgrind's permission, the real childhood of freedom and imagination, which the older children had lost forever; she brightened the lives even of Mrs. and Mr. Gradgrind, and she helped to save Tom from the disgrace of his crime.

The closing picture of the book, one of the most beautiful Dickens ever painted, tells the story of Sissy's future:

> But happy Sissy's happy children loving her; all children loving her; she, grown learned in childish lore; thinking no innocent and pretty fancy ever to be despised; trying hard to know her humbler fellow-creatures, and to beautify their lives of machinery and reality with those imaginative graces and delights, without which the heart of infancy will wither up, the sturdiest physical manhood will be morally stark death, and the plainest national prosperity figures can show will be the Writing on the Wall—she holding this course as part of no fantastic vow, or bond, or brotherhood, or sisterhood, or pledge, or covenant, or fancy dress, or fancy fair; but simply as a duty to be done. Did Louisa see these things of herself? These things were to be!
>
> Dear reader! It rests with you and me whether, in our two fields of action, similar things shall be or not. Let them be! We shall sit with lighter bosoms on the hearth, to see the ashes of our fires turn gray and cold.

And the educational Gradgrinds of the present time sneer at Dickens because he puts the early training of a circus above the early training of a Christian home like Mr. Gradgrind's. "The logical consequence of such reasoning," they say, "would be that all children should be trained in circuses."

Oh, no! Dickens did not recommend a circus as a good place to train children. But he did believe that even a circus is a thousand times better than a so-called Christian home for the true and complete development of a child, if in the circus the child is free and happy, and is allowed full play for her imagination, and is not arrested in her development by rote storing of facts and too early drill in arithmetic, and has the rich productive love of even one parent, and has blessed opportunities for loving service for her pets and her friends; and if in the so-called Christian home she is robbed of these privileges even in the name of religion.

Sissy had a blessed, free childhood. She lived in her own imaginary world most of the time; she had the deep love of her kind-hearted father and of Merrylegs, the dog; she read poetry and fairy tales; she attended to her father's needs; she had many opportunities to show her love in loving service for Merrylegs and her father; and she was not dwarfed by fact cramming and formal drill. Her chances of reaching a true womanhood were excellent, and when she got the opportunity for the revelation of character, she had character to reveal, and her character developed in its revelation for the benefit and happiness of others. Hers was the true Christian training after all. Homes and schools with such training are centres of great power.

One of the strongest pleas ever made for the cultivation of the imagination, "the fancies and affections," and for the teaching of literature, art, and music in the schools was given in Hard Times, which is an industrial as well as an educational story. Indeed, Dickens saw that the true solution of industrial questions was the proper training of the race. No attack on the meanness of utilitarianism and no exposition of its terrible dangers could be more incisive and philosophical than the following wonderful sentences:

> Utilitarian economists, skeletons of schoolmasters, commissioners of fact, genteel and used-up infidels, gabblers of many little dog's-eared creeds, the poor you will have always with you. Cultivate in them, while there is yet time, the utmost graces of the fancies and affections, to adorn their lives so much in need of ornament; or, in the moment of your triumph, when romance is utterly driven out of their souls, and they and a bare existence stand face to face, Reality will take a wolfish turn, and make an end of you!

Altogether Hard Times is one of the most remarkable educational books ever written.

Dickens made a plea for mental refreshment and recreation for the working classes in Nobody's Story, similar to that made in Hard Times:

> The workingman appealed to the Bigwig family, and said: "We are a labouring people, and I have a glimmering suspicion in me that labouring people of whatever condition were made—by a higher intelligence than yours, as I poorly understand it—to be in need of mental refreshment and recreation. See what we fall into, when we rest without it. Come! Amuse me harmlessly, show me something, give me an escape!"

Beautiful Lizzie Hexam, one of the latest and highest creations of Dickens, longed to read, but she did not learn to do so because her father objected so bitterly, and she wished to avoid everything that would weaken the bond of love between them, lest she might lose her influence for good over him.

Her brother Charley said to her:

> "You said you couldn't read a book, Lizzie. Your library of books is the hollow down by the flare, I think."
>
> "I should be very glad to be able to read real books. I feel my want of learning very much, Charley. But I should feel it much more, if I didn't know it to be a tie between me and father."

Dickens was revealing the strange fact that at first many poor and ignorant parents strenuously objected to their children being educated; and he was at the same time showing that great character growth could take place even without the power to read. Lizzie's self-sacrifice for her father and Charley was a true revelation of the divinity in her nature. Though she had not read books, she had read a great deal by her imagination from "the hollow down by the flare."

As Dickens grew older he saw more clearly the value of the dreaming of childhood while awake, of the deep reveries into which young people often fall, and ought to fall, so that they become oblivious to their environment, and sweep through the universe in strange imaginings, that after all are very real. He was fond of drawing pictures of young people giving free rein to their imaginations, unchecked by intermeddling adulthood, while they watched the glowing fire, or the ashes falling away from the dying coals. Lizzie's library from which she got her culture was in "the hollow down by the flare."

Crippled little Jenny Wren, the doll's dressmaker, said to Lizzie Hexam one day, when Eugene Wrayburn was visiting them:

> "I wonder how it happens that when I am work, work, working here, all alone in the summer time, I smell flowers."
>
> "As a commonplace individual, I should say," Eugene suggested languidly—for he was growing weary of the person of the house—"that you smell flowers because you *do* smell flowers."
>
> "No, I don't," said the little creature, resting one arm upon the elbow of her chair, resting her chin upon that hand, and looking vacantly before her; "this is not a flowery neighbourhood. It's anything but that. And yet, as I sit at work, I smell miles of flowers. I smell roses till I think I see the rose leaves lying in heaps, bushels, on the floor. I smell fallen leaves till I put down my hand—so—and expect to make them rustle. I smell the white and the pink May in the hedges, and all sorts of flowers that I never was among. For I have seen very few flowers indeed in my life."
>
> "Pleasant fancies to have, Jennie dear!" said her friend, with a glance toward Eugene as if she would have asked him whether they were given the child in compensation for her losses.
>
> "So I think, Lizzie, when they come to me. And the birds I hear! Oh!" cried the little creature, holding out her hand and looking upward, "how they sing!"

How life in any stage might be filled with richness and joy, if imaginations were stored with apperceptive elements and allowed to reconstruct the universe in our fancies! How truly real our fancies might become!

In A Child's Dream of a Star Dickens gives an exquisite picture of the influence of imagination in spiritual evolution.

> There was once a child, and he strolled about a good deal, and thought of a number of things. He had a sister, who was a child

> too, and his constant companion. These two used to wonder all day long. They wondered at the beauty of the flowers; they wondered at the height and blueness of the sky; they wondered at the depth of the bright water; they wondered at the goodness and the power of God who made the lovely world.
>
> They used to say to one another, sometimes, Supposing all the children upon earth were to die, would the flowers, and the water, and the sky be sorry? They believed they would be sorry. For, said they, the buds are the children of the flowers, and the little playful streams that gambol down the hillsides are the children of the water; and the smallest bright specks playing at hide and seek in the sky all night, must surely be the children of the stars; and they would all be grieved to see their playmates, the children of men, no more.
>
> There was one clear shining star that used to come out in the sky before the rest, near the church spire, above the graves. It was larger and more beautiful, they thought, than all the others, and every night they watched for it, standing hand in hand at a window. Whoever saw it first cried out, "I see the star!" And often they cried out both together, knowing so well when it would rise, and where. So they grew to be such friends with it, that, before lying down in their beds, they always looked out once again to bid it good night; and when they were turning round to sleep they used to say, "God bless the star!"
>
> But while she was still very young, oh very, very young, the sister drooped, and came to be so very weak that she could no longer stand in the window at night; and then the child looked sadly out by himself, and when he saw the star, turned round and said to the patient pale face on the bed, "I see the star!" and then a smile would come upon the face, and a little weak voice used to say, "God bless my brother and the star!"

Dickens had shown his recognition of the inestimable value of the imagination, and the importance of giving it free play and of doing everything possible to stimulate its activity by freedom, and story, and play, and literature, music, and art, but his description of Jemmy Jackman Lirriper's training shows a keener appreciation than any of his other writings of the value of the child's games in which personation is the leading characteristic; in which spools, or spoons, or blocks, or sticks are people or animals, with regular names and distinct characteristics and responsible duties, and in which chairs and tables and boxes are coaches, or steamboats, or railway trains. No friends are ever more real than those of the child's creative imagination, with things to represent them; no rides ever give greater delight than those rides in trains that move only in the imaginations of the children, who construct them by placing the chairs in a row, and who act as engineers, conductors, and brakemen. Such games form the best elements out of which the child's life power can be made, especially if the adulthood of his home sympathizes with him in his enterprises. They afford an outlet for his imaginative plans. In them he forms new worlds of his own, which are adapted to his stage of development, and in which he can be the creator and the centre of executive influence.

Jemmy Jackman Lirriper's training was ideal in most of his home life, though he had no father or mother to love and guide him.

> The miles and miles that me and the Major have travelled with Jemmy in the dusk between the lights are not to be calculated, Jemmy driving on the coach box, which is the Major's brass-bound writing desk on the table, me inside in the easy-chair, and the Major Guard up behind with a brown-paper horn doing it really wonderful. I do assure you, my dear, that sometimes when I have taken a few winks in my place inside the coach and have come half awake by the flashing light of the fire and have heard that precious pet driving and the Major blowing up behind to have the change of horses ready when we got to the Inn, I have believed we were on the old North Road that my poor Lirriper knew so well. Then to see that child and the Major both wrapped up getting down to warm their feet and going stamping about and having glasses of ale out of the paper match boxes on the chimney piece, is to see the Major enjoying it fully as much as the child I am very sure, and it's equal to any play when Coachee opens the coach door to look in at me inside and say "Wery 'past that 'tage.—'Prightened old lady?"

Such plays as Dickens here describes make one of the greatest differences between a real childhood and a barren childhood. The lack of opportunities for such perfect plays and such complete sympathy in their plays gives to the faces of orphan children brought up in institutions the distinctive look which marks them everywhere, so that they can be easily recognised by experienced students of happy childhood.

But Jemmy's make believe was not ruthlessly cut short with his early childhood. He continued his imaginative operations, or it might make it clearer to say his operative imaginations, after he went to school; and those beautiful old people, Mrs. Lirriper and Major Jackman, continued their interest, their real, perfectly sympathetic interest in his plans.

> Neither should I tell you any news, my dear, in telling you that the Major is still a fixture in the Parlours quite as much so as the roof of the house, and that Jemmy is of boys the best and brightest, and has ever had kept from him the cruel story of his poor pretty young mother, Mrs. Edson, being deserted in the second floor and dying in my arms, fully believing that I am his born Gran and him an orphan; though what with engineering since he took a taste for it, and him and the Major making Locomotives out of parasols, broken iron pots, and cotton reels, and them absolutely a-getting off the line and falling over the table and injuring

the passengers almost equal to the originals, it really is quite wonderful. And when I says to the Major, "Major, can't you by *any* means give us a communication with the guard?" the Major says, quite huffy, "No, madam, it's not to be done"; and when I says, "Why not?" the Major says, "That is between us who are in the Railway Interest, madam, and our friend, the Right Honourable Vice-President of the Board of Trade"; and if you'll believe me, my dear, the Major wrote to Jemmy at School to consult him on the answer I should have before I could get even that amount of unsatisfactoriness out of the man, the reason being that when we first began with the little model and the working signals beautiful and perfect (being in general as wrong as the real), and when I says, laughing, "What appointment am I to hold in this undertaking, gentlemen?" Jemmy hugs me round the neck and tells me, dancing, "You shall be the Public, Gran," and consequently they put upon me just as much as ever they like, and I sit a-growling in my easy-chair.

My dear, whether it is that a grown man as clever as the Major can not give half his heart and mind to anything—even a plaything—but must get into right down earnest with it, whether it is so or whether it is not so, I do not undertake to say; but Jemmy is far outdone by the serious and believing ways of the Major in the management of the United Grand Junction Lirriper and Jackman Great Norfolk Parlour Line, "for," says my Jemmy with the sparkling eyes when it was christened, "we must have a whole mouthful of name, Gran, or our dear old Public"—and there the young rogue kissed me—"won't stump up." So the Public took the shares—ten at ninepence, and immediately when that was spent twelve Preference at one and sixpence—and they were all signed by Jemmy and countersigned by the Major, and between ourselves much better worth the money than some shares I have paid for in my time. In the same holidays the line was made and worked and opened and ran excursions and collisions and had burst its boilers and all sorts of accidents and offences all most regular, correct, and pretty. The sense of responsibility entertained by the Major as a military style of station master, my dear, starting the down train behind time and ringing one of those little bells that you buy with the little coal scuttles off the tray round the man's neck in the street, did him honour; but noticing the Major of a night when he is writing out his monthly report to Jemmy at school of the state of the Rolling Stock and the Permanent Way, and all the rest of it (the whole kept upon the Major's sideboard and dusted with his own hands every morning before varnishing his boots), I notice him as full of thought and care, as full can be, and frowning in a fearful manner; but, indeed, the Major does nothing by halves, as witness his great delight in going out sur-

> veying with Jemmy when he has Jemmy to go with, carrying a chain and a measuring tape, and driving I don't know what improvements right through Westminster Abbey, and fully believed in the streets to be knocking everything upside down by Act of Parliament. As please Heaven will come to pass when Jemmy takes to that as a profession!

The Major's participation in the plans of Jemmy is a good illustration of the sympathy that Froebel and Dickens felt for childhood, a sympathy *with*, not *for*, the child. It meant more than approval—it meant co-operation, partnership.

Some educators would criticise Dickens for allowing the Major to make the locomotives with parasols, broken pots, and cotton reels. They teach that Jemmy should have made these himself. Dickens was away beyond such a narrow view as this. The child at first has much more power to plan than to execute. To leave him to himself means the failure of his plans and the irritation of his temper. It is a terrible experience for a child to get the habit of failure. The wise adult will enter into partnership with the child to aid in carrying out the child's plans. He will not even make suggestions of changes in plans when he sees how they might be improved. The plans and the leadership should be absolutely the child's own. The adult should be an assistant, and that only, when skill is required beyond that possessed by the child—either when the mechanical work is too difficult for the child or when more than one person is needed to execute his plan.

The adult may sometimes lead the child indirectly to a change of plan, but he should not do it by direct suggestion. The joy is lost for the child when he becomes conscious of the adult as interfering even sympathetically with his own personality. There is a great deal of well-intentioned dwarfing of childhood.

The consciousness of partnership, of unity, of sympathetic co-operation, is the best result of such blessed work as the Major did with Jemmy in carrying out Jemmy's plans. He is the child's best friend who most wisely and most thoroughly develops his imagination as a basis for all intellectual strength and clearness, and for the highest spiritual growth. He is the wealthiest man who sees diamonds in the dewdrops and unsullied gold in the sunset tints.

David Copperfield tells the names of the wonderful books he found in his father's blessed little room, and describes their influence upon his life.

> They kept alive my fancy and my hope of something beyond that place and time—they and the Arabian Nights and the Tales of the Genii. It is curious to me how I could ever have consoled myself under my small troubles (which were great troubles to me) by impersonating my favourite characters in them, as I did, and by putting Mr. and Miss Murdstone into all the bad ones, which I did, too. I have been Tom Jones—a child's Tom Jones, a harmless creature—for a week together. I have sustained my own idea of Roderick Random for a month at a stretch, I verily believe.
>
> "Let us end with the Boy's story," said Mrs. Lirriper, "for the Boy's story is the best that is ever told."

There are no other stories so enchanting, or so stimulating, as the stories that fill the imaginations of childhood.

CHAPTER IX.

SYMPATHY WITH CHILDHOOD.

The dominant element in Dickens's character was sympathy *with* childhood, not merely for it. He had the productive sympathy that feels and thinks from the child's standpoint.

The illustration just given of Major Jackman's co-operative sympathy with Jemmy Lirriper in the perfect carrying out of what to most people would have been only "the foolish ideas" of a child, as sincerely as if he had been executing commissions from the prime minister, is an excellent exemplification of the true ideal of sympathy in practice. The Major was not working for Jemmy's amusement merely; he was a very active and genuinely interested partner with Jemmy. "Jemmy was far outdone by the serious and believing ways of the Major" in the imaginative plays which were the most real life of Jemmy. Such was the sympathy of Dickens with his own children; such sympathy he believed to be the most productive power in the teacher or child trainer for beneficent influence on the character of the child.

There is no other characteristic of his writings so marked as his broad sympathy with childhood. Sympathy was the origin of all he wrote against coercion in all its dread forms, of all he wrote about robbing children of a real childhood, about the dwarfing of individuality, about the strangling of the imagination, about improper nutrition, about all forms of neglect, and cruelty, and bad training. The more fully his nature is known the more deeply he is loved, because of his great love for the child.

From the beginning of his educational work his overflowing, practical sympathy is revealed.

He tells us in the preface to Nickleby that his study of the Yorkshire schools and his delineation of the character of Squeers resulted from a resolution formed in childhood, which he was led to form by seeing a boy "with a suppurated abscess caused by its being ripped open by his Yorkshire guide, philosopher, and friend with an inky penknife."

The sympathy of Nicholas, and John Browdie, and the Cheeryble brothers with Smike and all suffering childhood are strong features of the book.

Dickens's own sympathy has cleared his mind of many fogs that still linger in some minds regarding a parent's rights in regard to his child, even though the parent has never recognised any of the child's rights. The movement in favour of the recognition of the rights of children even against their parents began with Dickens. When Nicholas discovered that Smike was the son of his uncle, Ralph Nickleby, he went to consult brother Charles Cheeryble in regard to his duty under the circumstances.

> He modestly, but firmly, expressed his hope that the good old gentleman would, under such circumstances as he described, hold him justified in adopting the extreme course of interfering between parent and child, and upholding the latter in his disobedience; even though his horror and dread of his father might seem, and would doubtless be represented, as a thing so repulsive and unnatural as to render those who countenanced him in it fit objects of general detestation and abhorrence.
>
> "So deeply rooted does this horror of the man appear to be," said Nicholas, "that I can hardly believe he really is his son. Nature does not seem to have implanted in his breast one lingering feeling of affection for him, and surely she can never err."
>
> "My dear sir," replied brother Charles, "you fall into the very common mistake of charging upon Nature matters with which she has not had the smallest connection, and for which she is in no way responsible. Men talk of Nature as an abstract thing, and lose sight of what is natural while they do so. Here is a poor lad who has never felt a parent's care, who has scarcely known anything all his life but suffering and sorrow, presented to a man who he is told is his father, and whose first act is to signify his intention of putting an end to his short term of happiness by consigning him to his old fate, and taking him from the only friend he has ever had—which is yourself. If Nature, in such a case, put into that lad's breast but one secret prompting which urged him toward his father and away from you, she would be a liar and an idiot."
>
> Nicholas was delighted to find that the old gentleman spoke so warmly, and in the hope that he might say something more to the same purpose, made no reply.
>
> "The same mistake presents itself to me, in one shape or other, at every turn," said brother Charles. "Parents who never showed their love complain of want of natural affection in their children; children who never showed their duty complain of want of natural feeling in their parents; lawmakers who find both so miserable that their affections have never had enough of life's sun to develop them are loud in their moralizings over parents and children too, and cry that the very ties of Nature are disregarded. Natural affections and instincts, my dear sir, are the most beautiful of the Almighty's works, but, like other beautiful works of his, they must be reared and fostered, or it is as natural that they should be wholly obscured, and that new feelings should usurp

> their place, as it is that the sweetest productions of the earth, left untended, should be choked with weeds and briers. I wish we could be brought to consider this, and, remembering natural obligations a little more at the right time, talk about them a little less at the wrong one."

It was chiefly to break the power of ignorant and cruel parenthood over suffering childhood that Ralph Nickleby was painted with such dark and repellent characteristics, and that poor Smike's sufferings were detailed with such minuteness. The sympathy of the world was aroused against the one and in favour of the other, as a basis for the climax of thought which brother Charles expressed so truly and so forcefully.

The same thought was driven home by the complaint of Squeers about one of the boys in Dotheboys Hall.

> "The juniorest Palmer said he wished he was in heaven. I really don't know, I do *not* know what's to be done with that young fellow; he's always a-wishing something horrid. He said once he wished he was a donkey, because then he wouldn't have a father as didn't love him! Pretty wicious that for a child of six!"

It required the genius of Dickens to make such a clear picture of an unloving father.

Even before Nicholas Nickleby was written Dickens had revealed his sympathetic nature. Oliver Twist's story was written to stir the hearts of his readers in favour of unfortunate children. What a contrast is made between the hardening effects of his treatment by Bumble and the "gentleman in the white waistcoat," and the humanizing influence of Rose Maylie's tear dropped on his cheek.

Surely no sensitive little boy ever submitted to more unsympathetic treatment than poor Oliver.

> When little Oliver was taken before "the gentlemen" that evening, and informed that he was to go that night as general house lad to a coffin maker's, and that if he complained of his situation, or ever came back to the parish again, he would be sent to sea, there to be drowned or knocked on the head, as the case might be, he evinced so little emotion that they by common consent pronounced him a hardened young rascal, and ordered Mr. Bumble to remove him forthwith.
>
> For some time Mr. Bumble drew Oliver along, without notice or remark; for the beadle carried his head very erect, as a beadle always should; and, it being a windy day, little Oliver was completely enshrouded by the skirts of Mr. Bumble's coat as they blew open and disclosed to great advantage his flapped waistcoat and drab plush knee breeches. As they drew near to their destination, however, Mr. Bumble thought it expedient to look down and see that the boy was in good order for inspection by his new

> master: which he accordingly did, with a fit and becoming air of gracious patronage.
>
> "Oliver!" said Mr. Bumble.
>
> "Yes, sir," replied Oliver in a low, tremulous voice.
>
> "Pull that cap off your eyes, and hold up your head, sir."
>
> Although Oliver did as he was desired at once, and passed the back of his unoccupied hand briskly across his eyes, he left a tear in them when he looked up at his conductor. As Mr. Bumble gazed sternly upon him, it rolled down his cheek. It was followed by another, and another. The child made a strong effort, but it was an unsuccessful one. Withdrawing his other hand from Mr. Bumble's, he covered his face with both, and wept until the tears sprung out from between his chin and bony fingers.
>
> "Well!" exclaimed Mr. Bumble, stopping short, and darting at his little charge a look of intense malignity. "Well! Of *all* the ungratefullest and worst-disposed boys as ever I see, Oliver, you are the— —"
>
> "No, no, sir," sobbed Oliver, clinging to the hand which held the well-known cane; "no, no, sir; I will be good indeed; indeed, indeed I will, sir! I am a very little boy, sir; and it is so—so— —"
>
> "So what?" inquired Mr. Bumble in amazement.
>
> "So lonely, sir! So very lonely!" cried the child. "Everybody hates me. Oh, sir, don't, don't, pray, be cross to me!" The child beat his hand upon his heart, and looked in his companion's face with tears of real agony.

The poor boy was put to bed by Sowerberry the first night. His master said, as they climbed the stairs:

> "Your bed's under the counter. You don't mind sleeping among the coffins, I suppose? But it doesn't much matter whether you do or don't, for you can't sleep anywhere else. Come, don't keep me here all night!"

Dickens pitied children for the terrors with which they were threatened, as Oliver was threatened by the board, and he pitied them also for the terrors that their imaginations brought to them at night. Sowerberry's lack of sympathy was as great as Bumble's. When one of his own children showed evidence of dread of retiring alone, Dickens sat upstairs with his family in the evenings afterward. He did not tell the child the reason, but she was saved from terror.

Oliver ran away from Sowerberry's, and when passing the workhouse he peeped between the bars of the gate into the garden. A very little boy was there who came to the gate to say "Good-bye" to him. He had been one of Oliver's little friends.

"Kiss me," said the child, climbing up the low gate and flinging his little arms round Oliver's neck: "Good-bye, dear! God bless you!"

The blessing was from a young child's lips, but it was the first that Oliver had ever heard invoked upon his head; and through the struggles and sufferings and troubles and changes of his after-life he never once forgot it.

When Oliver was taken to commit burglary by Bill Sykes, and was wounded and brought into the home he was assisting to rob, the good lady of the house sent for a doctor. The doctor dressed the arm, and when the boy fell asleep he brought Mrs. Maylie and Rose to see the criminal.

Rose sat down by Oliver's bedside and gathered his hair from his face.

As she stooped over him her tears fell upon his forehead.

The boy stirred and smiled in his sleep, as though these marks of pity and compassion had awakened some pleasant dream of a love and affection he had never known. Thus a strain of gentle music, or the rippling of water in a silent place, or the odour of a flower, or the mention of a familiar word, will sometimes call up sudden dim remembrances of scenes that never were in this life; which vanish like a breath; which some brief memory of a happier existence, long gone by, would seem to have awakened; which no voluntary exertion of the mind can ever recall.

"What can this mean?" exclaimed the elder lady. "This poor child can never have been the pupil of robbers!"

"Vice," sighed the surgeon, replacing the curtain, "takes up her abode in many temples; and who can say that a fair outside shall not enshrine her?"

"But at so early an age!" urged Rose.

"My dear young lady," rejoined the surgeon, mournfully shaking his head, "crime, like death, is not confined to the old and withered alone. The youngest and fairest are too often its chosen victims."

"But can you, oh, can you really believe that this delicate boy has been the voluntary associate of the worst outcasts of society?" said Rose.

The surgeon shook his head in a manner which intimated that he feared it was very possible, and, observing that they might disturb the patient, led the way into an adjoining apartment.

"But even if he has been wicked," pursued Rose, "think how young he is; think that he may never have known a mother's love, or the comfort of a home; that ill usage and blows, or the want of bread, may have driven him to herd with men who have forced

> him to guilt. Aunt, dear aunt, for mercy's sake think of this, before you let them drag this sick child to a prison, which in any case must be the grave of all his chance of amendment. Oh! as you love me, and know that I have never felt the want of parents in your goodness and affection, but that I might have done so, and might have been equally helpless and unprotected with this poor child, have pity upon him before it is too late!"
>
> "My dear love," said the elder lady, as she folded the weeping girl to her bosom, "do you think I would harm a hair of his head?"
>
> "Oh, no," replied Rose eagerly.
>
> "No, surely," said the old lady; "my days are drawing to their close, and may mercy be shown to me as I show it to others. What can I do to save him, sir?"

Dickens used the doctor to rebuke the large class of people who are ever ready to believe the worst about a boy, and who are always looking for his depravity instead of searching for the divinity in him.

Rose's plea for kind treatment for the boy, "even if he has been wicked," was a new doctrine propounded by Dickens. The worst boys at home or in school need most sympathy. Mrs. Maylie's attitude was in harmony with Christ's teaching, but quite out of harmony with much that was called Christian practice at the time Dickens wrote Oliver Twist. He taught the doctrine that children were turned into evil ways and confirmed in them through lack of sympathy. Poor Nancy said to Rose Maylie:

> "Lady," cried the girl, sinking on her knees, "dear, sweet, angel lady, you *are* the first that ever blessed me with such words as these; and if I had heard them years ago, they might have turned me from a life of sin and sorrow; but it is too late, it is too late!"

In The Old Curiosity Shop Dickens gave a beautiful picture of a sympathetic teacher in Mr. Marton. His school was not well lighted or properly ventilated, the furniture was poor, there was no apparatus except a dunce's cap, a cane, and a ruler, his methods were old-fashioned, but he possessed the greatest qualification of a good teacher, deep sympathy with childhood. This was shown by the erasure of the blot from the sick boy's writing; by his asking Nell to pray for the boy; by his appreciation of the boy's love; by his hoping for his recovery against the unfavourable reports; by his favourable interpretation of the worst signs; by his absent-mindedness in school; by his giving the boys a half holiday because he could not teach; by his asking them to go away quietly so as not to disturb the sick scholar; by his saying "I'm glad they didn't mind me" when the jolly boys went shouting away; by his telling the sick boy that the flowers missed him and were less gay on account of his absence; by his hanging the boy's handkerchief out of the window at his request, as a token of his remembrance of the boys playing on the green; by the loving way in which he embraced the dying boy, and held his cold hand in his after he was dead, chafing it, as if he could bring back the life into it.

Dombey and Son is full of appeals for the tender sympathy of adulthood for childhood. The story of Florence Dombey longing for the one look of tenderness, the one word of kindly interest, the one sympathetic caress from her father, which never came to her during her childhood, is one of the most touching stories ever written. It was written to show that children in the most wealthy homes need sympathy as much as any other children, and that they are often most cruelly neglected by their parents.

Floy pleaded to be allowed to lay her face beside her baby brother's because "she thought he loved her."

The love that is given back in exchange for loving interest is shown by Paul's loving gratitude to Floy for her interest in him, which led her to spend her pocket money in books, so that she might help him with his studies that confused him so.

> And high was her reward, when one Saturday evening, as little Paul was sitting down as usual to "resume his studies," she sat down by his side and showed him all that was rough made smooth, and all that was so dark made clear and plain, before him. It was nothing but a startled look in Paul's wan face—a flush—a smile—and then a close embrace; but God knows how her heart leaped up at this rich payment for her trouble.
>
> "Oh, Floy," cried her brother, "how I love you! How I love you, Floy!"
>
> "And I you, dear!"
>
> "Oh, I am sure, sure of that, Floy!"
>
> He said no more about it, but all that evening sat close by her, very quiet; and in the night he called out from his little room within hers, three or four times, that he loved her.

There is no higher reward than that of the sympathetic teacher who for the first time lets light into a dark mind or heart.

The lady whom Florence overheard talking to her little orphaned niece about her father's cruel coldness toward her truly said: "Not an orphan in the wide world can be so deserted as the child who is an outcast from a living parent's care."

As Dickens was one of the first to urge that children had rights, so he was one of the first to show that there had been altogether too much thought about the duty of children to parents, and too little about the duty of parents to children. Alice Marwood, one of the characters in Dombey and Son, said to Harriet Carker:

> "You brought me here by force of gentleness and kindness, and made me human by woman's looks and words and angel's deeds; I have felt, lying here, that I should like you to know this. It might explain, I have thought, something that used to help to harden me. I had heard so much, in my wrongdoing, of my neglected duty, that I took up with the belief that duty had not been done to me, and that as the seed was sown the harvest grew."

One other point in regard to sympathy was made in Dombey and Son, that a rough exterior may cover a sympathetic heart.

> Long may it remain in this mixed world a point not easy of decision, which is the more beautiful evidence of the Almighty's goodness: the delicate fingers that are formed for sensitiveness and sympathy of touch, and made to minister to pain and grief, or the rough, hard Captain Cuttle hand, that the heart teaches, guides, and softens in a moment!

In the model school of Dickens Doctor Strong is said to have been "the idol of the whole school"; and David adds, "it must have been a badly composed school if he had been anything else, for he was the kindest of men." Doctor Strong's wife, who had been his pupil in early life, said:

> "When I was very young, quite a little child, my first associations with knowledge of any kind were inseparable from a patient friend and teacher—the friend of my dead father—who was always dear to me. I can remember nothing that I know without remembering him. He stored my mind with its first treasures, and stamped his character upon them all. They never could have been, I think, as good as they have been to me, if I had taken them from any other hands."

David said, when telling the story of his first introduction to Mr. Murdstone:

> "God help me, I might have been improved for my whole life, I might have been made another creature, perhaps, for life, by a kind word at that season. A word of encouragement and explanation, of pity for my childish ignorance, of welcome home, of reassurance to me that it was home, might have made me dutiful to him in my heart henceforth, instead of in my hypocritical outside, and might have made me respect instead of hate him."

In Bleak House Dickens gave in Esther the most perfect type of human sympathy, and by his pathetic pictures of poor Jo, Phil, the Jellyby children, the Pardiggle children, and others, stirred a great wave of feeling, which led to a recognition of the duty of adulthood to childhood, and taught the value of sympathy in the training of children.

Esther laid down a new law, revealed by Froebel, but given to the English world by Dickens in the weighty sentence, "My comprehension is quickened when my affection is."

The lack of sympathy in adulthood is revealed for the condemnation of his readers in Mrs. Rachael's parting from Esther.

> Mrs. Rachael was too good to feel any emotion at parting, but I was not so good, and wept bitterly. I thought that I ought to have known her better after so many years, and ought to have made myself enough of a favourite with her to make her sorry then. When she gave me one cold parting kiss upon my forehead, like a

> thaw drop from the stone porch—it was a very frosty day—I felt so miserable and self-reproachful that I clung to her and told her it was my fault, I knew, that she could say good-bye so easily.
>
> "No, Esther!" she returned. "It is your misfortune!"

Poor child, she cried afterward because Mrs. Rachael was not sorry to part with her.

What a different parting she had when leaving the Miss Donnys' school, where for six years she had been a pupil, and for part of the time a teacher!

She received a letter informing her that she was to leave Greenleaf.

> Oh, never, never, never shall I forget the emotion this letter caused in the house! It was so tender in them to care so much for me; it was so gracious in that Father who had not forgotten me, to have made my orphan way so smooth and easy, and to have inclined so many youthful natures toward me, that I could hardly bear it. Not that I would have had them less sorry—I am afraid not; but the pleasure of it, and the pain of it, and the pride and joy of it, and the humble regret of it, were so blended, that my heart seemed almost breaking while it was full of rapture.
>
> The letter gave me only five days' notice of my removal. When every minute added to the proofs of love and kindness that were given me in those five days; and when at last the morning came, and when they took me through all the rooms that I might see them for the last time; and when some one cried, "Esther, dear, say good-bye to me here, at my bedside, where you first spoke so kindly to me!" and when others asked me only to write their names, "With Esther's love"; and when they all surrounded me with their parting presents, and clung to me weeping, and cried, "What shall we do when dear, dear Esther's gone!" and when I tried to tell them how forbearing and how good they had all been to me, and how I blessed and thanked them every one—what a heart I had!
>
> And when the two Miss Donnys grieved as much to part with me as the least among them; and when the maids said, "Bless you, miss, wherever you go!" and when the ugly lame old gardener, who I thought had hardly noticed me in all those years, came panting after the coach to give me a little nosegay of geraniums, and told me I had been the light of his eyes—indeed the old man said so!—what a heart I had then!

This was intended to show the results of her sympathy toward the pupils and everybody connected with the school.

Mrs. Jellyby is an immortal picture of the woman who neglects her family on account of her interest in Borrioboola Gha, or some other place for which her sympathy is aroused. Dickens held that a woman's first duty is to her children.

The wretched Mr. Jellyby, almost distracted by the poor meals, the disorder of his home, and the wild condition of his unfortunate family, said to his daughter, "Never have a mission, my dear."

Caddy emphasized the thought Dickens had given in Dombey and Son through Alice Marwood when she said to Esther:

> "Oh, don't talk of duty as a child, Miss Summerson; where's ma's duty as a parent? All made over to the public and Africa, I suppose! Then let the public and Africa show duty as a child; it's much more their affair than mine. You are shocked, I dare say! Very well, so am I shocked, too; so we are both shocked, and there's an end of it!"

On another occasion, overcome by emotion at the thought of her mother's neglect, she said to Esther:

> "I wish I was dead. I wish we were all dead. It would be a great deal better for us."
>
> In a moment afterward she kneeled on the ground at my side, hid her face in my dress, passionately begged my pardon, and wept. I comforted her, and would have raised her, but she cried, No, no; she wanted to stay there!
>
> "You used to teach girls," she said. "If you could only have taught me, I could have learned from you! I am so very miserable, and like you so much!"

How the Jellyby children loved and trusted Esther! How all children loved and trusted her for her true sympathy!

Poor Jo swept the steps at the graveyard where the friend who spoke kindly to him lay buried, and he always said of him, "He wos wery good to me, he wos."

And Jo's other friends, Mr. Snagsby, whose sympathy drew half crowns from his pocket, and Mr. George, and Doctor Woodcourt, and Mr. Jarndyce, and Esther, showed their kindly sympathy for the wretched boy so fully that the reading world loved them as real friends, and this loving admiration led the Christian world to think more clearly in regard to Christ's teachings about the little ones.

No heart can resist the plea for sympathy for such as Jo in the description of his last illness and death. When the end was very near, as Allan Woodcourt was watching the heavy breathing of the sufferer,

> After a short relapse into sleep or stupor he makes of a sudden a strong effort to get out of bed.
>
> "Stay, Jo! What now?"
>
> "It's time for me to go to that there berryin'-ground, sir," he returns with a wild look.
>
> "Lie down, and tell me. What burying-ground, Jo?"
>
> "Where they laid him as wos wery good to me, wery good

to me indeed, he wos. It's time fur me to go down to that there berryin'-ground, sir, and ask to be put along with him. I wants to go there and be berried. He used fur to say to me, 'I am as poor as you to-day, Jo,' he ses. I wants to tell him that I am as poor as him now, and have come there to be laid along with him."

"By and bye, Jo. By and bye."

"Ah! P'raps they wouldn't do it if I was to go myself. But will you promise to have me took there, sir, and laid along with him?"

"I will, indeed."

"Thank'ee, sir. Thank'ee, sir. They'll have to get the key of the gate afore they can take me in, for it's allus locked. And there's a step there, as I used for to clean with my broom.—It's turned wery dark, sir. Is there any light a-comin'?"

"It is coming fast, Jo."

Fast. The cart is shaken all to pieces, and the rugged road is very near its end.

"Jo, my poor fellow!"

"I hear you, sir, in the dark, but I'm a-gropin'—a-gropin'—let me catch hold of your hand."

"Jo, can you say what I say?"

"I'll say anythink as you say, sir, for I knows it's good."

"OUR FATHER."

"Our Father!—yes, that's wery good, sir."

"WHICH ART IN HEAVEN."

"Art in Heaven—is the light a-comin', sir?"

"It is close at hand. HALLOWED BE THY NAME!"

"Hallowed be—thy— —"

The light is come upon the dark benighted way. Dead!

Dead, your majesty. Dead, my lords and gentlemen. Dead, right reverends and wrong reverends of every order. Dead, men and women, born with heavenly compassion in your hearts. And dying thus around us every day.

One of the best of Dickens's illustrations of gratitude for sympathy is the case of Phil Squod, Mr. George's assistant in the shooting gallery. He was a mere child in everything but years of hard experiences, but he was devoted heart and soul to Mr. George for a kindly word of hearty sympathy. So devoted was he that he attached himself to Mr. George and became his faithful servant, and found his truest happiness in his service of love.

Phil recalled the story to Mr. George.

"It was after the case-filling blow-up when I first see you, commander. You remember?"

"I remember, Phil. You were walking along in the sun."

"Crawling, guv'ner, again a wall——"

"True, Phil—shouldering your way on——"

"In a nightcap!" exclaims Phil, excited.

"In a nightcap——"

"And hobbling with a couple of sticks!" cries Phil, still more excited.

"With a couple of sticks. When——"

"When you stops, you know," cries Phil, putting down his cup and saucer, and hastily removing his plate from his knees, "and says to me, 'What, comrade! You have been in the wars!' I didn't say much to you, commander, then, for I was took by surprise that a person so strong and healthy and bold as you was should stop to speak to such a limping bag of bones as I was. But you says to me, says you, delivering it out of your chest as hearty as possible, so that it was like a glass of something hot: 'What accident have you met with? You have been badly hurt. What's amiss, old boy? Cheer up, and tell us about it!' Cheer up! I was cheered already! I says as much to you, you says more to me, I says more to you, you says more to me, and here I am, commander! Here I am, commander!" cries Phil, who has started from his chair and unaccountably begun to sidle away. "If a mark's wanted, or if it will improve the business, let the customers take aim at me. They can't spoil *my* beauty. *I'm* all right. Come on! If they want a man to box at, let 'em box at me. Let 'em knock me well about the head. *I* don't mind! if they want a light weight, to be throwed for practice, Cornwall, Devonshire, or Lancashire, let 'em throw me. They won't hurt *me*. I have been throwed all sorts of styles all my life!"

Pip said in Great Expectations:

> It is not possible to know how far the influence of any amiable, honest-hearted, duty-doing man flies out into the world; but it is very possible to know how it has touched one's self in going by, and I know right well that any good that intermixed itself with my apprenticeship came of plain contented Joe, and not of restless aspiring discontented me.

Dear, simple-hearted Joe Gargery! When every one else was abusing Pip at the great dinner party, he showed his sympathy for him by putting some more gravy on his plate.

In Our Mutual Friend Lizzie Hexam, sympathizing with her father so much that she would not learn to read because he was bitterly prejudiced against education, but sympathizing so much with her brother Charley that she had him educated secretly so that he might become a teacher, is an illustration of nearly perfect sympathy.

The happiness of the little "minders" at old Betty Higden's is in sharp contrast to the misery of the boarders of the respectable (?) establishment of Mrs. Pipchin. In the one case was abject poverty and loving sympathy, in the other plenty and cruel selfishness. When Mr. and Mrs. Boffin were adopting Johnnie from Betty Higden's care, the brave old woman said:

> "If I could have kept the dear child without the dread that's always upon me of his coming to that fate I have spoken of, I could never have parted with him, even to you. For I love him, I love him, I love him! I love my husband long dead and gone, in him; I love my children dead and gone, in him; I love my young and hopeful days dead and gone, in him. I couldn't sell that love, and look you in your bright kind face. It's a free gift."
>
> Betty was not a logically reasoning woman, but God is good, and hearts may count in heaven as high as heads.

Dickens spoke with great enthusiasm in his American Notes of the practical sympathy of Doctor Howe with all afflicted children, especially with blind children, closing his sketch of the wonderful work he had done with the sentence: "There are not many persons, I hope and believe, who after reading these passages can ever hear that name with indifference." He noted that Laura Bridgman had a special desire for sympathy.

> She is fond of having other children noticed and caressed by the teachers, and those whom she respects; but this must not be carried too far, or she becomes jealous. She wants to have her share, which, if not the lion's, is the greater part; and if she does not get it, she says, "*My mother will love me.*"

Dickens's types of sympathy with children grew more perfect as he grew older. In his later years his head began to catch up with his heart. Major Jackman, Mrs. Lirriper, and Doctor Marigold are among his most wonderfully sympathetic characters.

What an ideal sending away to school Jemmy Lirriper had!

> So the Major being gone out and Jemmy being at home, I got the child into my little room here and I stood him by my chair and I took his mother's own curls in my hand and I spoke to him loving and serious. And when I had reminded the darling how that he was now in his tenth year, and when I had said to him about his getting on in life pretty much what I had said to the Major, I broke to him how that we must have this same parting, and there I was forced to stop, for there I saw of a sudden the well-remembered lip with its tremble, and it so brought back that time! But with the spirit that was in him he controlled it soon, and he says gravely,

> nodding through his tears: "I understand, Gran—I knew it *must* be, Gran—go on, Gran, don't be afraid of *me*." And when I had said all that ever I could think of, he turned his bright steady face to mine, and he says just a little broken here and there: "You shall see, Gran, that I can be a man, and that I can do anything that is grateful and loving to you; and if I don't grow up to be what you would like to have me—I hope it will be—because I shall die." And with that he sat down by me, and I went on to tell him of the school, of which I had excellent recommendations, and where it was and how many scholars, and what games they played as I had heard, and what length of holidays, to all of which he listened bright and clear. And so it came that at last he says: "And now, dear Gran, let me kneel down here where I have been used to say my prayers, and let me fold my face for just a minute in your gown and let me cry, for you have been more than father—more than mother—more than brothers, sisters, friends—to me!" And so he did cry, and I too, and we were both much the better for it.

Dear old Doctor Marigold, the travelling auctioneer, in his tender sympathy for his little girl when her mother was so cruel to her, whispering comforting words in her ear as he was calling for bids on his wares while she was dying, and afterward loving the deaf-mute child whom he adopted in memory of his own child whom he had lost, has made thousands more kindly sympathetic with children.

In the novel that he was writing when he died Dickens makes Canon Crisparkle say to Helena Landless: "You have the wisdom of Love, and it was the highest wisdom ever known upon this earth, remember."

David Copperfield said, "I hope that real love and truth are stronger in the end than any evil or misfortune in the world."

The effect of lack of true sympathy on the heart that should have felt and shown it is revealed in what Sydney Carton said to Mr. Lorry: "If you could say with truth to your own solitary heart to-night, 'I have secured to myself the love and attachment, the gratitude and respect, of no human creature; I have won myself a tender place in no regard; I have done nothing good or serviceable to be remembered by,' your seventy-eight years would be seventy-eight curses; would they not?"

The contrast between the coldness and heartlessness of his parents or guardians and the encouraging sympathy of his teacher is one of the strongest features in the story of Barbox Brothers (Mugby Junction).

> "You remember me, Young Jackson?"
>
> "What do I remember if not you? You are my first remembrance. It was you who told me that was my name. It was you who told me that on every 20th of December my life had a penitential anniversary in it called a birthday. I suppose the last communication was truer than the first!"

"What am I like, Young Jackson?"

"You are like a blight all through the year to me. You hard-lined, thin-lipped, repressive, changeless woman with a wax mask on! You are like the Devil to me—most of all when you teach me religious things, for you make me abhor them."

"You remember me, Mr. Young Jackson?" In another voice from another quarter:

"Most gratefully, sir. You are the ray of hope and prospering ambition in my life. When I attended your course I believed that I should come to be a great healer, and I felt almost happy—even though I was still the one boarder in the house with that horrible mask, and ate and drank in silence and constraint with the mask before me every day. As I had done every, every, every day through my school time and from my earliest recollection."

"What am I like, Mr. Young Jackson?"

"You are like a Superior Being to me. You are like Nature beginning to reveal herself to me. I hear you again as one of the hushed crowd of young men kindling under the power of your presence and knowledge, and you bring into my eyes the only exultant tears that ever stood in them."

"You remember Me, Mr. Young Jackson?" In a grating voice from quite another quarter:

"Too well. You made your ghostly appearance in my life one day, and announced that its course was to be suddenly and wholly changed. You showed me which was my wearisome seat in the Galley of Barbox Brothers. You told me what I was to do, and what to be paid; you told me afterward, at intervals of years, when I was to sign for the Firm, when I became a partner, when I became the Firm. I know no more of it, or of myself."

"What am I like, Mr. Young Jackson?"

"You are like my father, I sometimes think. You are hard enough and cold enough so to have brought up an acknowledged son. I see your scanty figure, your close brown suit, and your tight brown wig; but you, too, wear a wax mask to your death. You never by a chance remove it; it never by a chance falls off; and I know no more of you."

CHAPTER X.

CHILD STUDY AND CHILD NATURE.

Dickens was a profound student of children, and he revealed his consciousness of the need of a general study of childhood in all he wrote about the importance of a free childhood, individuality, the imagination, coercion, cramming, and wrong methods of training children.

He criticised the blindness of those who saw boys as a class or in a limited number of classes, distinguished by external and comparatively unimportant characteristics, in Mr. Grimwig, "who never saw any difference in boys, and only knew two sorts of boys, mealy boys and beef-faced boys."

He exposed the ignorance—the wilful ignorance—of vast numbers of parents and teachers who indignantly resent the suggestion that they need to study children, in Jane Murdstone. When Jane was interfering in the management of David, and with her brother totally misunderstanding him and misrepresenting him, his timid mother ventured to say:

> "I beg your pardon, my dear Jane, but are you quite sure—I am certain you'll excuse me, my dear Jane—that you quite understand Davy?"
>
> "I should be somewhat ashamed of myself, Clara," returned Miss Murdstone, "if I could not understand the boy, or any boy. I don't profess to be profound, but I do lay claim to common sense."

Many Jane Murdstones still claim that it is not necessary to study so common a thing as a boy. Yet a child is the most wonderful thing in the world, and, whether the Jane Murdstones in the schools and homes like it or not, the wise people *are* studying the child with a view to finding out what he should be guided to do in the accomplishment of his own training.

Richard Carstone had been eight years at school, and he was a miserable failure in life, although a man of good ability.

"It had never been anybody's business to find out what his natural bent was, or where his failings lay, or to adapt any kind of knowledge to him." Esther wisely said: "I did doubt whether Richard would not have profited by some one studying him a little, instead of his studying Latin verses so much."

Dickens studied every subject about which he wrote with great care and discrimination. As an instance of this careful study it may be stated that medical authorities say that the description of Smike's sickness and death is the best description of consumption ever written. Dickens had a wonderful imagination, but he never relied on his imagination for his facts or his philosophy. It is therefore reasonable to believe that as he wrote more about children than any other man or woman, he was the greatest and most reverent student of childhood that England has produced.

In addition to the revelations of his conclusions given in the evolution of his child characters, and in the many illustrations of good and of bad training, he continually makes direct statements in regard to child nature and how to deal with it in its varied manifestations.

His central motive was expressed by the old gentleman who found Little Nell astray in London: "I love these little people; and it is not a slight thing when they, who are so fresh from God, love us."

His ideal of unperverted child nature was entirely different from that which had been taught by theology and psychology. He believed the child to be pure and good, and that even when heredity was bad, its baneful influences need not blight the divinity in his life, if he was wisely trained and had a free life of self-activity, a suitable environment, and truly sympathetic friends.

> "It would be a curious speculation," said I, after some restless turns across and across the room, "to imagine her in her future life, holding her solitary way among a crowd of wild, grotesque companions, the only pure, fresh, youthful object in the throng."

To keep children pure and fresh was the chief aim of his life work. He had no respect for those who treated children as if they were grown-up, reasonable beings; who judged children as they would judge adults, and therefore misjudged them. He always remembered that a child was a little stranger in a new world, and that his complex nature had to adjust itself to its environment. He had a perfect, reverent, considerate sympathy for the timid young soul venturing to look out upon its new conditions. One of the most pathetic things in the world to him was the fact that children are nearly universally misunderstood and misinterpreted. How he longed to tear down the barriers of formalism, and conventionality, and indifference, and misconception from the lives of parents and teachers, so that timid children might be true to their better natures in their presence.

> When little Florence timidly presented herself, Mr. Dombey stopped in his pacing up and down and looked toward her. Had he looked with greater interest and with a father's eye, he might have read in her keen glance the impulses and fears that made her waver; the passionate desire to run clinging to him, crying, as she hid her face in his embrace, "Oh, father, try to love me! there's no one else!" the dread of a repulse; the fear of being too bold, and of offending him; the pitiable need in which she stood of some assurance and encouragement; and how her overcharged young heart was wandering to find some natural resting place for its sorrow and affection.
>
> But he saw nothing of this. He saw her pause irresolutely at

the door and look toward him; and he saw no more.

"Come in," he said, "come in; what is the child afraid of?"

She came in, and after glancing round her for a moment with an uncertain air, stood pressing her small hands hard together, close within the door.

"Come here, Florence," said her father coldly. "Do you know who I am?"

"Yes, papa."

"Have you nothing to say to me?"

The tears that stood in her eyes as she raised them quickly to his face were frozen by the expression it wore. She looked down again and put out her trembling hand.

Mr. Dombey took it loosely in his own, and stood looking down upon her for a moment, as if he knew as little as the child what to say or do.

"There! Be a good girl," he said, patting her on the head, and regarding her, as it were, by stealth with a disturbed and doubtful look. "Go to Richards. Go!"

His little daughter hesitated for another instant as though she would have clung about him still, or had some lingering hope that he might raise her in his arms and kiss her. She looked up in his face once more. He thought how like her expression was then to what it had been when she looked round at the doctor—that night—and instinctively dropped her hand and turned away.

It was not difficult to perceive that Florence was at a great disadvantage in her father's presence. It was not only a constraint upon the child's mind, but even upon the natural grace and freedom of her actions.

The child, in her grief and neglect, was so gentle, so quiet and uncomplaining, was possessed of so much affection that no one seemed to care to have, and so much sorrowful intelligence that no one seemed to mind or think about the wounding of, that Polly's heart was sore when she was left alone again.

The same lesson was given to parents and teachers in Murdstone's treatment of Davy. The sensitive, shy boy was regarded as sullen, and treated "like a dog" in consequence. Oh, what bitterness it puts into a child's life to be misunderstood by its dearest friends! If there were no other reason for the co-operative study of children by parents and teachers, it would be a sufficient reason that they might be understood and appreciated. Many lives are made barren and wicked by the failure of parents and teachers to understand them.

It is so easy for children to get the impression that they are not liked by adults.

When Walter started life in Mr. Dombey's great warehouse, his uncle, old Solomon Gills, with whom he lived, asked him on his return from work the first day:

> "Has Mr. Dombey been there to-day?"
>
> "Oh, yes! In and out all day."
>
> "He didn't take any notice of you, I suppose?"
>
> "Yes, he did. He walked up to my seat—I wish he wasn't so solemn and stiff, uncle—and said, 'Oh! you are the son of Mr. Gills, the ships' instrument maker.' 'Nephew, sir,' I said. 'I said nephew, boy,' said he. But I could take my oath he said son, uncle."
>
> "You're mistaken, I dare say. It's no matter."
>
> "No, it's no matter, but he needn't have been so sharp, I thought. There was no harm in it, though he did say son. Then he told me that you had spoken to him about me, and that he had found me employment in the house accordingly, and that I was expected to be attentive and punctual, and then he went away. I thought he didn't seem to like me much."
>
> "You mean, I suppose," observed the instrument maker, "that you didn't seem to like him much."
>
> "Well, uncle," returned the boy, laughing, "perhaps so; I never thought of that."

This short selection reveals the disrespect for childhood which leads adulthood to flatly contradict what a child says, whether he is making a statement of fact or of opinion. This is most inconsiderate, and naturally leads to a corresponding disrespect for adulthood on the part of the child. The selection clearly intimates that childhood would be more happy, and like adulthood better, if adulthood was not so "solemn and stiff." Parents and teachers should learn from Solomon's philosophy that a child's feelings toward an adult partly determine his impressions regarding the attitude of adulthood toward him.

The first thing necessary in training a child to be his real, best self is to win his affectionate regard and confidence. One has to be very true, very unconventional, and very joyous, to do this fully.

Dickens pitied the child because, even when he is understood, his wishes, plans, and decisions are not treated with respect. This is a gross injustice to the child's nature. As Pip so truly said: "It may be only small injustice that the child can be exposed to; but the child is small, and its world is small, and its rocking horse stands as many hands high, according to scale, as a big-boned Irish hunter."

Adulthood needs to learn no lesson more than that childhood lives a life of its own, that that life should not be tested by the scales and tape lines of adulthood, and that within its range of action its choice should be respected, and its opinions treated with reverent consideration.

Mrs. Lirriper said that when she used to read the Bible to Mrs. Edson, when that lady was dying, "though she took to all I read to her, I used to fancy that next to what was taught upon the Mount she took most of all to his gentle compassion for us poor women, and to his young life, and to how his mother was proud of him, and treasured his sayings in her heart."

The divinity in any child will grow more rapidly if his mother "treasures his sayings in her heart." We need more reverence for the child.

Dickens tried to make parents regard the child as a sacred thing, which should always be the richest joy of his parents.

Speaking of Mrs. Darnay, in The Tale of Two Cities, he says:

> The time passed, and her little Lucie lay on her bosom. Then, among the advancing echoes, there was the tread of her tiny feet and the sound of her prattling words. Let greater echoes resound as they would, the young mother at the cradle side could always hear those coming. They came, and the shady house was sunny with a child's laugh, and the divine Friend of children, to whom in her trouble she had confided hers, seemed to take her child in his arms, as he took the child of old, and made it a sacred joy to her.

Dickens had profound faith in children whose true development had not been arrested.

> Doctor Strong had a simple faith in him that might have touched the stone hearts of the very urns upon the wall.... He appealed in everything to the honour and good faith of the boys, and relied on their possession of those qualities unless they proved themselves unworthy.

Reliance begets reliance. Faith increases the qualities that merit faith.

David said the doctor's reliance on the boys "worked wonders." No wonder it worked wonders. We can help a boy to grow no higher than our faith in him can reach.

CHAPTER XI.

BAD TRAINING.

In addition to the bad training found in so many of his best-known schools, to show the evils of coercion in all forms, of the child depravity ideal, of the loss of a free, real, rich childhood, of the dwarfing of individuality, of the deadening of the imagination, and other similar evils, Dickens's books, from Oliver Twist to Edwin Drood, contain many illustrations of utterly wrong methods of training children.

The mean and cruel way in which children used to be treated by the managers of institutions is described in Oliver Twist. Dickens said that when Oliver was born he cried lustily.

> If he could have known that he was an orphan, left to the tender mercies of church wardens and overseers, perhaps he would have cried the louder.
>
> "Bow to the board," said Bumble, when he was brought before that august body. Oliver brushed away two or three tears that were lingering in his eyes, and seeing no board but the table, fortunately bowed to that.
>
> "What's your name, boy?" said the gentleman in the high chair.
>
> Oliver was frightened at the sight of so many gentlemen, which made him tremble; and the beadle gave him another tap behind, which made him cry. These two causes made him answer in a very low and hesitating voice; whereupon a gentleman in a white waistcoat said he was a fool. Which was a capital way of raising his spirits and putting him quite at his ease.
>
> "Boy," said the gentleman in the high chair, "listen to me. You know you're an orphan, I suppose?"
>
> "What's that, sir?" inquired poor Oliver.
>
> "The boy is a fool—I thought he was," said the gentleman in the white waistcoat.
>
> "Hush!" said the gentleman who had spoken first. "You know you've got no father or mother, and that you were brought up by the parish, don't you?"
>
> "Yes, sir," replied Oliver, weeping bitterly.

> "What are you crying for?" inquired the gentleman in the white waistcoat. And, to be sure, it was very extraordinary. What *could* the boy be crying for?
>
> "I hope you say your prayers every night," said another gentleman in a gruff voice, "and pray for the people who feed and take care of you—like a Christian."
>
> "Yes, sir," stammered the boy. The gentleman who spoke last was unconsciously right. It would have been *very* like a Christian, and a marvellously good Christian, too, if Oliver had prayed for the people who fed and took care of *him*.

The dreadful practices of first making children self-conscious and apparently dull by abuse and formalism, and then calling them "fools," or "stupid," or "dunces," are happily not so common now.

In Barnaby Rudge he makes Edward Chester complain to his father about the way he had been educated.

> From my childhood I have been accustomed to luxury and idleness, and have been bred as though my fortune were large and my expectations almost without a limit. The idea of wealth has been familiarized to me from my cradle. I have been taught to look upon those means by which men raise themselves to riches and distinction as being beyond my breeding and beneath my care. I have been, as the phrase is, liberally educated, and am fit for nothing.

Dickens was in terrible earnest to kill all the giants that preyed on the lifeblood of the joy, the hope, the freedom, the selfhood, and the imagination of childhood. He waged unceasing warfare against the system which he described as

> The excellent and thoughtful old system, hallowed by long prescription, which has usually picked out from the rest of mankind the most dreary and uncomfortable people that could possibly be laid hold of, to act as instructors of youth.

The selfish and mercenary ideal and its consequences are dealt with in the training of Jonas Chuzzlewit:

> The education of Mr. Jonas had been conducted from his cradle on the strictest principles of the main chance. The very first word he learned to spell was "gain," and the second one (when he got into two syllables) "money." But for two results, which were not clearly foreseen perhaps by his watchful parent in the beginning, his training may be said to have been unexceptionable. One of these flaws was, that having been long taught by his father to overreach everybody, he had imperceptibly acquired a love of overreaching that venerable monitor himself. The other, that from his early habits of considering everything as a question of property, he had gradually come to look with impatience on his parent

> as a certain amount of personal estate which had no right whatever to be going at large, but ought to be secured in that particular description of iron safe which is commonly called a coffin, and banked in the grave.

When Charity Pecksniff reproved Jonas for speaking irreverently of her father, he said:

> "Ecod, you may say what you like of *my* father, then, and so I give you leave," said Jonas. "I think it's liquid aggravation that circulates through his veins, and not regular blood. How old should you think my father was, cousin?"
>
> "Old, no doubt," replied Miss Charity; "but a fine old gentleman."
>
> "A fine old gentleman!" repeated Jonas, giving the crown of his hat an angry knock. "Ah! It's time he was thinking of being drawn out a little finer, too. Why, he's eighty!"
>
> "Is he, indeed?" said the young lady.
>
> "And ecod," cried Jonas, "now he's gone so far without giving in, I don't see much to prevent his being ninety; no, nor even a hundred. Why, a man with any feeling ought to be ashamed of being eighty, let alone more. Where's his religion, I should like to know, when he goes flying in the face of the Bible like that? Threescore and ten's the mark; and no man with a conscience, and a proper sense of what's expected of him, has any business to live longer."

When Jonas was particularly brutal in the treatment of Chuffey, the old clerk, his father seemed to enjoy his son's sharpness.

> It was strange enough that Anthony Chuzzlewit, himself so old a man, should take a pleasure in these gibings of his estimable son at the expense of the poor shadow at their table; but he did, unquestionably, though not so much—to do him justice—with reference to their ancient clerk, as in exultation at the sharpness of Jonas. For the same reason, that young man's coarse allusions, even to himself, filled him with a stealthy glee, causing him to rub his hands and chuckle covertly, as if he said in his sleeve, "*I* taught him. *I* trained him. This is the heir of my bringing up. Sly, cunning, and covetous, he'll not squander my money. I worked for this; I hoped for this; it has been the great end and aim of my life."
>
> What a noble end and aim it was to contemplate in the attainment, truly! But there be some who manufacture idols after the fashion of themselves, and fail to worship them when they are made; charging their deformity on outraged Nature. Anthony was better than these at any rate.

Exaggerated! Slightly exaggerated, but terribly true to Nature. Centring the life of a child on one base materialistic aim is certain to make a degraded if not a dangerous character. Every noble energy that should have given spiritual strength and beauty is devoured by the material monster as he grows in the heart. Respect for age, even for parents, is lost with all other virtues, and humanity becomes not a brotherhood to be co-operated with for noble purposes, but a horde to be entrapped and cheated. Jonas delighted his father with his rule in business: "Here's the rule for bargains—'Do other men, for they would do you.' That's the true business precept. All others are counterfeits."

Speaking of the conversation heard by Martin Chuzzlewit at the boarding house in New York, he said:

> It was rather barren of interest, to say the truth; and the greater part of it may be summed up in one word: Dollars. All their cares, hopes, joys, affections, virtues, and associations seemed to be melted down into dollars. Whatever the chance contributions that fell into the slow cauldron of their talk, they made the gruel thick and slab with dollars. Men were weighed by their dollars, measures gauged by their dollars; life was auctioneered, appraised, put up, and knocked down for its dollars. The next respectable thing to dollars was any venture having their attainment for its end. The more of that worthless ballast, honour and fair dealing, which any man cast overboard from the ship of his good name and good intent, the more ample stowage room he had for dollars. Make commerce one huge lie and mighty theft. Deface the banner of the nation for an idle rag; pollute it star by star; and cut out stripe by stripe as from the arm of a degraded soldier. Do anything for dollars! What is a flag to *them*!

This was a solemn warning against the training of a race with such low ideals.

In the preface to Martin Chuzzlewit Dickens shows that he deliberately planned Jonas Chuzzlewit as a psychological study. He says:

> I conceive that the sordid coarseness and brutality of Jonas would be unnatural, if there had been nothing in his early education, and in the precept and example always before him, to engender and develop the vices that make him odious. But, so born and so bred—admired for that which made him hateful, and justified from his cradle in cunning, treachery, and avarice—I claim him as the legitimate issue of the father upon whom those vices are seen to recoil. And I submit that their recoil upon that old man, in his unhonoured age, is not a mere piece of poetical justice, but is the extreme exposition of a direct truth.

Mrs. Pipchin was described as a child trainer of great respectability. She adopted the business of child training because her husband lost his money. Dickens did great service to the world by ridiculing the outrageous practice of sending children to be trained by women or taught by men whose only qualification for the most sacred of all duties was the fact that they had lost their money, and were therefore likely to be bad tempered and severe. He had already introduced Squeers to the world, but he knew that many people who shuddered at Squeers would send their own children to such as Mrs. Pipchin, because she was respectable and poor. He wished to alarm such people; hence Mrs. Pipchin.

Mrs. Chick, Mr. Dombey's sister, and Miss Tox called Mr. Dombey's attention to Mrs. Pipchin's establishment.

> "Mrs. Pipchin, my dear Paul," returned his sister, "is an elderly lady—Miss Tox knows her whole history—who has for some time devoted all the energies of her mind, with the greatest success, to the study and treatment of infancy, and who has been extremely well connected."
>
> This celebrated Mrs. Pipchin was a marvellous, ill-favoured, ill-conditioned old lady, of a stooping figure, with a mottled face like bad marble, a hook nose, and a hard gray eye that looked as if it might have been hammered at on an anvil without sustaining any injury. Forty years at least had elapsed since the Peruvian mines had been the death of Mr. Pipchin; but his relict still wore black bombazine, of such a lustreless, deep, dead, sombre shade that gas itself couldn't light her up after dark, and her presence was a quencher to any number of candles. She was generally spoken of as "a great manager" of children; and the secret of her management was, to give them everything that they didn't like and nothing that they did—which was found to sweeten their dispositions very much.

When Paul and Florence were taken to Mrs. Pipchin's establishment, Mrs. Pipchin gave them an opportunity to study her disciplinary system as soon as Mrs. Chick and Miss Tox went away. "Master Bitherstone was divested of his collar at once, which he had worn on parade," and Miss Pankey, the only other little boarder at present, was walked off to the castle dungeon (an empty apartment at the back, devoted to correctional purposes), for having sniffed thrice in the presence of visitors.

> At one o'clock there was a dinner, chiefly of the farinaceous and vegetable kind, when Miss Pankey (a mild little blue-eyed morsel of a child, who was shampooed every morning, and seemed in danger of being rubbed away altogether) was led in from captivity by the ogress herself, and instructed that nobody who sniffed before visitors ever went to heaven. When this great truth had been thoroughly impressed upon her, she was regaled with rice; and subsequently repeated the form of grace established in the castle, in which there was a special clause thanking Mrs. Pipchin for a good dinner. Mrs. Pipchin's niece, Berinthia, took cold pork. Mrs. Pipchin, whose constitution required warm nourishment, made a special repast of mutton chops, which were

brought in hot and hot, between two plates, and smelled very nice.

As it rained after dinner and they couldn't go out walking on the beach, and Mrs. Pipchin's constitution required rest after chops, they went away with Berry (otherwise Berinthia) to the dungeon—an empty room looking out upon a chalk wall and a water butt, and made ghastly by a ragged fireplace without any stove in it. Enlivened by company, however, this was the best place after all; for Berry played with them there, and seemed to enjoy a game at romps as much as they did; until Mrs. Pipchin knocking angrily at the wall, like the Cock Lane Ghost revived, they left off, and Berry told them stories in a whisper until twilight.

For tea there was plenty of milk and water, and bread and butter, with a little black teapot for Mrs. Pipchin and Berry, and buttered toast unlimited for Mrs. Pipchin, which was brought in, hot and hot, like the chops. Though Mrs. Pipchin got very greasy outside over this dish, it didn't seem to lubricate her internally at all; for she was as fierce as ever, and the hard gray eye knew no softening.

After tea, Berry brought out a little workbox, with the Royal Pavilion on the lid, and fell to working busily; while Mrs. Pipchin, having put on her spectacles and opened a great volume bound in green baize, began to nod. And whenever Mrs. Pipchin caught herself falling forward into the fire, and woke up, she filliped Master Bitherstone on the nose for nodding too.

At last it was the children's bedtime, and after prayers they went to bed. As little Miss Pankey was afraid of sleeping alone in the dark, Mrs. Pipchin always made a point of driving her upstairs herself, like a sheep; and it was cheerful to hear Miss Pankey moaning long afterward, in the least eligible chamber, and Mrs. Pipchin now and then going in to shake her. At about half-past nine o'clock the odour of a warm sweetbread (Mrs. Pipchin's constitution wouldn't go to sleep without sweetbread) diversified the prevailing fragrance of the house, which Mrs. Wickam said was "a smell of building," and slumber fell upon the castle shortly after.

The breakfast next morning was like the tea overnight, except that Mrs. Pipchin took her roll instead of toast, and seemed a little more irate when it was over. Master Bitherstone read aloud to the rest a pedigree from Genesis (judiciously selected by Mrs. Pipchin), getting over the names with the ease and clearness of a person tumbling up the treadmill. That done, Miss Pankey was borne away to be shampooed, and Master Bitherstone to have something else done to him with salt water, from which he always returned very blue and dejected. Paul and Florence went out in the meantime on the beach with Wickam—who was constantly in tears—and at about noon Mrs. Pipchin presided over some Early Readings. It being a part of Mrs. Pipchin's system not to encourage a child's mind to develop and expand itself like a young flower, but to open it by force like an oyster, the moral of these lessons was usually of a violent and stunning character; the hero—a naughty boy—seldom, in the mildest catastrophe, being finished off by anything less than a lion or a bear.

Sunday evening was the most melancholy evening in the week; for Mrs. Pipchin always made a point of being particularly cross on Sunday nights. Miss Pankey was generally brought back from an aunt's at Rottingdean, in deep distress; and Master Bitherstone, whose relatives were all in India, and who was required to sit, between the services, in an erect position with his head against the parlour wall, neither moving hand nor foot, suffered so acutely in his young spirits that he once asked Florence, on a Sunday night, if she could give him any idea of the way back to Bengal.

But it was generally said that Mrs. Pipchin was a woman of system with children; and no doubt she was. Certainly the wild ones went home tame enough, after sojourning for a few months beneath her hospitable roof.

At this exemplary old lady Paul would sit staring in his little armchair by the fire for any length of time. He never seemed to know what weariness was when he was looking fixedly at Mrs. Pipchin. He was not fond of her; he was not afraid of her; but in those old, old moods of his, she seemed to have a grotesque attraction for him. There he would sit, looking at her, and warming his hands, and looking at her, until he sometimes quite confounded Mrs. Pipchin, ogress as she was. Once she asked him, when they were alone, what he was thinking about.

"You," said Paul, without the least reserve.

"And what are you thinking about me?" asked Mrs. Pipchin.

"I'm thinking how old you must be," said Paul.

"You mustn't say such things as that, young gentleman," returned the dame. "That'll never do."

"Why not?" asked Paul.

"Because it's not polite," said Mrs. Pipchin snappishly.

"Not polite?" said Paul.

"No."

"It's not polite," said Paul innocently, "to eat all the mutton chops and toast, Wickam says."

"Wickam," retorted Mrs. Pipchin, colouring, "is a wicked, impudent, bold-faced hussy."

"What's that?" inquired Paul.

"Never you mind, sir," retorted Mrs. Pipchin. "Remember the story of the little boy that was gored to death by a mad bull for asking questions."

"If the bull was mad," said Paul, "how did he know that the boy had asked questions? Nobody can go and whisper secrets to a mad bull. I don't believe that story."

"You don't believe it, sir?" repeated Mrs. Pipchin, amazed.

"No," said Paul.

"Not if it should happen to have been a tame bull, you little infidel?" said Mrs. Pipchin.

"Berry's very fond of you, ain't she?" Paul once asked Mrs. Pipchin when they were sitting by the fire with the cat.

"Yes," said Mrs. Pipchin.

"Why?" asked Paul.

"Why?" returned the disconcerted old lady. "How can you ask such things, sir? Why are you fond of your sister Florence?"

"Because she's very good," said Paul. "There's nobody like Florence."

"Well!" retorted Mrs. Pipchin shortly, "and there's nobody like me, I suppose."

"Ain't there really, though?" asked Paul, leaning forward in his chair, and looking at her very hard.

"No," said the old lady.

"I am glad of that," observed Paul, rubbing his hands thoughtfully. "That's a very good thing."

To which every one would say "Amen," if they could believe Mrs. Pipchin's statement to be actually true.

Mrs. Pipchin combined in her "system" many of the evils of child training.

She was not good-looking, and those who train children should be decidedly good-looking. They need not be handsome; they ought to be winsome. Her "mottled face like bad marble, and hard grey eye" meant danger to childhood.

She was gloomy in appearance, in manner, and in dress, all disqualifications for any position connected with child development.

She was "a bitter old lady," and children should be surrounded with an atmosphere of sweetness and joyousness.

Her one diabolical rule was "to give children everything they didn't like and nothing they did like." This rule is the logical limit of the doctrine of child depravity.

She was generally spoken of as a "great manager," simply because she compelled children to do her bidding by fear of punishment in the "dungeon," or of being sent to bed, or robbed of their meals, or by some other mean form of contemptible coercion. These processes were praised as excellent till Dickens destroyed their respectability. His title "child-queller" is admirable, and full of philosophy. Many a man has been able to form a truer conception regarding child freedom through the influence of the word "child-queller." Every teacher should ask himself every day, "Am I a child-queller?" It will be a blessed thing for the children when there shall be no more Pipchinny teachers.

The environment of the ogress was not attractive. The gardens grew only marigolds, snails were on the doors, and bad odours in the house. "In the winter time the air couldn't be got out of the castle, and in the summer time it couldn't be got in." Dickens knew that the environment of children has a direct influence on their characters, and that ventilation is essential to good health. These lessons were needed fifty years ago.

Mrs. Pipchin made children dishonest by putting on collars for parade.

"The farinaceous and vegetable" diet, the "regaled with rice" criticisms show that Dickens anticipated by half a century the present interest in the study of nutrition as one of the most important educational subjects.

The combination of coercion and religion is ridiculed in the theological constraint of Mrs. Pipchin, when she told little Miss Pankey "that nobody who sniffed before visitors ever went to heaven."

The outrageous selfishness of adulthood was exposed by the description of Mrs. Pipchin's anger at the play of the children in the back room when it was raining and they could not go out.

The injustice of the "child-queller" was shown because she filliped Master Bitherstone on the nose for nodding in the evening, whenever she woke up from her own nodding.

The sacrilege of having prayers between two processes of cruelty is worthy of note. Religion should never be associated in the mind of a child with injustice, cruelty, or any meanness.

The dreadful practice of driving timid children to sleep in the dark was another of Mrs. Pipchin's accomplishments. The retiring hour of childhood should be made the happiest and most nerve soothing of the day. Wise and sympathetic adulthood, especially motherhood, can then reach the central nature of the child most successfully.

The formal reading of a meaningless selection from the Bible by Bitherstone tended to prevent the development of a true interest in that most interesting of all books.

The Early Readings, with the bad boy in the story "being finished off generally by a lion or a bear," were a fit accompaniment to a system in which no child's mind was encouraged to expand like a flower naturally, but to be opened by force like an oyster.

Dickens began with Mrs. Pipchin his revelation of the great blunder of checking the questions of children. "Remember the story of the little boy that was gored to death by a mad bull for asking questions," she said to Paul. The same evil is pointed out in the training of Pip in Great Expectations.

Another common error is revealed by Mrs. Pipchin, when she called Paul "a little infidel," because he did not accept her statement about the mad bull, although she knew it to be false herself. Even when children doubt the truth they should not be called "infidels," unless, indeed, it is desired to make them definitely and consciously sceptical.

The Puritan Sabbath was a part of Mrs. Pipchin's quelling system too.

It was little wonder, therefore, that the wild children went home tame enough after a few months in her awful institution.

Few men who have ever lived have studied the child and his training so thoroughly as to be able to condense into such brief space so many of the evils of bad training.

Mrs. Pipchin and Mr. Squeers have been made to do good work for childhood.

Biler was so badly treated at the grinders' school that he played hookey, but that was not the worst feature of his education. They did not feel any responsibility for character development in the school of the Charitable Grinders.

> But they never taught honour at the grinders' school, where the system that prevailed was particularly strong in the engendering of hypocrisy; insomuch that many of the friends and masters of past grinders said, if this were what came of education for the common people, let us have none. Some more rational said, Let us have a better one; but the governing powers of the grinders' company were always ready for *them*, by picking out a few boys who had turned out well in spite of the system, and roundly asserting that they could have only turned out well because of it. Which settled the business of those objectors out of hand, and established the glory of the grinders' institution.

In David Copperfield, Uriah Heep, utterly detestable in character, is the natural product of the system of training under which both he and his father were brought up. Uriah said:

> "Father and me was both brought up at a foundation school for boys; and mother, she was likewise brought up at a public, sort of charitable, establishment. They taught us all a deal of um-

> bleness—not much else that I know of—from morning to night. We was to be umble to this person, and umble to that; and to pull off our caps here, and to make bows there; and always to know our place, and abase ourselves before our betters. And we had such a lot of betters! Father got the monitor medal by being umble. So did I. Father got made a sexton by being umble. He had the character, among the gentlefolks, of being such a well-behaved man that they were determined to bring him on. 'Be umble, Uriah,' says father, 'and you'll get on. It was what was always being dinned into you and me at school; it's what goes down best. Be umble,' says father, 'and you'll do!' And really it ain't done bad!"
>
> It was the first time it had ever occurred to me that this detestable cant of false humility might have originated out of the Heep family. I had seen the harvest, but had never thought of the seed. I had never doubted his meanness, his craft and malice; but I fully comprehended now, for the first time, what a base, unrelenting, and revengeful spirit must have been engendered by this early, and this long, suppression.

David himself tells how he suffered after the death of his mother from the cold neglect of Mr. Murdstone and Jane Murdstone. No child can be so destitute as the child who is neglected through dislike.

> And now I fell into a state of neglect, which I can not look back upon without compassion. I fell at once into a solitary condition—apart from all friendly notice, apart from the society of all other boys of my own age, apart from all companionship but my own spiritless thoughts—which seems to cast its gloom upon this paper as I write.
>
> What would I have given to have been sent to the hardest school that ever was kept! to have been taught something, anyhow, anywhere! No such hope dawned upon me. They disliked me, and they sullenly, sternly, steadily overlooked me. I think Mr. Murdstone's means were straitened at about this time; but it is little to the purpose. He could not bear me; and in putting me from him he tried, as I believe, to put away the notion that I had any claim upon him—and succeeded.
>
> I was not actively ill used. I was not beaten or starved; but the wrong that was done to me had no intervals of relenting, and was done in a systematic, passionless manner. Day after day, week after week, month after month, I was coldly neglected. I wonder sometimes, when I think of it, what they would have done if I had been taken with an illness—whether I should have lain down in my lonely room and languished through it in my usual solitary way, or whether anybody would have helped me out.

But the greatest lesson in wrong training given in David Copperfield is the character development of Steerforth. He was ruined by the misdirected love of his mother, and his life is a fine psychological study.

He was a boy of unusually good ability and great attractiveness. He possessed by nature every element of power and grace required to make him a strong, true, and very successful man; but the love of his mother degenerated to pride and admiration, indulgence was substituted for guidance, and the strong woman became weak at the vital point of training her boy. She allowed him to become selfish and vain by yielding to his caprices. She thought she was making his character strong by allowing no restraint to be put upon it. She failed to distinguish between license and liberty. She had conceived the ideal of the need of freedom, but she knew naught of the true harmony between control and spontaneity. She allowed the spontaneity, and gloried in his resistance to control. She was blind to the balancing element in "the perfect law of liberty." She made her boy a powerful engine without a governor valve. So his selfhood became selfishness, and his character was wrecked. Among other immoral opinions that he gained from his mother's training was the idea that he belonged to a select class superior to common humanity. How Dickens hated this thought! Rosa Dartle asked Steerforth about

> "That sort of people—are they really animals and clods, and beings of another order? I want to know so much."
>
> "Why, there's a pretty wide separation between them and us," said Steerforth, with indifference. "They are not to be expected to be as sensitive as we are. Their delicacy is not to be shocked or hurt very easily. They are wonderfully virtuous, I dare say—some people contend for that, at least, and I am sure I don't want to contradict them; but they have not very fine natures, and they may be thankful that, like their coarse, rough skins, they are not easily wounded."

He was trained to despise work, which is a good start toward the utter loss of character. A boy who despises his fellow-beings whom he assumes to rank below him, and who also despises work, instead of recognising the duty of every man to be a producer or a distributor of power, may easily fall into moral degeneracy.

> "Help yourself, Copperfield!" said Steerforth. "We'll drink the daisies of the field, in compliment to you; and the lilies of the valley that toil not, neither do they spin, in compliment to me—the more shame for me!"

His character lacked seriousness. He had the fatal levity that led him to discuss the most sacred subjects in a flippant manner.

His mother knew that Creakle's school was not a proper place for him, but she wished to make him conscious of his superiority even over his teacher, and she knew that Creakle, tyrannical bully though he was, would yield to Steerforth, because his mother was wealthy.

> "It was not a fit school generally for my son," said she; "far from it; but there were particular circumstances to be considered

at the time, of more importance even than that selection. My son's high spirit made it desirable that he should be placed with some man who felt its superiority, and would be content to bow himself before it; and we found such a man there."

What a perversion of the ideal of freedom in the development of character, to suppose that it could only reach perfection by a consciousness of superiority; by having some one who should control him bow down before him! No man in the world is truly free who has a desire to dominate some one else—another man, a woman, or a child. Yet Mrs. Steerforth sacrificed her son's education in order that his manly spirit might be cultivated by the subordination of the man who should have governed him. She showed better judgment in deciding that a coercive tyrant like Creakle would make a subservient sycophant.

"My son's great capacity was tempted on there by a feeling of voluntary emulation and conscious pride," the fond lady went on to say. "He would have risen against all constraint; but he found himself the monarch of the place, and he haughtily determined to be worthy of his station. It was like himself."

As Steerforth began consciously to feel his better nature surrendering to his sensuality, he experienced the pangs that all strong natures feel at the loss of moral power, and one time when he and David were visiting Mr. Peggotty at Yarmouth he seemed to be moody and disposed to sadness. He said suddenly to David when they were alone one day:

"David, I wish to God I had had a judicious father these last twenty years!"

"My dear Steerforth, what is the matter?"

"I wish with all my soul I had been better guided!" he exclaimed. "I wish with all my soul I could guide myself better!"

There was a passionate dejection in his manner that quite amazed me. He was more unlike himself than I could have supposed possible.

"It would be better to be this poor Peggotty, or his lout of a nephew," he said, getting up and leaning moodily against the chimney piece, with his face toward the fire, "than to be myself, twenty times richer and twenty times wiser and be the torment to myself that I have been, in this Devil's bark of a boat, within the last half hour!"

He had already begun to poison the fountains of little Emily's purity.

When Steerforth, after running away with Emily and deserting her, was drowned and brought home, Rosa Dartle, who had loved him, charged his mother with his ruin. She had a scar on her lip, made by a hammer thrown by Steerforth when he was a boy.

"Do you remember when he did this?" she proceeded. "Do

> you remember when in his inheritance of your nature, and in your pampering of his pride and passion, he did this, and disfigured me for life? Look at me, marked until I die with his high displeasure, and moan and groan for what you made him!"
>
> "Miss Dartle," I entreated her, "for Heaven's sake— —"
>
> "I *will* speak," she said, turning on me with her lightning eyes. "Be silent you! Look at me, I say, proud mother of a proud false son! Moan for your nurture of him, moan for your corruption of him, moan for your loss of him, moan for mine!"
>
> She clinched her hand, and trembled through her spare, worn figure, as if her passion were killing her by inches.
>
> "You resent his self-will!" she exclaimed. "You injured by his haughty temper! You, who opposed to both, when your hair was gray, the qualities which made both when you gave him birth! You, who from his cradle reared him to be what he was, and stunted what he should have been! Are you rewarded, *now*, for your years of trouble?"
>
> "Miss Dartle," said I, "if you can be so obdurate as not to feel for this afflicted mother— —"
>
> "Who feels for me?" she sharply retorted. "She has sown this. Let her moan for the harvest that she reaps to-day!"

To show that the seed for the harvest had been sown by his mother was Dickens's aim in the delineation of his character. Yet she loved him as a part of her own life. She said to Mr. Peggotty, when he came to plead with her for Emily:

> "My son, who has been the object of my life, to whom its every thought has been devoted, whom I have gratified from a child in every wish, from whom I have had no separate existence since his birth."

There was a double sadness in David's soliloquy about Steerforth, who had been his friend:

> In the keen distress of the discovery of his unworthiness, I thought more of all that was brilliant in him, I softened more toward all that was good in him, I did more justice to the qualities that might have made him a man of a noble nature and a great name, than ever I had done in the height of my devotion to him.

In Bleak House a great deal of attention is paid to child training.

Esther's sadness because of her neglected birthday touches a tender chord.

> It was my birthday. There were holidays at school on other birthdays; none on mine. There were rejoicings at home on other birthdays, as I knew from what I heard the girls relate to one another; there were none on mine. My birthday was the most melan-

choly day at home in the whole year.

There is more than mere sentiment in birthday celebrations both at home and in school. It develops a pleasant consciousness of individuality and community—two of the greatest educational ideals.

The cruelty of telling children of any supposed blight of heredity or of any other shadow that arrogant conventionality dares to throw over them, is criticised in the hard, gloomy way in which Esther's godmother referred to her mother.

Even worse than this in the refinement of its cruelty was her parting injunction. It is a shameful thing to make a child believe that she is different from other children in any sense of either badness or goodness.

> "Submission, self-denial, diligent work, are the preparations for a life begun with such a shadow on it. You are different from other children, Esther, because you were not born, like them, in common sinfulness and wrath. You are set apart."
>
> I went up to my room and crept to bed, and laid my doll's cheek against mine wet with tears, and holding that solitary friend upon my bosom cried myself to sleep. Imperfect as my understanding of my sorrow was, I knew that I had brought no joy, at any time, to anybody's heart, and that I was to no one upon earth what Dolly was to me.

Dickens evidently meant to reveal more than her godmother's cruelty in her closing moralizings. She made the mistake of using self-denial and diligent work as curses instead of blessings. They were for the time none the less curses to the child, however.

The gross negligence of parents in regard to the sacredness of the children's retiring hour is exposed in the management of the Jellyby children. Indeed, Mrs. Jellyby may be regarded as several volumes of treatises on how not to train children. Caddy expressed her views of the training they received by saying: "I wish I was dead. I wish we were all dead. It would be a great deal better for us." She wisely added: "Oh, don't talk of duty as a child! where's ma's duty as a parent?" Esther said wisely:

> It struck me that if Mrs. Jellyby had discharged her own natural duties and obligations before she swept the horizon with a telescope in search of others, she would have taken the best precautions against becoming absurd; but I need scarcely observe that I kept this to myself.

Esther describes the process of putting the children to bed one evening she was visiting at the Jellyby home:

> Mrs. Jellyby stopped for a moment her conversation with Mr. Quale, on the Brotherhood of Humanity, long enough to order the children to bed.
>
> As Peepy cried for me to take him to bed, I carried him up-

> stairs, where the young woman with the flannel bandage charged into the midst of the little family like a dragon, and overturned them into cribs.
>
> Peepy was the unfortunate child who had fallen downstairs, who now interrupted the correspondence by presenting himself with a slip of plaster on his forehead, to exhibit his wounded knees, in which Ada and I did not know which to pity most, the bruises or the dirt. Mrs. Jellyby merely added, with the serene composure with which she said everything, "Go along, you naughty Peepy!" and fixed her fine eyes on Africa again.

Here Mrs. Jellyby was guilty of two wrongs, one of commission, the other of omission. She did a positive wrong in unjustly calling the child "naughty" when he was merely unfortunate. Even if children are so badly guided that they do wrong, it is a serious mistake to make them feel consciously "bad" by calling them unpleasant names. It is always wrong to define in the child's consciousness a passing wave of evil.

Mrs. Jellyby's sin of omission was her neglect of the opportunity of sympathizing with the suffering boy, and of training him to bear suffering bravely by the suggestion that he was "a brave little soldier home from the war."

Mr. Jarndyce, in speaking of Harold Skimpole's children, said, when Richard Carstone asked if he had any children:

> "Yes, Rick! Half a dozen. More! Nearer a dozen, I should think. But he has never looked after them. How could he? He wanted somebody to look after *him*. He is a child, you know!" said Mr. Jarndyce.
>
> "And have the children looked after themselves at all, sir?" inquired Richard.
>
> "Why, just as you may suppose," said Mr. Jarndyce, his countenance suddenly falling. "It is said that the children of the very poor are not brought up, but dragged up. Harold Skimpole's children have tumbled up somehow or other— —"

Again Dickens was impressing the responsibility of parents for the care and proper training of their children.

Mr. Jarndyce accounted for the utterly unpractical nature of Mr. Skimpole by saying:

> "Why, he is all sentiment, and—and susceptibility, and—and sensibility—and—and imagination. And these qualities are not regulated in him, somehow. I suppose the people who admired him for them in his youth attached too much importance to them, and too little to any training that would have balanced and adjusted them; and so he became what he is."

Mrs. Pardiggle was given as a type of the philanthropic woman who does *not* neglect her children, but whose training is worse—much worse than Mrs. Jellyby's neglect. The Jellyby children had as much motherly sympathy as the Pardiggles, and they had freedom. There is always this advantage in neglect. Louisa Gradgrind gave utterance to a philosophical principle when she said to her father: "Oh! if you had only neglected me, what a much better and much happier creature I should have been." Dickens did not teach that neglect is good training, but he did teach that it is a lighter curse than the Gradgrind or Pardiggle training.

The Jellyby children had a slight chance to turn out moderately well, but the Pardiggle children were certain to be morose, hypocritical, and vicious. They were certain to hate all forms of Christian philanthropy. Mrs. Pardiggle's intentions were undoubtedly good, but she destroyed the character of her children, nevertheless.

> "These, young ladies," said Mrs. Pardiggle with great volubility, after the first salutations, "are my five boys. You may have seen their names in a printed subscription list (perhaps more than one) in the possession of our esteemed friend Mr. Jarndyce. Egbert, my eldest (twelve), is the boy who sent out his pocket money, to the amount of five and threepence to the Tockahoopo Indians. Oswald, my second (ten and a half), is the child who contributed two and ninepence to the Great National Smithers Testimonial. Francis, my third (nine), one and sixpence halfpenny; Felix, my fourth (seven), eightpence to the Superannuated Widows; Alfred, my youngest (five), has voluntarily enrolled himself in the Infant Bonds of Joy, and is pledged never through life to use tobacco in any form."
>
> We had never seen such dissatisfied children. It was not merely that they were weazened and shrivelled—though they were certainly that too—but they looked absolutely ferocious with discontent. At the mention of the Tockahoopo Indians I could really have supposed Egbert to be one of the most baleful members of that tribe, he gave me such a savage frown. The face of each child as the amount of his contribution was mentioned darkened in a peculiarly vindictive manner, but his was by far the worst. I must except, however, the little recruit into the Infant Bonds of Joy, who was stolidly and evenly miserable.
>
> "You have been visiting, I understand," said Mrs. Pardiggle, "at Mrs. Jellyby's?"
>
> We said yes, we had passed one night there.
>
> "Mrs. Jellyby is a benefactor to society, and deserves a helping hand. My boys have contributed to the African project—Egbert, one and six, being the entire allowance of nine weeks; Oswald, one and a penny halfpenny, being the same; the rest, according to their little means. Nevertheless, I do not go with Mrs. Jellyby in all things. I do not go with Mrs. Jellyby in her treatment of

> her young family. It has been noticed. It has been observed that her young family are excluded from participation in the objects to which she is devoted. She may be right, she may be wrong; but, right or wrong, this is not my course with *my* young family. I take them everywhere."
>
> I was afterward convinced (and so was Ada) that from the ill-conditioned eldest child these words extorted a sharp yell. He turned it off into a yawn, but it began as a yell.
>
> "They attend matins with me (very prettily done) at half past six o'clock in the morning all the year round, including, of course, the depth of winter," said Mrs. Pardiggle rapidly, "and they are with me during the revolving duties of the day. I am a school lady, I am a visiting lady, I am a reading lady, I am a distributing lady; I am on the local linen box committee, and many general committees; and my canvassing alone is very extensive—perhaps no one's more so. But they are my companions everywhere; and by these means they acquire that knowledge of the poor, and that capacity of doing charitable business in general—in short, that taste for the sort of thing—which will render them in after life a service to their neighbours, and a satisfaction to themselves. My young family are not frivolous; they expend the entire amount of their allowance in subscriptions, under my direction; and they have attended as many public meetings, and listened to as many lectures, orations, and discussions as generally fall to the lot of few grown people. Alfred (five), who, as I mentioned, has of his own election joined the Infant Bonds of Joy, was one of the very few children who manifested consciousness on one occasion, after a fervid address of two hours from the chairman of the evening."
>
> Alfred glowered at us as if he never could, or would, forgive the injury of that night.
>
> "You may have observed, Miss Summerson," said Mrs. Pardiggle, "in some of the lists to which I have referred, in the possession of our esteemed friend Mr. Jarndyce, that the names of my young family are concluded with the name of O. A. Pardiggle, F. R. S., one pound. That is their father. We usually observe the same routine. I put down my mite first; then my young family enrol their contributions, according to their ages and their little means; and then Mr. Pardiggle brings up the rear. Mr. Pardiggle is happy to throw in his limited donation, under my direction; and thus things are made, not only pleasant to ourselves, but, we trust, improving to others."

Mrs. Pardiggle invited Esther and Ada to go out with her to visit a "wicked brickmaker" in the neighbourhood. Ada walked ahead with Mrs. Pardiggle and Esther followed with the five children. She had an interesting experience.

> I am very fond of being confided in by children, and am happy in being usually favoured in that respect, but on this occasion it gave me great uneasiness. As soon as we were out of doors, Egbert, with the manner of a little footpad, demanded a shilling of me, on the ground that his pocket money was "boned" from him. On my pointing out the great impropriety of the word, especially in connection with his parent (for he added sulkily "By her!"), he pinched me and said, "Oh, then! Now! Who are you? *You* wouldn't like it, I think! What does she make a sham for, and pretend to give me money, and take it away again? Why do you call it *my* allowance, and never let me spend it?" These exasperating questions so inflamed his mind, and the minds of Oswald and Francis, that they all pinched me at once, and in a dreadfully expert way; screwing up such little pieces of my arms that I could hardly forbear crying out. Felix at the same time stamped upon my toes. And the Bond of Joy, who, on account of always having the whole of his little income anticipated, stood, in fact, pledged to abstain from cakes as well as tobacco, so swelled with grief and rage when we passed a pastry-cook shop, that he terrified me by becoming purple. I never underwent so much, both in body and mind, in the course of a walk with young people, as from these unnaturally constrained children, when they paid me the compliment of being natural.

In the brickmaker's hovel they heard something of how the very poor brought up children, or failed to bring them up, in Dickens's time. The brickmaker was lying at full length on the floor, smoking his pipe. He gave them no welcome.

> I wants a end of these liberties took with my place. I wants a end of being drawed like a badger. Now you are a-going to pollpry and question according to custom—I know what you're a-going to be up to. Well! You haven't got no occasion to be up to it. I'll save you the trouble. Is my daughter a-washin'? Yes, she is a-washin'. Look at the water. Smell it! That's wot we drinks. How do you like it, and what do you think of gin, instead? An't my place dirty? Yes, it is dirty—it's nat'rally dirty, and it's nat'rally onwholesome; and we've had five dirty and onwholesome children, as is all dead infants, and so much the better for them, and for us besides.

The utter carelessness of some "society gentlemen" in regard to the education of their children is referred to in the description Caddy Jellyby gave of her lover, the son of the great Turveydrop.

> Caddy told me that her lover's education had been so neglected that it was not always easy to read his notes. She said if he were not so anxious about his spelling, and took less pains to make it clear, he would do better; but he put so many unnecessary letters into short words that they sometimes quite lost their En-

> glish appearance. "He does it with the best intention," observed Caddy, "but it hasn't the effect he means, poor fellow!" Caddy then went on to reason how could he be expected to be a scholar when he had passed his whole life in the dancing school, and had done nothing but teach and fag, fag and teach, morning, noon, and night! And what did it matter? She could write letters enough for both, as she knew to her cost, and it was far better for him to be amiable than learned. "Besides, it's not as if I was an accomplished girl, who had any right to give herself airs," said Caddy. "I know little enough, I am sure, thanks to ma!"

The products of the fashionable education of Dickens's time (there is not so much of it now, thanks largely to Dickens) were shown in the cousins of Sir Leicester Dedlock.

> The rest of the cousins are ladies and gentlemen of various ages and capacities; the major part, amiable and sensible, and likely to have done well enough in life if they could have overcome their cousinship; as it is, they are almost all a little worsted by it, and lounge in purposeless and listless paths, and seem to be quite as much at a loss how to dispose of themselves as anybody else can be how to dispose of them.

In Little Dorrit Mrs. General is used as a type of two varieties of false training. Her pupils were never to be allowed to know that there was anything vulgar or wrong in the world. She believed the good old theory, that adulthood had two duties in developing purity of character, one to prevent children knowing that there was any evil, the other to chain them back or beat them back from evil, if they accidentally found it and wished to investigate it. She never thought of training a child to do its part in reducing the evil around him. Seclusion and exclusion took the place of community in her perverted philosophy.

She believed, too, in educating the surface. She did not work from within intellectually or spiritually. She varnished the surface that it might receive the proper society polish, therefore neither heart nor head required much attention. According to her theory, young ladies should never be so unladylike as to have great purposes or great ideas. Unfortunately some of her descendants are still living.

> "Fanny," observed Mrs. General, "at present forms too many opinions. Perfect breeding forms none, and is never demonstrative.
>
> "I have conversed with Amy several times since we have been residing here on the general subject of the formation of a demeanour. She has expressed herself to me as wondering exceedingly at Venice. I have mentioned to her that it is better not to wonder."

Her father sent for Amy to reprove her for her lack of what Mrs. General regarded as true culture, and Amy said:

> "I think, father, I require a little time."

> "Papa is a preferable mode of address," observed Mrs. General. "Father is rather vulgar, my dear. The word papa, besides, gives a pretty form to the lips. Papa, potatoes, poultry, prunes, and prism are all very good words for the lips; especially prunes and prism. You will find it serviceable, in the formation of a demeanour, if you sometimes say to yourself in company—on entering a room, for instance—papa, potatoes, poultry, prunes and prism, prunes and prism.
>
> "If Miss Amy Dorrit will direct her own attention to, and will accept of my poor assistance in, the formation of a surface, Mr. Dorrit will have no further cause of anxiety. May I take this opportunity of remarking, as an instance in point, that it is scarcely delicate to look at vagrants with the attention which I have seen bestowed upon them by a very dear young friend of mine? They should not be looked at. Nothing disagreeable should ever be looked at. Apart from such a habit standing in the way of that graceful equanimity of surface which is so expressive of good breeding, it hardly seems compatible with refinement of mind. A truly refined mind will seem to be ignorant of the existence of anything that is not perfectly proper, placid, and pleasant."

Great Expectations has numerous illustrations of bad training. Mrs. Gargery had many of the worst characteristics of disrespectful and coercive adulthood. She abused Pip for asking questions, scolded him, thimbled him, and sent him to bed in the dark. She told him he was on the way to commit murder and a great variety of crimes, because criminals always "begin by asking questions." She kept him in a state of constant terror. She tried in every possible way to lower his opinion of himself, which is a crime against childhood. One of the worst features of the old education was its teaching of a spurious humility, a depreciation of selfhood. One of the greatest weaknesses of humanity is the general lack of true faith of men and women in their own powers. He was told that he was "naterally wicious," and made the butt of all the observations relating to boys who possessed any vices whatever.

Dickens revealed all these characteristics to condemn them.

Pip discussed a very grave question for students of children when he was accounting for the fact that he deliberately misstated facts so systematically in answering the questions of his sister and Mr. Pumblechook, in regard to Miss Havisham and the peculiarities of her mysterious home.

> When I reached home my sister was very curious to know all about Miss Havisham's, and asked a number of questions. And I soon found myself getting heavily bumped from behind in the nape of the neck and the small of the back, and having my face ignominiously shoved against the kitchen wall, because I did not answer those questions at sufficient length.
>
> If a dread of not being understood be hidden in the breasts of

> other young people to anything like the extent to which it used to be hidden in mine—which I consider probable, as I have no particular reason to suspect myself of having been a monstrosity—it is the key to many reservations. I felt convinced that if I described Miss Havisham's as my eyes had seen it I should not be understood.
>
> Whitewash on the forehead hardens the brain into a state of obstinacy perhaps. Anyhow, with whitewash from the wall on my forehead, my obstinacy was adamantine.

Two thoughts are worthy of note in this part of Pip's training: abuse, especially of the thumping, bumping, shaking variety, makes a child obstinate; and many of childhood's difficulties arise from not being understood, or the fear of being misunderstood.

Pip resented, as all children do, more than they can show, the unpleasant habit of taking patronizing liberties with them.

> And here I may remark that when Mr. Wopsle referred to me, he considered it a necessary part of such reference to rumple my hair and poke it into my eyes. I can not conceive why everybody of his standing who visited at our house should always have put me through the same inflammatory process under similar circumstances. Yet I do not call to mind that I was ever in my earlier youth the subject of remark in our social family circle, but some large-handed person took some such ophthalmic steps to patronize me.

And Mr. Pumblechook! What could a boy do but hate him?

> Meanwhile, councils went on in the kitchen at home, fraught with almost insupportable aggravation to my exasperated spirit. That ass, Pumblechook, used often to come over of a night for the purpose of discussing my prospects with my sister; and I really do believe (to this hour with less penitence than I ought to feel) that if these hands could have taken a linchpin out of his chaise cart, they would have done it. The miserable man was a man of that confined stolidity of mind that he could not discuss my prospects without having me before him—as it were, to operate upon—and he would drag me up from my stool (usually by the collar) where I was quiet in a corner, and, putting me before the fire as if I were going to be cooked, would begin by saying, "Now, mum, here is this boy! Here is this boy which you brought up by hand. Hold up your head, boy, and be forever grateful unto them which so did so. Now, mum, with respections to this boy!" And then he would rumple my hair the wrong way—which from my earliest remembrance, as already hinted, I have in my soul denied the right of any fellow-creature to do—and would hold me before him by the sleeve: a spectacle of imbecility only to be equalled by himself.

Mrs. Pocket's training was given as an illustration of the folly of giving girls no practical education.

> Her father had directed Mrs. Pocket to be brought up from her cradle as one who, in the nature of things, must marry a title, and who was to be guarded from the acquisition of plebeian domestic knowledge.
>
> So successful a watch and ward had been established over the young lady by this judicious parent, that she had grown up highly ornamental, but perfectly helpless and useless.

Her home proved that she had grown up a credit to her training. There never was a family more utterly without order, management, or system than Mrs. Pocket's. Servants and children indulged in unending turmoil and conflict. Dickens added a grim humour to the picture by saying:

> Mr. Pocket was out lecturing; for he was a most delightful lecturer on domestic economy, and his treatises on the management of children and servants were considered the very best text-books on those themes. But Mrs. Pocket was at home and was in a little difficulty, on account of the baby's having been accommodated with a needle-case to keep him quiet during the unaccountable absence (with a relative in the Foot Guards) of Millers. And more needles were missing than it could be regarded as quite wholesome for a patient of such tender years either to apply externally or to take as a tonic.

Mrs. Pocket continued to read her one book about the dignities of the titled aristocracy, and prescribed "Bed" as a sovereign remedy for baby.

Dickens believed a mother should find her highest joy and most sacred duty in training her own children. Mrs. Pocket was a type to be avoided.

The description of the dinner at Mr. Pocket's, after which the six children were brought in, and Mrs. Pocket attempted to mind the baby, is one of the raciest bits of Dickens's humour. One observation in connection with the dinner is worth studying.

> After dinner the children were introduced, and Mrs. Coiler made admiring comments on their eyes, noses, and legs—a sagacious way of improving their minds.

How few yet clearly understand this profound criticism of bad training! How many children are still made vain and frivolous by having their attention directed especially to their physical attributes and their dress, rather than to the things that would yield them much greater immediate happiness and a much truer basis for future development!

In his last book, Edwin Drood, Dickens showed that he still hated the tyranny that dwarfs and distorts the souls of children.

Neville Landless described his own training to his tutor, who had won his confidence as it had never been won before.

> "We lived with a stepfather there. Our mother died there, when we were little children. We have had a wretched existence. She made him our guardian, and he was a miserly wretch who grudged us food to eat and clothes to wear.
>
> "This stepfather of ours was a cruel brute as well as a grinding one. It was well he died when he did, or I might have killed him."
>
> Mr. Crisparkle stopped short in the moonlight and looked at his hopeful pupil in consternation.
>
> "I surprise you, sir?" he said, with a quick change to a submissive manner.
>
> "You shock me; unspeakably shock me."
>
> The pupil hung his head for a little while, as they walked on, and then said: "You never saw him beat your sister. I have seen him beat mine, more than once or twice, and I never forgot it.
>
> "I have had, sir, from my earliest remembrance, to suppress a deadly and bitter hatred. This has made me secret and revengeful. I have been always tyrannically held down by the strong hand. This has driven me, in my weakness, to the resource of being false and mean. I have been stinted of education, liberty, money, dress, the very necessaries of life, the commonest pleasures of childhood, the commonest possessions of youth. This has caused me to be utterly wanting in I do not know what emotions, or remembrances, or good instincts—I have not even a name for the thing, you see—that you have had to work upon in other young men to whom you have been accustomed."

Hatred instead of love; product, a secret and revengeful character. "Tyrannically held down by a strong hand"; product, falseness and meanness. "Stinted of education, liberty, money, dress, the very necessaries of life, the commonest pleasures of childhood, the commonest possessions of youth"; product, a manhood utterly barren in true emotions, or pleasant memories, or good instincts.

No other writer has described so many phases of bad training as Dickens.

CHAPTER XII.

GOOD TRAINING.

Dickens wrote much less about good training than about bad training. It was the part of a true philosopher and a profound student of human nature to do so. Pictures of wrong treatment of children accomplished a double purpose. They made men hate the wrong, and made them more clearly conscious of the right than pictures of the right alone could have done. Descriptions of ideal conditions can not make as deep impressions as descriptions of utterly bad conditions in the present stage of human evolution.

His revelation of cruel tyranny, of will breaking, of cramming, of dwarfing of individuality, of distorting of imagination, of harshness, of lack of sympathy, of evil in a hundred hideous forms, made men more conscious of their corresponding opposites than attempts to reveal these opposites by direct effort could have done; and in addition it stirred in human hearts everywhere the determination to remove or remedy the wrong.

Little Nell's grandfather gave her a good training. Omitting poverty and loneliness, and some strange companionships, she had a training calculated to make her the supremely pure and attractive child she was. Her grandfather loved her passionately; he had never been unkind to her, he had taught her carefully in the virtues that are learned by the unselfish performance of duty; she had the opportunity for simple, loving service, and she was trained to have profound reverence for and true faith in God.

Her grandfather left her alone every night, yet she was never afraid. Dickens describes their usual parting in the evening.

> Then she ran to the old man, who folded her in his arms and bade God bless her.
>
> "Sleep soundly, Nell," he said in a low voice, "and angels guard thy bed! Do not forget thy prayers, my sweet."
>
> "No, indeed," answered the child fervently, "they make me feel so happy!"
>
> "That's well; I know they do; they should," said the old man. "Bless thee a hundred times! Early in the morning I shall be home."
>
> "You'll not ring twice," returned the child. "The bell wakes me, even in the middle of a dream."

The Toodle family is painted in direct contrast to the Dombey family in the relationship of parents to children. Mrs. Toodle came to nurse Paul Dombey when his mother died. Mr. Toodle himself came too, and Mr. Dombey called him in to speak to him.

> He was a strong, loose, round-shouldered, shuffling, shaggy fellow, on whom his clothes sat negligently; with a good deal of hair and whisker, deepened in its natural tint, perhaps, by smoke and coal-dust; hard knotty hands; and a square forehead, as coarse in grain as the bark of an oak. A thorough contrast in all respects to Mr. Dombey, who was one of those close-shaved, close-cut moneyed gentlemen who are glossy and crisp like new bank notes, and who seem to be artificially braced and tightened as by the stimulating action of golden shower baths.
>
> "You have a son, I believe?" said Mr. Dombey.
>
> "Four on 'em, sir. Four hims and a her. All alive!"
>
> "Why, it's as much as you can afford to keep them!" said Mr. Dombey.
>
> "I couldn't hardly afford but one thing in the world less, sir."
>
> "What is that?"
>
> "To lose 'em, sir."
>
> "Can you read?" asked Mr. Dombey.
>
> "Why, not partick'ler, sir."
>
> "Write?"
>
> "With chalk, sir?"
>
> "With anything?"
>
> "I could make shift to chalk a little bit, I think, if I was put to it," said Toodle, after some reflection.
>
> "And yet," said Mr. Dombey, "you are two or three and thirty, I suppose?"
>
> "Thereabout, I suppose, sir," answered Toodle, after more reflection.
>
> "Then why don't you learn?" asked Mr. Dombey.
>
> "So I'm agoing to, sir. One of my little boys is agoing to learn me, when he's old enough, and been to school himself."

What a beautiful picture of the true relationship that should exist between a mother and her children is given in the reception to Mrs. Toodle when she went home to visit her family!

> "Why, Polly!" cried her sister. "You! what a turn you *have* given me! who'd have thought it! come along in, Polly! How well

> you do look, to be sure! The children will go half wild to see you, Polly, that they will."
>
> That they did, if one might judge from the noise they made, and the way in which they dashed at Polly and dragged her to a low chair in the chimney corner, where her own honest apple face became immediately the centre of a bunch of smaller pippins, all laying their rosy cheeks close to it, and all evidently the growth of the same tree. As to Polly, she was full as noisy and vehement as the children; and it was not until she was quite out of breath, and her hair was hanging all about her flushed face, and her new christening attire was very much dishevelled, that any pause took place in the confusion. Even then, the smallest Toodle but one remained in her lap, holding on tight with both arms round her neck; while the smallest Toodle but two mounted on the back of the chair, and made desperate efforts, with one leg in the air, to kiss her round the corner.

Unfortunately the eldest Toodle, nicknamed Biler, was sent to the grinders' school by Mr. Dombey, and he was so badly treated that he played truant and got into bad company; but his mother clung to him and treated him kindly, and hoped for him still. Mr. Carker went home with Biler to satisfy himself in regard to his family.

> "This fellow," said Mr. Carker to Polly, giving him a gentle shake, "is your son, eh, ma'am?"
>
> "Yes, sir," sobbed Polly, with a courtesy; "yes, sir."
>
> "A bad son, I am afraid?" said Mr. Carker.
>
> "Never a bad son to me, sir," returned Polly.
>
> "To whom, then?" demanded Mr. Carker.
>
> "He has been a little wild, sir," replied Polly, checking the baby, who was making convulsive efforts with his arms and legs to launch himself on Biler, through the ambient air, "and has gone with wrong companions; but I hope he has seen the misery of that, sir, and will do well again."
>
> When Mr. Carker had concluded his visit, as he made his way among the crowding children to the door, Rob retreated on his mother, and took her and the baby in the same repentant hug.
>
> "I'll try hard, dear mother, now. Upon my soul I will!" said Rob.
>
> "Oh, do, my dear boy! I am sure you will, for our sakes and your own!" cried Polly, kissing him. "But you're coming back to speak to me, when you have seen the gentleman away?"
>
> "I don't know, mother." Rob hesitated, and looked down. "Father—when's he coming home?"

> "Not till two o'clock to-morrow morning."
>
> "I'll come back, mother, dear!" cried Rob. And passing through the shrill cry of his brothers and sisters in reception of this promise, he followed Mr. Carker out.
>
> "What!" said Mr. Carker, who had heard this. "You have a bad father, have you?"
>
> "No, sir!" returned Rob, amazed. "There ain't a better nor a kinder father going than mine is."
>
> "Why don't you want to see him, then?" asked his patron.
>
> "There's such a difference between a father and a mother, sir," said Rob, after faltering for a moment. "He couldn't hardly believe yet that I was going to do better—though I know he'd try to; but a mother—*she* always believes what's good, sir; at least I know my mother does, God bless her!"

It was not the fault of his home that Biler went astray.

Nor did Dickens fail to give a picture for the fathers too. Mr. Toodle was a workman on a train, and great was the joy in the family when father came home.

> "Polly, my gal," said Mr. Toodle, with a young Toodle on each knee and two more making tea for him, and plenty more scattered about—Mr. Toodle was never out of children, but always kept a good supply on hand—"you ain't seen our Biler lately, have you?"
>
> "No," replied Polly, "but he's almost certain to look in tonight. It's his right evening, and he's very regular."
>
> "I suppose," said Mr. Toodle, relishing his meal infinitely, "as our Biler is a-doin' now about as well as a boy *can* do, eh, Polly?"
>
> "Oh! he's a-doing beautiful!" responded Polly.
>
> "He ain't got to be at all secretlike—has he, Polly?" inquired Mr. Toodle.
>
> "No!" said Mrs. Toodle plumply.
>
> "I'm glad he ain't got to be at all secretlike, Polly," observed Mr. Toodle in his slow and measured way, and shovelling in his bread and butter with a clasp knife, as if he were stoking himself, "because that don't look well; do it, Polly?"
>
> "Why, of course, it don't, father. How can you ask?"
>
> "You see, my boys and gals," said Mr. Toodle, looking round upon his family, "wotever you're up to in a honest way, it's my opinion as you can't do better than be open. If you find yourselves in cuttings or in tunnels, don't you play no secret games. Keep your whistles going, and let's know where you are."

> The rising Toodles set up a shrill murmur, expressive of their resolution to profit by the paternal advice.
>
> "But what makes you say this along of Rob, father?" asked his wife anxiously.
>
> "Polly, old 'ooman," said Mr. Toodle, "I don't know as I said it partickler along o' Rob, I'm sure. I starts light with Rob only; I comes to a branch; I takes on what I finds there; and a whole train of ideas gets coupled on to him afore I knows where I am, or where they comes from. What a Junction a man's thoughts is," said Mr. Toodle, "to be sure!"
>
> This profound reflection Mr. Toodle washed down with a pint mug of tea, and proceeded to solidify with a great weight of bread and butter; charging his young daughters meanwhile to keep plenty of hot water in the pot, as he was uncommon dry, and should take the indefinite quantity of "a sight of mugs" before his thirst was appeased.

And as the jolly old fellow ate his supper he was surrounded by all his smaller children, some on his knees, and others under his arms, and all getting bites of bread and butter and sups of tea in turn, although they had had their own supper before he came home.

Dickens did not wish to teach that such relationships should exist between parents and children in the homes of the labouring classes only. He used Toodle and his family as representing one extreme of society, as at present constituted, in sharp contrast with Mr. Dombey's family at the other extreme. How happy the one home with barely enough to secure the necessaries of life! how miserable the other with unlimited wealth! And the best things in the Toodle home were the children, and the love and unconventional freedom between them and their parents. With such a feeling of community and love in all homes, and with schools of a proper character, the children will be trained for higher, and progressively advancing manhood and womanhood.

David Copperfield's training was not all coercive and degrading. Before the Murdstones came to blight his young life he had joy and sympathy to stimulate all that was good in him. His mother and Peggotty were kind and true. The three had perfect faith in each other. They formed a blessed unity. "The memory of his lessons in those happy days recalled no feeling of disgust or reluctance. On the contrary, he seemed to have walked along a path of flowers, and to have been cheered by the gentleness of his mother's voice and manner all the way."

Again, after the Murdstone interval of terror and cruelty, David was kindly treated and well trained by his aunt. Her relationship toward him throughout his whole youth is well presented in her parting words, as she left him at Mr. Wickfield's house, where he was to live while at Doctor Strong's school.

> She told me that everything would be arranged for me by Mr. Wickfield, and that I should want for nothing, and gave me the

> kindest words and the best advice.
>
> "Trot," said my aunt in conclusion, "be a credit to yourself, to me, and Mr. Dick, and Heaven be with you!"
>
> I was greatly overcome, and could only thank her again and again, and send my love to Mr. Dick.
>
> "Never," said my aunt, "be mean in anything; never be false; never be cruel. Avoid these three vices, Trot, and I can always be hopeful of you."

In Mr. Wickfield's home and in Doctor Strong's school he had ideal conditions of development. He received respectful consideration, fatherly interest, wise counsel, and generous hospitality from Mr. Wickfield. With Agnes he had the most delightful relationship of sympathetic and stimulating friendship. There is no better influence in the life of a boy opening into young manhood than the true friendship of a girl of the character of Agnes.

In Doctor Strong's school David met with the best conditions of good training yet revealed by the "new education."

The boys were taught politeness, courtesy, and consideration for the feelings of others in Doctor Strong's school.

> About five-and-twenty boys were studiously engaged at their books when we went in, but they rose to give the Doctor good morning, and remained standing when they saw Mr. Wickfield and me.
>
> "A new boy, young gentlemen," said the Doctor; "Trotwood Copperfield."
>
> One Adams, who was the head boy, then stepped out of his place and welcomed me. He looked like a young clergyman, in his white cravat, but he was very affable and good-humoured; and he showed me my place, and presented me to the masters in a gentlemanly way that would have put me at my ease if anything could.

Physical education received due attention at Doctor Strong's school. "We had noble games out of doors." These outdoor sports have done more than anything else to develop the strength and energy of the British character. Thoughtful educators everywhere recognise the value of play in the development of the physical, the intellectual, and the spiritual nature as taught by Froebel. The love of play has been one of the distinctive elements of the British people.

Doctor Strong's personal influence was good. "He was the idol of the whole school." He was not coercive nor restrictive; he was an inspiration to effort and to manliness of conduct. "He was the kindest of men," full of sympathy with boyhood and with individual boys. "He had a simple faith in him that might have touched the stone hearts of the very urns upon the wall." Mr. Wickfield told David that he feared some of the boys might take advantage of his kindness and faith, but boys do not abuse the confidence of such teachers. "He appealed in everything to the honour and good faith of the boys, and avowed his intention to rely on the possession of these qualities unless they proved themselves unworthy." David says this "worked wonders." He had no spies in schoolroom or grounds. He trusted his boys in a frank, unconventional way, and they proved themselves worthy of trust. In such an atmosphere a boy grows to be reliable. He does not need to be hypocritical or false. "The boys all became warmly attached to the school—I am sure I did for one, and I never knew, in all my time, of any other boy being otherwise—and learned with a good will, desiring to do it credit."

They had independent self-activity. "We had plenty of liberty." Without this no child can reach his best growth. The boys did not abuse their privilege. They respected themselves more because they had liberty. "As I remember, we were well spoken of in the town, and rarely did any disgrace, by our appearance or manner, to the reputation of Doctor Strong and Doctor Strong's boys."

The community ideal was wrought into the lives of the boys by their experience in this model school. "We all felt that we had a part in the management of the place, and in sustaining its character and dignity." The highest work of schools, colleges, and universities is to fill the lives of men and women with the apperceptive centres of the community ideal. Christian community can not be made clear by books or teaching or sermons unless its foundations are laid by experience, by "sharing in the management" of the conditions of the life of the boy, or girl, or student. Froebel pleaded for a college and university education in which students should "share in the management." Dickens applied this high ideal.

There is another most important element in Doctor Strong's influence. He was not "a human barrel organ," like Mr. Feeder, "playing a little list of Greek and Latin tunes over and over again without any variation." He was an original investigator. He was preparing a dictionary of Greek roots. He was not merely an accumulator of knowledge as it had been prepared by some one else. He was not a mere canal through which knowledge slowly flowed through artificial channels, nor a marsh in which knowledge had become confused and stagnant, nor a dead sea into which knowledge flowed, but from which there was no outlet. He was a fresh fountain from which knowledge came clear and pure. So the boys gained knowledge readily from him, but, far beyond knowledge, they learned incidentally the habit of work, and were filled with the desire to add to the store of knowledge as a basis for the progressive evolution of humanity.

What a farce it is to say that Dickens was not conscious of the pedagogic value of his work. He had great facility in learning, but he was also a hard student. No one could have written so much and so wisely about education unless he had studied carefully the thought of the most advanced educators.

David's aunt had the wisdom to try to develop in him the characteristics of excellence that were lacking in his parents. This is a thought that is slowly making its way in the minds of educators.

> "But what I want you to be, Trot," resumed my aunt—"I don't mean physically, but morally; you are very well physically—is a firm fellow. A fine firm fellow, with a will of your own.

> With resolution," said my aunt, shaking her cap at me, and clinching her hand. "With determination. With character, Trot—with strength of character that is not to be influenced, except on good reason, by anybody, or by anything. That's what I want you to be. That's what your father and mother might both have been, Heaven knows, and been the better for it."
>
> I intimated that I hoped I should be what she described.
>
> "That you may begin, in a small way, to have a reliance upon yourself, and to act for yourself," said my aunt, "I shall send you upon your trip alone."
>
> In pursuance of my aunt's kind scheme, I was shortly afterward fitted out with a handsome purse of money and a portmanteau, and tenderly dismissed upon my expedition. At parting, my aunt gave me some good advice and a good many kisses; and said that as her object was that I should look about me, and should think a little, she would recommend me to stay a few days in London, if I liked it, either on my way down into Suffolk, or in coming back. In a word, I was at liberty to do as I would for three weeks or a month; and no other conditions were imposed upon my freedom than the before-mentioned thinking and looking about me, and a pledge to write three times a week and faithfully report myself.

Betsy Trotwood may safely be taken as a model in dealing with boys during the adolescent period, and with young men just about to start in the real work of life.

Dickens puts into the words of David Copperfield a statement of the elements of character which he regarded as most essential to success in life, and which he would take pains to develop by the training in homes and schools.

> I will only add to what I have already written of my perseverance at this time of my life, and of a patient and continuous energy which then began to be matured within me, and which I know to be the strong part of my character, if it have any strength at all, that there, on looking back, I find the source of my success. I have been very fortunate in worldly matters; many men have worked much harder, and not succeeded half so well; but I never could have done what I have done without the habits of punctuality, order, and diligence, without the determination to concentrate myself on one object at a time, no matter how quickly its successor should come upon its heels, which I then formed. My meaning simply is, that whatever I have tried to do in life, I have tried with all my heart to do well; that whatever I have devoted myself to, I have devoted myself to completely; that, in great aims and in small, I have always been thoroughly in earnest. I have never believed it possible that any natural or improved ability

> can claim immunity from the companionship of the steady, plain, hard-working qualities, and hope to gain its end. There is no such thing as such fulfilment on this earth. Some happy talent, and some fortunate opportunity, may form the two sides of the ladder on which some men mount, but the rounds of that ladder must be made of stuff to stand wear and tear; and there is no substitute for thoroughgoing, ardent, and sincere earnestness. Never to put one hand to anything on which I could throw my whole self and never to affect depreciation of my work, whatever it was, I find, now, to have been my golden rules.

Bleak House, which is so rich in illustrations of bad training, contains little direct teaching regarding the proper training of children.

The value of a doll in the training of a girl is shown in Esther's early experience. The doll had a real personal relationship to her. She made it her confidant, and in various ways gave it a distinct personal standing. She could pour out to it the joys and sorrows of her heart more fully than to any real person. The doll was an outlet for the pent-up emotions that were checked in their flow by the adults with whom she was associated. A doll is more than a mere plaything to a child; or perhaps it would be more exact to say play with a doll means much more than most people believe. Dickens was able to sympathize with even a little girl.

Esther says:

> I can remember, when I was a very little girl indeed, I used to say to my doll, when we were alone together, "Now, Dolly, I am not clever, you know very well, and you must be patient with me, like a dear!" And so she used to sit propped up in a great armchair, with her beautiful complexion and rosy lips, staring at me—or not so much at me, I think, as at nothing—while I busily stitched away, and told her every one of my secrets.
>
> My dear old doll! I was such a shy little thing that I seldom dared to open my lips, and never dared to open my heart, to anybody else. It almost makes me cry to think what a relief it used to be to me, when I came home from school of a day, to run upstairs to my room, and say "Oh you dear faithful Dolly, I knew you would be expecting me!" and then to sit down on the floor, leaning on the elbow of her great chair, and tell her all I had noticed since we parted. I had always rather a noticing way—not a quick way, oh, no!—a silent way of noticing what passed before me, and thinking I should like to understand it better. I have not by any means a quick understanding. When I love a person very tenderly indeed, it seems to brighten.

When on her lonely birthday she had been told by her godmother that a shadow hung over her life she says:

> I went up to my room, and crept to bed, and laid my doll's cheek against mine wet with tears; and holding that solitary

friend upon my bosom cried myself to sleep.

Dear, dear, to think how much time we passed alone together afterward, and how often I repeated to the doll the story of my birthday, and confided to her that I would try, as hard as ever I could, to repair the fault I had been born with (of which I confessedly felt guilty and yet innocent), and would strive as I grew up to be industrious, contented, and kind-hearted, and to do some good to some one, and win some love to myself if I could.

Mr. Jarndyce emphasized the opinion of David Copperfield when he gave advice to Richard Carstone:

"Trust in nothing but in Providence and your own efforts. Never separate the two, like the heathen wagoner. Constancy in love is a good thing; but it means nothing, and is nothing, without constancy in every kind of effort. If you had the abilities of all the great men, past and present, you could do nothing well without sincerely meaning it and setting about it. If you entertain the supposition that any real success, in great things or in small, ever was or could be, ever will or can be, wrested from fortune by fits and starts, leave that wrong idea here."

Mr. George gave Woolwich Bagnet kindly counsel regarding his duty to his mother:

"The time will come, my boy," pursues the trooper, "when this hair of your mother's will be gray, and this forehead all crossed and recrossed with wrinkles—and a fine old lady she'll be then. Take care, while you are young, that you can think in those days, '*I* never whitened a hair of her dear head—*I* never marked a sorrowful line in her face!' For of all the many things that you can think of when you are a man, you had better have *that* by you, Woolwich!"

Mr. Meagles in Little Dorrit, good, kind Mr. Meagles, explained why Little Dorrit, amid all her trials and all her difficulties, had grown to be so true a woman, loved by so many people.

If she had constantly thought of herself, and settled with herself that everybody visited this place upon her, turned it against her, and cast it at her, she would have led an irritable and probably a useless existence. Yet I have heard tell, Tattycoram, that her young life has been one of active resignation, goodness, and noble service. Shall I tell you what I consider those eyes of hers that were here just now, to have always looked at, to get that expression?

"Yes, if you please, sir."

"Duty, Tattycoram. Begin it early, and do it well; and there is no antecedent to it, in any origin or station, that will tell against us with the Almighty, or with ourselves."

Although Mr. Pocket was not able to manage his own household and family, chiefly owing to the hopeless incompetence of Mrs. Pocket, he was an excellent teacher, and knew how to treat his pupils. Pip found him a most satisfactory guide.

> He advised my attending certain places in London for the acquisition of such mere rudiments as I wanted, and my investing him with the functions of explainer and director of all my studies. He hoped that with intelligent assistance I should meet with little to discourage me, and should soon be able to dispense with any aid but his. Through his way of saying this, and much more to similar purpose, he placed himself on confidential terms with me in an admirable manner: and I may state at once that he was always so zealous and honourable in fulfilling his compact with me that he made me zealous and honourable in fulfilling mine with him. If he had shown indifference as a master, I had no doubt I should have returned the compliment as a pupil; he gave me no such excuse, and each of us did the other justice.

In Our Mutual Friend Betty Higden and Mrs. Boffin are given as true types of the proper spirit of adulthood toward childhood. Betty, poor as she was, wept at the thought of parting from Johnny, and Mrs. Boffin said to her:

> "If you trust the dear child to me he shall have the best of homes, the best of care, the best of education, the best of friends. Please God, I will be a true good mother to him!"

Jemmy Lirriper had an ideal training in many ways. He had freedom and love, and his imagination and individuality were developed as fully as Mrs. Lirriper and the Major could secure these desirable results. His boyish personality received respectful consideration. The Major's method of revealing mathematical conceptions and processes, while it did not fully reveal Froebel's processes in reaching the same results (even the great mathematicians have been slow in doing that), was much in advance of the pedagogy of his time, and it shows the spirit in which Dickens would have the child treated, and this is much more important than mathematics.

Mrs. Lirriper tells the story:

> My dear, the system upon which the Major commenced, and, as I may say, perfected Jemmy's learning when he was so small that if the dear was on the other side of the table you had to look under it instead of over it to see him with his mother's own bright hair in beautiful curls, is a thing that ought to be known to the Throne and Lords and Commons, and then might obtain some promotion for the Major, which he well deserves, and would be none the worse for (speaking between friends, L. S. D-ically). When the Major first undertook his learning he says to me:
>
> "I'm going, Madam," he says, "to make our child a Calculating Boy."

"Major," I says, "you terrify me, and may do the pet a permanent injury you would never forgive yourself."

"Madam," says the Major, "I would regret if this fine mind was not early cultivated. But mark me, Madam," says the Major, holding up his forefinger, "cultivated on a principle that will make it a delight."

"Major," I says, "I will be candid with you and tell you openly that if ever I find the dear child fall off in his appetite I shall know it is his calculations, and shall put a stop to them at two minutes' notice. Or if I find them mounting to his head," I says, "or striking anyways cold to his stomach or leading to anything approaching flabbiness in his legs, the result will be the same, but, Major, you are a clever man and have seen much, and you love the child and are his own godfather, and if you feel a confidence in trying, try."

"Spoken, Madam," says the Major, "like Emma Lirriper. All I have to ask, Madam, is that you will leave my godson and myself to make a week or two's preparations for surprising you, and that you will give leave to have up and down any small articles not actually in use that I may require from the kitchen."

"From the kitchen, Major!" I says, half feeling as if he had a mind to cook the child.

"From the kitchen," says the Major, and smiles and swells, and at the same time looks taller.

So I passed my word, and the Major and the dear boy were shut up together for half an hour at a time through a certain while, and never could I hear anything going on betwixt them but talking and laughing and Jemmy clapping his hands and screaming out numbers, so I says to myself "It has not harmed him yet," nor could I, on examining the dear find any signs of it anywhere about him, which was likewise a great relief. At last one day Jemmy brings me a card in joke in the Major's neat writing "The Messrs. Jemmy Jackman," for we had given him the Major's other name too, "request the honour of Mrs. Lirriper's company at the Jackman Institution in the front parlour this evening at five, military time, to witness a few slight feats of elementary arithmetic." And, if you'll believe me, there in the front parlour at five punctually to the moment was the Major behind the Pembroke table with both leaves up and a lot of things from the kitchen tidily set out on old newspapers spread atop of it, and there was the Mite stood up on a chair, with his rosy cheeks flushing and his eyes sparkling clusters of diamonds.

"Now, Gran," says he, "oo tit down and don't oo touch ler people"—for he saw with every one of those diamonds of his that I was going to give him a squeeze.

"Very well, sir," I says, "I am obedient in this good company, I am sure." And I sits down in the easy-chair that was put for me, shaking my sides.

But picture my admiration when the Major, going on almost as quick as if he was conjuring, sets out all the articles he names, and says, "Three saucepans, an Italian iron, a hand bell, a toasting fork, a nutmeg grater, four potlids, a spice box, two egg cups, and a chopping board—how many?" and when that Mite instantly cries "Tifteen, tut down tive and carry ler 'topping board," and then claps his hands, draws up his legs, and dances on his chair!

My dear, with the same astonishing ease and correctness, him and the Major added up the tables, chairs, and sofy, the picters, fender and fire irons, their own selves, me and the cat, and the eyes in Miss Wozenham's head, and whenever the sum was done Young Roses and Diamonds claps his hands and draws up his legs and dances on his chair.

The pride of the Major! ("*Here's* a mind, Ma'am!" he says to me behind his hand.)

Then he says aloud, "We now come to the next elementary rule—which is called——"

"Umtraction!" cries Jemmy.

"Right," says the Major. "We have here a toasting fork, a potato in its natural state, two potlids, one egg-cup, a wooden spoon, and two skewers, from which it is necessary, for commercial purposes, to subtract a sprat gridiron, a small pickle jar, two lemons, one pepper castor, a black-beetle trap, and a knob of the dresser drawer—what remains?"

"Toatin fork!" cries Jemmy.

"In numbers, how many?" says the Major.

"One!" cries Jemmy.

("*Here's* a boy, Ma'am!" says the Major to me, behind his hand.)

"We now approach the next elementary rule—which is entitled——"

"Tickleication," cries Jemmy.

"Correct," says the Major.

But, my dear, to relate to you in detail the way in which they multiplied fourteen sticks of firewood by two bits of ginger and a larding needle, or divided pretty well everything else there was on the table by the heater of the Italian iron and a chamber candlestick, and got a lemon over, would make my head spin round

> and round and round, as it did at the time. So I says, "If you'll excuse my addressing the chair, Professor Jackman, I think the period of the lecture has now arrived when it becomes necessary that I should take a good hug of this young scholar." Upon which Jemmy calls out from his station on the chair, "Gran, oo open oor arms and me'll make a 'pring into 'em." So I opened my arms to him, as I had opened my sorrowful heart when his poor young mother lay a-dying, and he had his jump and we had a good long hug together, and the Major, prouder than any peacock, says to me behind his hand, "You need not let him know it, Madam" (which I certainly need not, for the Major was quite audible), "but he is a boy!"

Doctor Marigold's training of the little deaf-mute girl and "Old Cheeseman's" treatment of children are revelations of the mature ideals of Dickens regarding the proper attitude of adulthood toward childhood.

CHAPTER XIII.

COMMUNITY.

While the opinions of Dickens on the subject of community may not seem very advanced to some of the most progressive men and women of the present, they were much ahead of his own time, and they are beyond the practice of our time.

> I have had my share of sorrows—more than the common lot, perhaps, but I have borne them ill. I have broken where I should have bent; and have mused and brooded, when my spirit should have mixed with all God's great creation. The men who learn endurance are they who call the whole world brother. I have turned *from* the world, and I pay the penalty.

Thus spoke Mr. Haredale to Edward Chester, in Barnaby Rudge.

No one who has lived since the time of Dickens could write a more striking statement of the responsibility of every man for his brother, and of the terrific consequences of neglect of the duties of brotherhood both to him who is neglected and to him who neglects, than Dickens wrote in Dombey and Son. There is no phase of sociology that has stepped beyond the position taken by Dickens in the following selection:

> Was Mr. Dombey's master vice, that ruled him so inexorably, an unnatural characteristic? It might be worth while, sometimes to inquire what Nature is, and how men work to change her, and whether, in the enforced distortions so produced, it is not natural to be unnatural. Coop any son or daughter of our mighty mother within narrow range, and bind the prisoner to one idea, and foster it by servile worship of it on the part of the few timid or designing people standing round, and what is Nature to the willing captive who has never risen up upon the wings of a free mind—drooping and useless soon—to see her in her comprehensive truth!
>
> Alas! are there so few things in the world about us most unnatural, and yet most natural in being so! Hear the magistrate or judge admonish the unnatural outcast of society; unnatural in brutal habits, unnatural in want of decency, unnatural in losing and confounding all distinctions between good and evil; unnatural in ignorance, in vice, in recklessness, in contumacy, in mind, in looks, in everything. But follow the good clergyman or doctor, who, with his life imperilled at every breath he draws, goes down

into their dens, lying within the echoes of our carriage wheels and daily tread upon the pavement stones. Look round upon the world of odious sights—millions of immortal creatures have no other world on earth—at the lightest mention of which humanity revolts, and dainty delicacy living in the next street, stops her ears, and lisps, "I don't believe it!" Breathe the polluted air, foul with every impurity that is poisonous to health and life; and have every sense conferred upon our race for its delight and happiness, offended, sickened, and disgusted, and made a channel by which misery and death alone can enter. Vainly attempt to think of any simple plant, or flower, or wholesome weed that, set in this fetid bed, could have its natural growth or put its little leaves off to the sun as God designed it. And then, calling up some ghastly child, with stunted form and wicked face, hold forth on its unnatural sinfulness, and lament its being so early far away from heaven—but think a little of its having been conceived, and born and bred, in hell!

Those who study the physical sciences, and bring them to bear upon the health of man, tell us that if the noxious particles that rise from vitiated air were palpable to the sight, we should see them lowering in a dense black cloud above such haunts, and rolling slowly on to corrupt the better portions of a town. But if the moral pestilence that rises with them, and in the eternal laws of outraged nature, is inseparable from them, could be made discernible too, how terrible the revelation! Then should we see depravity, impiety, drunkenness, theft, murder, and a long train of nameless sins against the natural affections and repulsions of mankind, overhanging the devoted spots, and creeping on, to blight the innocent and spread contagion among the pure. Then should we see how the same poisoned fountains that flow into our hospitals and lazar houses, inundate the jails, and make the convict ships swim deep, and roll across the seas, and overrun vast continents with crime. Then should we stand appalled to know that where we generate disease to strike our children down and entail itself on unborn generations, there also we breed, by the same certain process, infancy that knows no innocence, youth without modesty or shame, maturity that is mature in nothing but in suffering and guilt, blasted old age that is a scandal on the form we bear. Unnatural humanity! When we shall gather grapes from thorns, and figs from thistles; when fields of grain shall spring up from the offal in the byways of our wicked cities, and roses bloom in the fat churchyards that they cherish; then we may look for natural humanity and find it growing from such seed.

Oh, for a good spirit who would take the housetops off, with a more potent and benignant hand than the lame demon in the

> tale, and show a Christian people what dark shapes issue from amidst their homes, to swell the retinue of the destroying angel as he moves forth among them! For only one night's view of the pale phantoms rising from the scenes of our too long neglect; and from the thick and sullen air where vice and fever propagate together, raining the tremendous and social retributions which are ever pouring down, and ever coming thicker! Bright and blessed the morning that should rise on such a night; for men, delayed no more by stumbling-blocks of their own making, which are but specks of dust upon the path between them and eternity, would then apply themselves, like creatures of one common origin, owing one duty to the father of one family, and tending to one common end to make the world a better place!
>
> Not the less bright and blessed would that day be for rousing some who never have looked out upon the world of human life around them to a knowledge of their own relation to it, and for making them acquainted with a perversion of Nature in their own contracted sympathies and estimates; as great and yet as natural in its development when once begun as the lowest degradation known.

This selection is worth rereading. The most advanced thinkers will understand it best.

Dickens showed that he understood clearly that a man becomes marred and degraded by shutting the world out of his heart, even though the reason for the exclusion may in itself be good. Love is the highest of all sentiments, and Dickens used it in the case of Mr. Wickfield to show that even the tender love he had for his dead wife became a source of evil to him, when it made him cease to think of the sorrows of his fellows, and only of his own affliction. Either in joy or sorrow the benefit to the individual results from a deepening of his consciousness of unity with the whole of humanity. Mr. Wickfield said to David:

> "Weak indulgence has ruined me. Indulgence in remembrance and indulgence in forgetfulness. My natural grief for my child's mother turned to disease; my natural love for my child turned to disease. I have infected everything I touched. I have brought misery on what I dearly love, I know—*You* know! I thought it possible that I could truly love one creature in the world, and not love the rest; I thought it possible that I could truly mourn for one creature gone out of the world, and not have some part in the grief of all who mourned. Thus the lessons of my life have been perverted! I have preyed on my own morbid coward heart, and it has preyed on me. Sordid in my grief, sordid in my love, sordid in my miserable escape from the darker side of both, oh, see the ruin I am, and hate me, shun me!"

In Tom Tiddler's Ground Dickens attacks the ideal that there may be merit in seclusion. Mr. Traveller visits the hermit who had become famous, and who was so vain on account of his dirt and simplicity of living, and he tells him some plain truths regarding himself and the duty of man to his fellow-men.

> "Now," said he, "that a man—even behind bars, in a blanket and a skewer—should tell me that he can see from day to day any orders or conditions of men, women, or children, who can by any possibility teach him that it is anything but the miserablist drivelling for a human creature to quarrel with his social nature—not to go so far as to say, to renounce his common human decency, for that is an extreme case, or who can teach him that he can in any wise separate himself from his kind and the habits of his kind, without becoming a deteriorated spectacle calculated to give the Devil (and perhaps the monkeys) pleasure—is something wonderful!"
>
> "You think yourself profoundly wise," said the Hermit.
>
> "Bah," returned Mr. Traveller, "there is little wisdom in knowing that every man must be up and doing, and that all mankind are made dependent on one another.
>
> "It is a moral impossibility," continued Mr. Traveller, "that any son or daughter of Adam can stand on this ground that I put my foot on, or on any ground that mortal treads, and gainsay the healthy tenure on which we hold our existence."
>
> "Which is," sneered the Hermit, "according to you— —"
>
> "Which is," returned the Traveller, "according to Eternal Providence, that we must arise and wash our faces and do our gregarious work and act and react on each other, leaving only the idiot and the palsied to sit blinking in the corner."

Dickens saves Little Emily from her great sorrow, and lifts the load of "shame" from her heart by giving her the opportunity of helping to care for others.

> But theer was some poor folks aboard as had illness among 'em, and she took care of *them;* and theer was the children in our company, and she took care of *them;* and so she got to be busy, and to be doing good, and that helped her.

And in the same great book he ridicules the misuse of the sacred word "society" by applying it to the sham and mockery of all that should be truly helpful and ennobling in the social intercourse of mankind.

> Or perhaps this *is* the Desert of Sahara! for, though Julia has a stately house, and mighty company, and sumptuous dinners every day, I see no green growth near her; nothing that can ever come to fruit or flower. What Julia calls "society," I see among it Mr. Jack Maldon, from his Patent Place, sneering at the hand that gave it to him, and speaking to me of the Doctor, as "so charmingly antique."

> But when society is the name of such hollow gentlemen and ladies, Julia, and when its breeding is professed indifference to everything that can advance or can retard mankind, I think we must have lost ourselves in the same Desert of Sahara, and had better find the way out.

When he spoke of Little Dorrit as "inspired" he proceeded to say:

> She was inspired to be something which was not what the rest were, and to be that something, different and laborious, for the sake of the rest. Inspired? Yes. Shall we speak of the inspiration of a poet or a priest, and not of the heart impelled by love and self-devotion to the lowliest work in the lowliest way of life!

Dickens had reached the great conception that the duty of every individual is to add something by his life to the general good. That we should not leave the world as we found it; that our work is not done well if we spend our lives in digging among the richest treasures of the past and revealing them unselfishly to our fellow-men, but that each should make some existing thing or condition better, or reveal some new thought or principle, or plan, or process, so that humanity may climb more easily and more certainly from the mists and shadows to the higher glory of the clearer light.

> Mr. Doyce had made an invention, but had met with almost insuperable difficulties in getting it before the people.
>
> "It is much to be regretted," said Clennam, "that you ever turned your thoughts that way, Mr. Doyce."
>
> "True, sir, true, to a certain extent. But what is a man to do? If he has the misfortune to strike out something serviceable to the nation, he must follow where it leads him."
>
> "Hadn't he better let it go?" asked Clennam.
>
> "He can't do it," said Doyce, shaking his head, with a thoughtful smile. "It's not put into his head to be buried. It's put into his head to be made useful. You hold your life on the condition that to the last you shall struggle hard for it. Every man holds a discovery on the same terms."
>
> "That is to say," said Arthur, with a growing admiration of his quiet companion, "you are not fully discouraged even now?"
>
> "I have no right to be, if I am," returned the other. "The thing is as true as it ever was."

Throughout his writings Dickens vigorously condemns the class distinctions that separate mankind into sections, and thus destroy the bond of unity and brotherhood that should exist between them.

Miss Monflathers, in Old Curiosity Shop, drew the line very definitely between genteel children and the children of the poor.

Mr. Dombey pompously consented to have the children of the poor educated, because "it is necessary that the inferior classes should continue to be taught to know their position." Fancy using education to prevent the unity of men, when its highest function should be the revelation of community and the qualification of individuals for the functions of brotherhood.

In David Copperfield the pathetic side of the evil of class distinctions is shown by the appeals of Mr. Peggotty to Mrs. Steerforth that she would consent to her son's marriage with Little Emily, and her indignant refusal to allow her son to do so.

In Bleak House Sir Leicester Dedlock was amazed at the audacity of Mr. Rouncewell's democratic ideas, and his mind was filled with gloomy forebodings of the evil that such principles as those held by Mr. Rouncewell would work in the social organization as planned and fixed by the Dedlock class. These were his thoughts:

> From the village school of Chesney Wold, intact as it is this minute, to the whole framework of society; from the whole framework of society, to the aforesaid framework receiving tremendous cracks in consequence of people (ironmasters, lead mistresses, and what not) not minding their catechism, and getting out of the station unto which they are called—necessarily and forever, according to Sir Leicester's rapid logic, the first station in which they happen to find themselves; and from that, to their educating other people out of *their* stations, and so obliterating the landmarks, and opening the flood gates, and all the rest of it; this is the swift progress of the Dedlock mind.

In American Notes, after describing at length the admirable co-operative arrangements, and the varied means of culture, amusement, and refinement enjoyed by the young women in the factories at Lowell, Mass., he says:

> The large class of readers, startled by these facts, will exclaim with one voice, "How very preposterous!" On my deferentially inquiring why, they will answer, "These things are above their station." In reply to that objection, I would beg to ask what their station is.
>
> It is their station to work. And they *do* work. They labour in these mills, upon an average, twelve hours a day, which is unquestionably work. And pretty tight work too. Perhaps it is above their station to indulge in such amusements on any terms. Are we quite sure that we in England have not formed our ideas of the "station" of working people from accustoming ourselves to the contemplation of that class as they are, and not as they might be? I think that if we examine our own feelings, we shall find that the pianos, and the circulating libraries, and even the Lowell Offering, startle us with their novelty, and not by their bearing upon any abstract question of right or wrong.

> For myself, I know no station in which, the occupation of to-day cheerfully done and the occupation of to-morrow cheerfully looked to, any one of these pursuits is not most humanizing and laudable. I know no station which is rendered more endurable to the person in it, or more safe to the person out of it, by having ignorance for its associate. I know no station which has a right to monopolize the means of mutual instruction, improvement, and rational entertainment; or which has ever continued to be a station very long, after seeking to do so.

Walter Wilding planned an ideal relationship between employer and employed in No Thoroughfare. He advertised for a housekeeper so that he "might sit daily at the head of the table at which the people in my employment eat together, and may eat of the same roast and boiled, and drink of the same beer, and one and all form a kind of family."

He planned, too, to train his employees to sing "Handel, Mozart, Haydn, Kent, Purcell, Doctor Arne, Greene, Mendelssohn, to make music a part of the bond between us. We will form a Choir in some quiet church near the Corner."

He touched the true chord of community when Joey Ladle used the word "they." Joey asked, when Mr. Wilding unfolded his plan:

> "Is all to live in the house, Young Master Wilding? The two other cellarmen, the three porters, the two 'prentices, and the odd men?"
>
> "Yes. I hope we shall all be a united family, Joey."
>
> "Ah!" said Joey. "I hope they may be."
>
> "They? Rather say *we*, Joey."

Not many employers have reached the ideals of Dickens yet.

CHAPTER XIV.

NUTRITION AS A FACTOR IN EDUCATION.

The influence of diet in the development not only of physical power, but of intellectual and spiritual power also, has now begun to attract general attention. There is no longer any doubt that the character of the bones, of the muscles, of the nerves, and of the brain itself, is decided to a considerable extent by the food that is eaten. There is no longer any doubt that many children have been urged to do work which becomes destructive beyond the fatigue point of their little brains, when their brains have not been properly nourished, either from lack of proper food or of properly cooked food, or from eating too much or too little.

The deterioration of the physical system, and especially the deterioration of the neurological system, is one of the most startling subjects within the range of view of educators and psychologists. One of the most attractive departments of child study is that which investigates the means of deciding from external manifestations of form, proportion, action, voice, and attitude the nature and condition of the brain and neurological system of the child. When this discovery has been made, however, it but prepares the way for further investigation to discover in what way abnormal or weak systems may be helped to become normal and strong.

One of the fundamental things to be done by scientists and educators is to discover the kinds of food adapted to different stages of the child's growth, and to the varied functions of study and work required of him. By proper nutrition and by proper exercise much may be done to increase the power and efficiency of the body and the brain and the rest of the neurological system.

Dickens saw the need of attention to the problems of nutrition very clearly. He began to write about it in Oliver Twist.

He first exposed the horrors of baby farming, with its terrible percentage of deaths, resulting almost entirely from the villainous indifference to the diet of the children. Children yet die in homes from similar causes, or, if they do not die, they go through life weakened and dwarfed.

> For the next eight or ten months Oliver was the victim of a systematic course of treachery and deception. He was brought up by hand. The hungry and destitute situation of the infant orphan was duly reported by the workhouse authorities to the parish authorities. The parish authorities inquired with dignity of the workhouse authorities whether there was no female then domiciled "in the house" who was in a situation to impart to Ol-

> iver Twist the consolation and nourishment of which he stood in need. The workhouse authorities replied with humility that there was not. Upon this the parish authorities magnanimously and humanely resolved that Oliver should be "farmed," or, in other words, that he should be despatched to a branch workhouse some three miles off, where twenty or thirty other juvenile offenders against the poor laws rolled about the floor all day, without the inconvenience of too much food or too much clothing, under the parental superintendence of an elderly female, who received the culprits at and for the consideration of sevenpence halfpenny per small head per week. Sevenpence halfpenny's worth per week is a good round diet for a child; a great deal may be got for sevenpence halfpenny, quite enough to overload its stomach, and make it uncomfortable. The elderly female was a woman of wisdom and experience; she knew what was good for children; and she had a very accurate perception of what was good for herself. So she appropriated the greater part of the weekly stipend to her own use, and consigned the rising parochial generation to even a shorter allowance than was originally provided for them. Thereby finding in the lowest depth a deeper still; and proving herself a very great experimental philosopher.

The system did not work well for the children.

> For at the very moment when a child had contrived to exist upon the smallest possible portion of the weakest possible food, it did perversely happen in eight and a half cases out of ten, either that it sickened from want or cold, or fell into the fire from neglect, or got half-smothered by accident; in any one of which cases, the miserable little being was usually summoned into another world, and there gathered to the fathers it had never known in this.
>
> It can not be expected that this system of farming would produce any very extraordinary or luxuriant crop. Oliver Twist's ninth birthday found him a pale, thin child, somewhat diminutive in stature, and decidedly small in circumference. It *was* his ninth birthday; and he was keeping it in the coal cellar with a select party of two other young gentlemen, who, after participating with him in a sound thrashing, had been locked up for atrociously presuming to be hungry.

The famous meal in the workhouse when Oliver asked for more was intended to direct attention to the way children were fed and treated in institutions. The boys were fed on gruel.

> Of this festive composition each boy had one porringer, and no more—except on occasions of great public rejoicing, when he had two ounces and a quarter of bread besides. The bowls never wanted washing. The boys polished them with their spoons till

they shone again; and when they had performed this operation (which never took very long, the spoons being nearly as large as the bowls), they would sit staring at the copper, with such eager eyes, as if they could have devoured the very bricks of which it was composed; employing themselves, meanwhile, in sucking their fingers most assiduously, with the view of catching up any stray splashes of gruel that might have been cast thereon. Boys have generally excellent appetites. Oliver Twist and his companions suffered the tortures of slow starvation for three months; at last they got so voracious and wild with hunger that one boy who was tall for his age, and hadn't been used to that sort of thing (for his father had kept a small cookshop), hinted darkly to his companions that unless he had another basin of gruel *per diem*, he was afraid he might some night happen to eat the boy who slept next to him, who happened to be a weakly youth of tender age. He had a wild, hungry eye; and they implicitly believed him. A council was held; lots were cast who should walk up to the master after supper that evening, and ask for more; and it fell to Oliver Twist.

The evening arrived; the boys took their places. The master, in his cook's uniform, stationed himself at the copper; his pauper assistants ranged themselves behind him; the gruel was served out; and a long grace was said over a short commons. The gruel disappeared; the boys whispered each other and winked at Oliver; while his next neighbours nudged him. Child as he was, he was desperate with hunger and reckless with misery. He rose from the table; and advancing to the master, basin and spoon in hand, said, somewhat alarmed at his own temerity:

"Please, sir, I want some more."

The master was a fat, healthy man; but he turned very pale. He gazed in stupefied astonishment on the small rebel for some seconds, and then clung for support to the copper. The assistants were paralyzed with wonder; the boys with fear.

"What!" said the master at length, in a faint voice.

"Please, sir," replied Oliver, "I want some more."

The master aimed a blow at Oliver's head with the ladle; pinioned his arms; and shrieked aloud for the beadle.

The board were sitting in solemn conclave, when Mr. Bumble rushed into the room in great excitement, and addressing the gentleman in the high chair, said:

"Mr. Limbkins, I beg your pardon, sir! Oliver Twist has asked for more."

There was a general start. Horror was depicted in every countenance.

> "For *more*!" said Mr. Limbkins. "Compose yourself, Bumble, and answer me distinctly. Do I understand that he asked for more, after he had eaten the supper allotted by the dietary?"
>
> "He did, sir," replied Bumble.
>
> "That boy will be hung," said the gentleman in the white waistcoat. "I know that boy will be hung."

Having shown how infants were starved in "farming," and how boys were starved in the workhouses, he next directed attention to the way apprentices were treated.

Mr. Sowerberry was an undertaker, who decided to take Oliver from the workhouse. He took Oliver "upon liking," which meant that "if he could get enough work out of him without putting too much food into him, he should keep him for a term of years to do what he liked with him."

When Oliver had been driven to desperation by Noah Claypole, and had punished him as he deserved, Mrs. Sowerberry sent for Mr. Bumble. When Mr. Bumble asked Oliver if he was not afraid of him, Oliver bravely answered "No!" The Beadle was petrified with amazement, and he accounted for Oliver's wickedness by saying:

> "It's meat."
>
> "What?" exclaimed Mrs. Sowerberry.
>
> "Meat, ma'am, meat," replied Bumble, with stern emphasis. "You've overfed him, ma'am. You've raised a artificial soul and spirit in him, ma'am, unbecoming a person of his condition; as the board, Mrs. Sowerberry, who are practical philosophers, will tell you. What have paupers to do with soul or spirit? It's quite enough that we let 'em have live bodies. If you had kept the boy on gruel, ma'am, this would never have happened."
>
> "Dear, dear!" ejaculated Mrs. Sowerberry, piously raising her eyes to the kitchen ceiling; "this comes of being liberal!"
>
> The liberality of Mrs. Sowerberry to Oliver had consisted in a profuse bestowal upon him of all the dirty odds and ends which nobody else would eat.

By this conversation Dickens meant to teach that a well-fed child is a different type from one who is not properly nourished; that food has an influence on the spirit, as well as on the body. He did not disapprove of Oliver's spirit, but he heartily commended him for resenting the way he was treated. This lesson was needed too, as children were expected to submit uncomplainingly to those who were their legal guardians, whether strangers or parents. Now, largely through Dickens, children are not only encouraged to defend themselves against cruel and tyrannical guardians or parents, and to run away from them, but the state itself will take them away, if cruelty is proved against those who should be their protectors.

Dickens also revealed by this incident the meanness of adults not only in institutions but in homes, in giving to the children the "odds and ends," the scraps, the parts of the fowl or the meat that older people do not care for. He brought the matter up again in Great Expectations. At the Christmas dinner Pip "was regaled with the scaly tips of the drumsticks of the fowls, and with those obscure corners of pork of which the pig, when living, had least reason to be vain."

One of the reasons given by Snawley to Squeers to induce him to take his stepsons at a lower rate was that "they were not great eaters."

The selfishness of adulthood toward childhood, and the stupidity of the general idea, that children do not require good food because they are young and do not have to work hard, were held up to deserved ridicule, in Squeers's manner of breakfasting in London, and the food he provided for the five hungry little boys to strengthen them for their long ride to Yorkshire in cold weather.

> He found that learned gentleman sitting at breakfast, with the three little boys before noticed, and two others who had turned up by some lucky chance since the interview of the previous day, ranged in a row on the opposite seat. Mr. Squeers had before him a small measure of coffee, a plate of hot toast, and a cold round of beef; but he was at that moment intent on preparing breakfast for the little boys.
>
> "This is two penn'orth of milk, is it, waiter?" said Mr. Squeers, looking down into a large blue mug, and slanting it gently, so as to get an accurate view of the quantity of liquid contained in it.
>
> "That's two penn'orth, sir," replied the waiter.
>
> "What a rare article milk is, to be sure, in London!" said Mr. Squeers with a sigh. "Just fill that mug up with lukewarm water, William, will you?"
>
> "To the wery top, sir?" inquired the waiter. "Why, the milk will be drownded."
>
> "Never you mind that," replied Mr. Squeers. "Serve it right for being so dear. You ordered that thick bread and butter for three, did you?"
>
> "Coming directly, sir."
>
> "You needn't hurry yourself," said Squeers; "there's plenty of time. Conquer your passions, boys, and don't be eager after vittles." As he uttered this moral precept, Mr. Squeers took a large bite out of the cold beef, and recognised Nicholas.
>
> "Sit down, Mr. Nickleby," said Squeers. "Here we are, a-breakfasting you see!"
>
> Nicholas did *not* see that anybody was breakfasting, except Mr. Squeers; but he bowed with all becoming reverence, and looked as cheerful as he could.

"Oh! that's the milk and water, is it, William?" said Squeers. "Very good; don't forget the bread and butter presently."

At this fresh mention of the bread and butter the five little boys looked very eager, and followed the waiter out, with their eyes; meanwhile Mr. Squeers tasted the milk and water.

"Ah!" said that gentleman, smacking his lips, "here's richness! Think of the many beggars and orphans in the streets that would be glad of this, little boys. A shocking thing hunger is, isn't it, Mr. Nickleby?"

"Very shocking, sir," said Nicholas.

"When I say number one," pursued Mr. Squeers, putting the mug before the children, "the boy on the left hand nearest the window may take a drink; and when I say number two, the boy next him will go in, and so till we come to number five, which is the last boy. Are you ready?"

"Yes, sir," cried the little boys with great eagerness.

"That's right," said Squeers, calmly getting on with his breakfast; "keep ready till I tell you to begin. Subdue your appetites, my dears, and you've conquered human natur. This is the way we inculcate strength of mind, Mr. Nickleby," said the schoolmaster, turning to Nicholas, and speaking with his mouth very full of beef and toast.

Nicholas murmured something—he knew not what—in reply; and the little boys, dividing their gaze between the mug, the bread and butter (which had by this time arrived), and every morsel which Mr. Squeers took into his mouth, remained with strained eyes in torments of expectation.

"Thank God for a good breakfast," said Squeers, when he had finished. "Number one may take a drink."

Number one received the mug ravenously, and had just drunk enough to make him wish for more, when Mr. Squeers gave the signal for number two, who gave up at the same interesting moment to number three; and the process was repeated until the milk and water terminated with number five.

"And now," said the schoolmaster, dividing the bread and butter for three into as many portions as there were children, "you had better look sharp with your breakfast, the horn will blow in a minute or two, and then every boy leaves off."

Permission being thus given to fall to, the boys began to eat voraciously, and in desperate haste, while the schoolmaster (who was in high good humour after his meal) picked his teeth with a fork, and looked smilingly on. In a very short time the horn was

> heard.
>
> "I thought it wouldn't be long," said Squeers, jumping up and producing a little basket from under the seat; "put what you haven't had time to eat in here, boys! You'll want it on the road!"

Young Wackford Squeers was fed on the fattest meats, so that he might be kept plump and energetic, in order that he might be taken to London to show intending patrons how well the boys were fed in Dotheboys Hall.

Again, in The Old Curiosity Shop, the starving of child servants is condemned by the way Sally Brass fed the Marchioness. Dick Swiveller's curiosity led him to peep through a crack in the kitchen door one day while Sally was giving the little servant her dinner.

> Everything was locked up; the coal cellar, the candle box, the salt box, the meat safe were all padlocked. There was nothing that a beetle could have lunched upon. The pinched and meagre aspect of the place would have killed a chameleon; he would have known, at the first mouthful, that the air was not eatable, and must have given up the ghost in despair.
>
> The small servant stood with humility in presence of Miss Sally, and hung her head.
>
> "Are you there?" said Miss Sally.
>
> "Yes, ma'am," was the answer, in a weak voice.
>
> "Go farther away from the leg of mutton, or you'll be picking it, I know," said Miss Sally.
>
> The girl withdrew into a corner, while Miss Brass took a key from her pocket, and opening the safe, brought from it a dreary waste of cold potatoes, looking as eatable as Stonehenge. This she placed before the small servant, ordering her to sit down before it, and then, taking up a great carving knife, made a mighty show of sharpening it upon the carving fork.
>
> "Do you see this?" said Miss Brass, slicing off about two square inches of cold mutton, after all this preparation, and holding it out on the point of the fork.
>
> The small servant looked hard enough at it with her hungry eyes to see every shred in it, small as it was, and answered, "Yes."
>
> "Then don't you ever go and say," retorted Miss Sally, "that you hadn't meat here. There, eat it up."
>
> This was soon done. "Now, do you want any more?" said Miss Sally.
>
> The hungry creature answered with a faint "No." They were evidently going through an established form.
>
> "You've been helped once to meat," said Miss Brass, summing

> up the facts; "you have had as much as you can eat, you're asked if you want any more, and you answer 'No!' Then don't you ever go and say you were allowanced, mind that."

Dickens showed the evil effects of eating too rapidly in his description of the dinner in Mrs. Pawkins's boarding house in New York, where Martin Chuzzlewit boarded for a short time after reaching America.

> It was a numerous company, eighteen or twenty perhaps. Of these, some five or six were ladies, who sat wedged together in a little phalanx by themselves. All the knives and forks were working away at a rate that was quite alarming; very few words were spoken; and everybody seemed to eat his utmost in self-defence, as if a famine were expected to set in before breakfast time to-morrow morning, and it had become high time to assert the first law of Nature. The poultry, which may perhaps be considered to have formed the staple of the entertainment—for there was a turkey at the top, a pair of ducks at the bottom, and two fowls in the middle—disappeared as rapidly as if every bird had had the use of its wings, and had flown in desperation down a human throat. The oysters, stewed and pickled, leaped from their capacious reservoirs, and slid by scores into the mouths of the assembly. The sharpest pickles vanished, whole cucumbers at once, like sugar-plums, and no man winked his eye. Great heaps of indigestible matter melted away as ice before the sun. It was a solemn and an awful thing to see. Dyspeptic individuals bolted their food in wedges; feeding not themselves, but broods of nightmares, who were continually standing at livery within them. Spare men, with lank and rigid cheeks, came out unsatisfied from the destruction of heavy dishes, and glared with watchful eyes upon the pastry. What Mrs. Pawkins felt each day at dinner time is hidden from all human knowledge. But she had one comfort. It was very soon over.

Dickens repeats this criticism of rapid eating in his American Notes, when specifying the causes of disease among American people. He says: "The custom of hastily swallowing large quantities of animal food three times a day and rushing back to sedentary pursuits after each meal must be changed."

Poor Paul Dombey was sacrificed to his father's pride. Mrs. Toodle was dismissed by Mr. Dombey because she dared to take his infant son with her when she went to see her own children. Paul was thus robbed of the natural food, which his sensitive nature needed so much. This was largely responsible for the fact that Paul was delicate. By first depriving him of proper food, and then sending him to Doctor Blimber's school "to learn everything," Mr. Dombey led directly to Paul's death. His pride and vanity overreached themselves.

In Mrs. Pipchin's meals Dickens tried to show two things: First, the selfishness of adulthood in regard to children's diet as compared with its own; second, the absolute insufficiency of the kind of food commonly supplied to children for building up strong, energetic, and well-developed men and women.

She regaled the children with a repast of "farinaceous and vegetable foods—chiefly rice," but she herself had a good hot dinner with mutton chops.

The children were required to repeat a form of grace thanking Mrs. Pipchin for a good dinner. Oliver was told he must be thankful to the kind gentlemen who provided food for him in the workhouse. The same mockery of religion by mixing it up with the starvation of childhood is made ridiculous in the letter which Squeers read to the unfortunate children in Dotheboys Hall, pretending that it had been written by the stepmother of Mobbs.

"Mobbs's stepmother," said Squeers, "took to her bed on hearing that he wouldn't eat fat, and has been very ill ever since. She wishes to know, by an early post, where he expects to go to if he quarrels with his vittles; and with what feelings he could turn up his nose at the cow's liver's broth, after his good master had asked a blessing on it." "Cow's liver's broth" would not be a very strengthening diet for children even with the blessing of so good a man as Squeers upon it.

Dickens makes a characteristic hit at the fashionable idea which was popular at one time, that it was rather indelicate, especially in a lady, to have a good robust constitution and a vigorous digestion in describing Mr. Vholes in Bleak House. "His digestion was impaired, which is always highly respectable."

Mrs. Cruncher, in A Tale of Two Cities, objected to the questionable ways in which Mr. Cruncher earned his money sometimes. Her husband charged her with flying in the face of Providence by refusing the "wittles and drink" he provided for her, and especially for neglecting to give it to their son. "With you flying into the face of your own wittles and drink! I don't know how scarce you mayn't make the wittles and drink here by your flopping tricks and your unfeeling conduct. Look at your boy: he is yourn, ain't he? He's as thin as a lath. Do you call yourself a mother, and not know a mother's first duty is to blow her son out."

Abel Magwitch, when describing the terrible training he received at the hands of a Christian community in the most advanced Christian civilization of the world, said that when he was in jail some philanthropists "measured his head to find out the cause of his wickedness," and added with great wisdom, "they had better a-measured my stomach."

The folly of hoping that healthy infants can be nourished by mothers who are compelled to labour continuously through long hours without rest is shown in the description of the child whose mother was a waitress, in Somebody's Luggage. Incidentally, too, Dickens reveals in this case the facts that the power of assimilation of little children is usually impaired, and that, as a consequence, they become more peevish, and therefore get shaken and otherwise abused for the ignorance of the adults responsible for their care. Speaking of the treatment of the baby, he says:

> You were conveyed—ere yet your dawning powers were otherwise developed than to harbour vacancy in your inside—you were conveyed by surreptitious means into a pantry adjoining

> the Admiral Nelson, Civic and General Dining-Rooms, there to receive by stealth that healthful sustenance which is the pride and boast of the British female constitution. Under the combined influence of the smells of roast and boiled, and soup, and gas, and malt liquors, you partook of your earliest nourishment; your unwilling grandmother sitting prepared to catch you when your mother was called and dropped you; your grandmother's shawl ever ready to stifle your natural complainings; your innocent mind surrounded by uncongenial cruets, dirty plates, dish covers, and cold gravy; your mother calling down the pipe for veals and porks, instead of soothing you with nursery rhymes. Under these untoward circumstances you were early weaned. Your unwilling grandmother, ever growing more unwilling as your food assimilated less, then contracted habits of shaking you till your system curdled, and your food would not assimilate at all.

The schoolmaster in Jemmy Lirriper's original story was captured and put into confinement for his treatment of the boys, and he was to have nothing to eat but the boys' dinners, and was to drink half a cask of their beer every day.

The schoolboy in The Schoolboy's Story describes the food given to the boys as one of the grievances they had against the institution.

> As to the beef, it's shameful. It's *not* beef. Regular beef isn't veins. You can chew regular beef. Besides which, there's gravy to regular beef, and you never see a drop to ours. Another of our fellows went home ill, and heard the family doctor tell his father that he couldn't account for his complaint unless it was the beer. Of course it was the beer, and well it might be!
>
> However, beef and Old Cheeseman are two different things. So is beer. It was Old Cheeseman I meant to tell about; not the manner in which our fellows get their constitutions destroyed for the sake of profit.
>
> Why, look at the pie crust alone. There's no flakiness in it. It's solid—like damp lead. Then our fellows get nightmares, and are bolstered for calling out and waking other fellows. Who can wonder!
>
> Old Cheeseman one night walked in his sleep, put his hat on over his nightcap, got hold of a fishing rod and a cricket bat, and went down into the parlour, where they naturally thought from his appearance he was a Ghost. Why, he never would have done that if his meals had been wholesome. When we all begin to walk in our sleeps, I suppose they'll be sorry for it.

At Doctor Blimber's school they used "to crib the boys' dinners." There is no more outrageous practice than that of depriving a child of food as a means of punishment.

Dickens ended his sketch entitled A Walk in a Workhouse with a plea on behalf of the inmates for "a little more liberty—and a little more bread," and even in his last book, Edwin Drood, he was still directing attention to the poor food supplied in boarding schools.

Mrs. Billickin was very plain in her hints about the poor board supplied to Rosa at Miss Twinkleton's when she received the schoolmistress in her own home. Referring to Rosa, who was now residing with Mrs. Billickin, she said:

> "I did think it well to mention to my cook, which I 'ope you will agree with, Miss Twinkleton, was a right precaution, that the young lady being used to what we should consider here but poor diet, had better be brought forward by degrees. For a rush from scanty feeding to generous feeding, and from what you may call messing to what you may call method, do require a power of constitution, which is not often found in youth, particularly when undermined by boarding school! I was put in youth to a very genteel boarding school, the mistress being no less a lady than yourself, of about your own age, or, it may be some years younger, and a poorness of blood flowed from the table which has run through my life."

CHAPTER XV.

MINOR SCHOOLS.

The schools of Squeers, Doctor Blimber, Mr. Creakle, Doctor Strong, and Mr. Gradgrind and Mr. M'Choakumchild are the most celebrated schools of Dickens, and they contain the greater part of his pedagogical teaching. His other schools are, however, worthy of very careful study.

One of the first of the Sketches by Boz described a man who had passed through many vicissitudes, and at length was reduced to such poverty that he applied to the parish board for charity. This led to his appointment as a school-master. Dickens clearly intended to teach the lesson, afterward emphasized in Nicholas Nickleby and other books, that poverty should not establish a claim to the position of a school-teacher.

Minerva Hall, also in Sketches by Boz, reveals "one of those public nuisances, a spoiled child," spoiled because his papa was too busy with public duties and his mamma with society duties to train him properly. It also shows the reason Mrs. Cornelius Brook Dingwall had for sending her daughter to school. She said: "One of my principal reasons for parting with my daughter is that she has lately acquired some sentimental ideas, which it is most desirable to eradicate from her young mind." Here the public nuisance fell out of a chair, and mamma and papa showed their usual mode of training him. Mamma called him "a naughty boy," and threatened "to send for James to take him away"—both name and threat being wrong. Papa merely excused the cherub on the ground of "his great flow of spirits." The school also shows the silly training of so-called "finishing schools," as chiefly intended to teach young ladies the small conventionalities of "society."

In The Old Curiosity Shop there are four schools: Mr. Marton's two schools, Mrs. Wackles's school, and Miss Monflathers's school. Mr. Marton's first school was introduced to reveal all the good qualities that Mr. Squeers lacked, especially sympathy. Mr. Marton was the immediate successor of Mr. Squeers, and they possessed directly opposite traits of character in their relationship to childhood. Mr. Squeers was coarse, unsympathetic, and coercive. Mr. Marton was kind, considerate, and a perfect type of true sympathy with the child. It is reasonable to believe that Mr. Marton and Mr. Squeers were drawn as companion pictures to illustrate and enforce the same truth—that sympathy with the child is the fundamental element in the character of a true teacher.

The old bachelor emphasized this when he said to Mr. Marton, "You are none the worse teacher for having learned humanity."

There is a great deal of food for psychological and pedagogical study in the introduction of the boys he was to teach in his second school, given by the bachelor to Mr. Marton. The bachelor was as full of genuine boyish spirit as it is possible for any adult to be, and was in some respects a more perfect type for an ideal teacher than Mr. Marton. Mr. Marton had the tender, spiritual sympathy of a true woman, the motherhood spirit that constitutes the atmosphere in which all right elements of childhood find their richest development; the bachelor had the perfect manly sympathy that enabled him to enter heartily into boy life. He had especially the power of recognising in the things for which boys are often rebuked the best evidences of their strength, and he could remember his own boyhood so well as to fully sympathize *with* the boys. Mr. Marton and the bachelor reveal the whole range of sympathetic possibilities.

> When nothing more was left to be done he charged the boy to run off and bring his schoolmates to be marshalled before their new master and solemnly reviewed.
>
> "As good a set of fellows, Marton, as you'd wish to see," he said, turning to the schoolmaster when the boy was gone; "but I don't let 'em know I think so. That wouldn't do at all."
>
> The messenger soon returned at the head of a long row of urchins, great and small, who, being confronted by the bachelor at the house door, fell into various convulsions of politeness; clutching their hats and caps, squeezing them into the smallest possible dimensions, and making all manner of bows and scrapes, which the little old gentleman contemplated with excessive satisfaction, and expressed his approval of by a great many nods and smiles. Indeed, his approbation of the boys was by no means so scrupulously disguised as he had led the schoolmaster to suppose, inasmuch as it broke out in sundry loud whispers and confidential remarks which were perfectly audible to them every one.
>
> "This first boy, schoolmaster," said the bachelor, "is John Owen; a lad of good parts, sir, and frank, honest temper; but too thoughtless, too playful, too light-headed by far. That boy, my good sir, would break his neck with pleasure, and deprive his parents of their chief comfort—and between ourselves, when you come to see him at hare and hounds, taking the fence and ditch by the finger post, and sliding down the face of the little quarry, you'll never forget it. It's beautiful!"
>
> John Owen having been thus rebuked, and being in perfect possession of the speech aside, the bachelor singled out another boy.
>
> "Now look at that lad, sir," said the bachelor. "You see that fellow? Richard Evans his name is, sir. An amazing boy to learn, blessed with a good memory and a ready understanding, and moreover with a good voice and ear for psalm singing, in which

he is the best among us. Yet, sir, that boy will come to a bad end; he'll never die in his bed; he's always falling asleep in sermon time—and to tell you the truth, Mr. Marton, I always did the same at his age, and feel quite certain that it was natural to my constitution, and I couldn't help it."

This hopeful pupil edified by the above terrible reproval, the bachelor turned to another.

"But if we talk of examples to be shunned," said he, "if we come to boys that should be a warning and a beacon to all their fellows, here's the one, and I hope you won't spare him. This is the lad, sir; this one with the blue eyes and light hair. This is a swimmer, sir, this fellow—a diver, Lord save us! This is a boy, sir, who had a fancy for plunging into eighteen feet of water, with his clothes on, and bringing up a blind man's dog, who was being drowned by the weight of his chain and collar, while his master stood wringing his hands upon the bank, bewailing the loss of his guide and friend. I sent the boy two guineas anonymously, sir," added the bachelor, in his peculiar whisper, "directly I heard of it; but never mention it on any account, for he hasn't the least idea that it came from me."

Having disposed of this culprit, the bachelor turned to another, and from him to another, and so on through the whole array, laying, for their wholesome restriction within due bounds, the same cutting emphasis on such of their propensities as were dearest to his heart, and were unquestionably referable to his own precept and example. Thoroughly persuaded, in the end, that he had made them miserable by his severity, he dismissed them with a small present, and an admonition to walk quietly home, without any leapings, scufflings, or turnings out of the way; which injunction, he informed the schoolmaster in the same audible confidence, he did not think he could have obeyed when he was a boy had his life depended on it.

What a model he was for teachers, this glorious bachelor, in his sympathy *with* the boys, and in his unconventionality! When teachers begin to feel the grip of formalism on their better natures and begin to lose faith in so-called bad boys, they should read this introduction of the pupils by the bachelor. Bless his memory! he will always rank among the greatest child trainers.

His pretence of not letting the boys know that he thought they were good fellows was a pleasant rebuke of the miserable old doctrine that a boy should always be told his faults, but never be spoken to about his virtues. This false doctrine having been so carefully applied in homes and schools for centuries as a religious duty, based on the unscriptural doctrine of child depravity, has made a large portion of humanity in Christian countries mere defect dodgers, instead of making them conscious of power to do independent work for God and their fellow-men.

Dickens had no faith in this doctrine, and he taught that one of the highest things a teacher can do for a child is to recognise and show honest appreciation of his best powers and qualities. When superintendents search as carefully for the good qualities and powers of their teachers as some yet do for their weaknesses, and when they are so unconventional as to be able to show genuine appreciation frankly to the teachers themselves, the schools will reach their proper rate of progressive development.

Through the whole series of criticisms of the boys, Dickens is showing the full rich sympathy of his own great heart for the whole race of boys in the unreasonable and unjust criticism to which they are subjected by forgetful and ignorant adulthood. Those who should be wisest in these matters—and especially many who think themselves wise—are still very forgetful of their own early life, and very ignorant of boyhood.

Mrs. Wackles's school was called a "Ladies' Seminary," but it was in reality "a very small day school for young ladies of proportionate dimensions."

> The several duties of instruction in this establishment were thus discharged: English grammar, composition, geography, and the use of the dumb-bells, by Miss Melissa Wackles; writing, arithmetic, dancing, music, and general fascination, by Miss Sophy Wackles; the art of needlework, marking, and samplery, by Miss Jane Wackles; corporal punishment, fasting, and other tortures and terrors, by Mrs. Wackles. Miss Melissa Wackles was the eldest daughter, Miss Sophy the next, and Miss Jane the youngest. Miss Melissa might have seen five-and-thirty summers or thereabout, and verged on the autumnal, Miss Sophy was a fresh, good-humoured, buxom girl of twenty; and Miss Jane numbered scarcely sixteen years. Mrs. Wackles was an excellent, but rather venomous old lady of threescore.

Mrs. Wackles's school is described to show the frivolous nature of such so-called private educational institutions, and to strike again the abominable practice of abusing children by "corporal punishment, fasting, and other tortures and terrors" by "a venomous old lady of threescore."

Miss Monflathers's school was a boarding establishment for young ladies, in which they were duly impressed with the dignity of their social position; with the terrible danger of yielding in any way to their natural impulses, all of which were assumed to be very wicked; with the sinfulness of sympathizing with or in any way recognising the lower classes; with the impropriety of knowing the fact that there was any wrong in the world to be righted or any suffering to be relieved; with the inestimable value of aristocratic birth; and with the most important truth that men are very dangerous animals, to be carefully shunned.

Little Nell was sent to the establishment of Miss Monflathers with notices of Mrs. Jarley's waxworks, being temporarily in the employ of that lady.

> Nell had no difficulty in finding out Miss Monflathers's Boarding and Day Establishment, which was a large house, with

a high wall, and a large garden gate with a large brass plate, and a small grating through which Miss Monflathers's parlour maid inspected all visitors before admitting them; for nothing in the shape of a man—no, not even a milkman—was suffered, without special license, to pass that gate. Even the taxgatherer, who was stout, and wore spectacles and a broadbrimmed hat, had the taxes handed through the grating. More obdurate than gate of adamant or brass, this gate of Miss Monflathers's frowned on all mankind. The very butcher respected it as a gate of mystery, and left off whistling when he rang the bell.

As Nell approached the awful door, it turned slowly upon its hinges with a creaking noise, and forth from the solemn grove beyond came a long file of young ladies, two and two, all with open books in their hands, and some with parasols likewise. And last of the goodly procession came Miss Monflathers, bearing herself a parasol of lilac silk, and supported by two smiling teachers, each mortally envious of the other, and devoted unto Miss Monflathers.

Confused by the looks and whispers of the girls, Nell stood with downcast eyes and suffered the procession to pass on, until Miss Monflathers, bringing up the rear, approached her, when she courtesied and presented her little packet; on receipt whereof Miss Monflathers commanded that the line should halt.

"You're the waxwork child, are you not?" said Miss Monflathers.

"Yes, ma'am," replied Nell, colouring deeply, for the young ladies had collected about her, and she was the centre on which all eyes were fixed.

"And don't you think you must be a very wicked little child," said Miss Monflathers, who was of rather uncertain temper, and lost no opportunity of impressing moral truths upon the tender minds of young ladies, "to be a waxwork child at all?"

Poor Nell had never viewed her position in this light, and not knowing what to say, remained silent, blushing more deeply than before.

"Don't you know," said Miss Monflathers, "that it's very naughty and unfeminine, and a perversion of the properties wisely and benignantly transmitted to us, with expansive powers to be roused from their dormant state through the medium of cultivation?"

"Don't you feel how naughty it is of you," resumed Miss Monflathers, "to be a waxwork child, when you might have the proud consciousness of assisting, to the extent of your infant powers, the manufactures of your country; of improving your mind by the constant contemplation of the steam engine; and of earning a comfortable and independent subsistence of from two and nine-pence to three shillings per week? Don't you know that the harder you are at work, the happier you are?"

"'How doth the little— —'" murmured one of the teachers in quotation from Dr. Watts.

"Eh?" said Miss Monflathers, turning smartly round. "Who said that?"

"The little busy bee," said Miss Monflathers, drawing herself up, "is applicable only to genteel children.

'In books, or work, or healthful play'

is quite right as far as they are concerned; and the work means painting on velvet, fancy needlework, or embroidery. In such cases as these," pointing to Nell with her parasol, "and in the case of all poor people's children, we should read it thus:

'In work, work, work. In work alway
Let my first years be passed,
That I may give for ev'ry day
Some good account at last.'"

Just then somebody happened to discover that Nell was crying, and all eyes were again turned toward her.

There were indeed tears in her eyes, and drawing out her handkerchief to brush them away, she happened to let it fall. Before she could stoop to pick it up, one young lady of about fifteen or sixteen, who had been standing a little apart from the others, as though she had no recognised place among them, sprang forward and put it in her hand. She was gliding timidly away again, when she was arrested by the governess.

"It was Miss Edwards who did that, I *know*," said Miss Monflathers predictively. "Now I am sure that was Miss Edwards."

It was Miss Edwards, and everybody said it was Miss Edwards, and Miss Edwards herself admitted that it was.

"Is it not," said Miss Monflathers, putting down her parasol to take a severer view of the offender, "a most remarkable thing, Miss Edwards, that you have an attachment to the lower classes which always draws you to their sides; or, rather, is it not a most extraordinary thing that all I say and do will not wean you from propensities which your original station in life has unhappily rendered habitual to you, you extremely vulgar-minded girl?"

"I really intended no harm, ma'am," said a sweet voice. "It was a momentary impulse, indeed."

"An impulse!" repeated Miss Monflathers scornfully. "I wonder that you presume to speak of impulses to me"—both the teachers assented—"I am astonished"—both the teachers were astonished—"I suppose it is an impulse which induces you to take the part of every grovelling and debased person that comes in your way"—both the teachers supposed so too.

"But I would have you know, Miss Edwards," resumed the governess, in a tone of increased severity, "that you can not be permitted—if it be only for the sake of preserving a proper example and decorum in this establishment—that you can not be permitted, and that you shall not be permitted, to fly in the face of your superiors in this extremely gross manner. If *you* have no reason to feel a becoming pride before waxwork children, there are young ladies here who have, and you must either defer to those young ladies or leave the establishment, Miss Edwards."

This young lady, being motherless and poor, was apprenticed at the school—taught for nothing—teaching others what she learned for nothing—boarded for nothing—lodged for nothing—and set down and rated as something immeasurably less than nothing, by all the dwellers in the house. The servant maids felt her inferiority, for they were better treated; free to come and go, and regarded in their stations with much more respect. The teachers were infinitely superior, for they had paid to go to school in their time, and were paid now. The pupils cared little for a companion who had no grand stories to tell about home; no friends to come with post horses, and be received in all humility, with cake and wine, by the governess; no deferential servant to attend and bear her home for the holidays; nothing genteel to talk about, and nothing to display. But why was Miss Monflathers always vexed and irritated with the poor apprentice how did that come to pass?

Why, the gayest feather in Miss Monflathers's cap, and the brightest glory of Miss Monflathers's school, was a baronet's daughter—the real live daughter of a real live baronet—who, by some extraordinary reversal of the laws of Nature, was not only plain in features but dull in intellect, while the poor apprentice had both a ready wit and a handsome face and figure. It seems incredible. Here was Miss Edwards, who only paid a small premium which had been spent long ago, every day outshining and excelling the baronet's daughter, who learned all the extras (or was taught them all), and whose half yearly bill came to double that of any other young lady's in the school, making no account of the honour and reputation of her pupilage. Therefore, and because she was a dependent, Miss Monflathers had a great dislike to Miss Edwards, and was spiteful to her, and aggravated by her, and, when she had compassion on Little Nell, verbally fell upon and maltreated her, as we have already seen.

"You will not take the air to-day, Miss Edwards," said Miss Monflathers. "Have the goodness to retire to your own room, and not to leave it without permission."

The poor girl was moving hastily away, when she was suddenly, in a nautical phrase, "brought to" by a subdued shriek from Miss Monflathers.

"She has passed me without any salute!" cried the governess, raising her eyes to the sky. "She has actually passed me without the slightest acknowledgment of my presence!"

The young lady turned and courtesied. Nell could see that she raised her dark eyes to the face of her superior, and that their expression, and that of her whole attitude for the instant, was one of mute but most touching appeal against this ungenerous usage. Miss Monflathers only tossed her head in reply, and the great gate closed upon a bursting heart.

In addition to the gross evils of such institutions already suggested, Dickens exposed the cruelty of Miss Monflathers, as a type of Christian rectitude, toward Nell, whom she assumed to be very wicked, and the tendency of society to treat teachers with contempt, if they are not rich. The standard based on mere wealth is happily changing.

The tone of Miss Monflathers's lofty criticism in language and thought, quite incomprehensible to the person admonished, is very true to the life in cases of conventional people, who take no pains to understand child nature or human nature in any phase, except its depravity.

The heartlessness of the distinction between the "genteel" children and poor children is clearly pointed out. There could scarcely be a more unchristlike thought than the one that would prohibit the children of the poor from the enjoyment of their natural tendency to play. No civilization in which either by deliberate purpose or by criminal negligence the children of the poorest are left without the privilege and the means for full free play should dare to call itself Christian. Yet Miss Monflathers's parody aptly represented the practical outworking of civilization at the time of Dickens, and long since, too, in regard to poor children.

Miss Monflathers told Miss Edwards majestically that she "must not take the air to-day," and contemptuously ordered her to remain in her room all day. This was written to condemn the common punishment of keeping children in at recess or confining them as a means of punishment. Dickens always thought it a crime against childhood to punish a child by robbing it of any of its natural rights to food, or fresh air, or free exercise.

The ecstasy of passion reached by Miss Monflathers because Miss Edwards passed her without saluting her showed Dickens's attitude toward those who insisted and still insist on obeisance from those whom they are pleased to regard as "inferiors." Public school education has been criticised because "it does not train poor children to courtesy to their superiors." Any system deserves the support of all right-thinking people if it trains the children of the poorest to hold their heads up respectfully, and look the world squarely in the face without a debasing consciousness of inferiority. The greatest aim of education, so far as the individual is concerned, is freedom—spiritual freedom. Respect for properly constituted authority should become a part of every child's consciousness, but this properly involves contempt for the arrogant assumption of certain people that certain other people should bow down in servile humility to them. Education must always be the enemy of tyranny, slavery, and all kinds of abasement.

The grinders' school was introduced to ridicule the practice of forcing all children in charitable institutions to wear a uniform dress, and to attack corporal punishment, neglect of moral training, and the practice of placing ignorant men in the high position of a teacher. The teacher in the grinders' school was "a superannuated old grinder of savage disposition, who had been appointed schoolmaster because he didn't know anything, and wasn't fit for anything, and for whose cruel cane all chubby little boys had a perfect fascination." The practice of dressing all children alike, and of dressing them all without taste, is continued in most homes for orphan children still. Surely the poor orphans have suffered enough without subjecting them to the indignity of tasteless dressing. There might at least be a difference of taste in colour, for instance, for the blondes and the brunettes.

The school taught by Agnes in David Copperfield is mentioned to show that if a teacher works with a true spirit (Agnes was a splendid character for women to study with great care), teaching is a pleasant instead of an unhappy profession.

David said: "It is laborious, is it not?" "The labour is so pleasant," she returned, "that it is scarcely grateful in me to call it by that name."

The school attended by Uriah Heep and his father before him was described as an attack on the practice of instilling into the minds of poor children the consciousness of subserviency. David says: "I fully comprehended now for the first time (after hearing Uriah describe his training at school) what a base, unrelenting, and revengeful spirit must have been engendered by this early, and this long, suppression."

The first school attended by Esther in Bleak House is apparently introduced to point out four evils in the social training of little children. The other children were all older than Esther; her godmother refused to allow her to accept invitations to go to the homes of the other girls; she was never allowed out to play; and while holidays were given on the birthdays of other girls, none were ever given on hers. The cruelty of two of these evils was made still more bitter by the revelation of the fact that she was not treated like other girls because of some wrong her mother was supposed to have done.

Miss Donny's school at Greenleaf was a charming place, conducted in a "precise, exact, and orderly way." Esther was taught well, and trained well. She was to be a governess, and so she taught as she learned. Her barren childhood made her sympathize with the girls whom she taught, especially the new girls, and she naturally won their love, and was therefore happy. Esther possessed every essential characteristic of a good teacher and a true woman. Miss Donny's school is one of the schools in which Dickens was approving, not condemning.

Mr. Cripple's academy is merely mentioned in Little Dorrit to complain about the habit of scribbling over buildings and on desks and walls in which boys used to indulge, and of which many evidences may yet be found on the fences and walls of the present day.

"The pupils of Mr. Cripple's appeared to have been making a copy book of the street door, it was so extensively scribbled over in pencil."

Pip's early education, in Great Expectations, was received in Mr. Wopsle's great-aunt's school.

> Mr. Wopsle's great-aunt kept an evening school in the village; that is to say, she was a ridiculous old woman of limited means and unlimited infirmity, who used to go to sleep from six to seven every evening, in the society of youth, who paid twopence per week each, for the improving opportunity of seeing her do it. She rented a small cottage, and Mr. Wopsle had the room upstairs, where we students used to overhear him reading aloud in a most dignified and terrific manner, and occasionally bumping on the ceiling. There was a fiction that Mr. Wopsle "examined" the scholars once a quarter. What he did on those occasions was to turn up his cuffs, stick up his hair, and give us Mark Antony's oration over the body of Cæsar.
>
> Much of my unassisted self, and more by the help of Biddy than of Mr. Wopsle's great-aunt, I struggled through the alphabet as if it had been a bramble bush; getting considerably worried and scratched by every letter. After that I fell among those thieves, the nine figures, who seemed every evening to do something new to disguise themselves and baffle recognition. But at last I began, in a purblind groping way, to read, write, and cipher on the very smallest scale.
>
> Biddy was Mr. Wopsle's great-aunt's granddaughter; I confessed myself quite unequal to the working out of the problem, what relation she was to Mr. Wopsle.
>
> The educational scheme or course established by Mr. Wopsle's great-aunt may be resolved into the following synopsis: The pupils ate apples and put straws down one another's backs, until Mr. Wopsle's great-aunt collected her energies, and made an indiscriminate totter at them with a birch rod. After receiving the charge with every mark of derision, the pupils formed in line and buzzingly passed a ragged book from hand to hand. The book had an alphabet in it, some figures and tables, and a little spelling—that is to say, it had had once. As soon as this volume began to circulate, Mr. Wopsle's great-aunt fell into a state of coma,

> arising either from sleep or a rheumatic paroxysm. The pupils then entered among themselves upon a competitive examination on the subject of boots, with the view of ascertaining who could tread the hardest upon whose toes. This mental exercise lasted until Biddy made a rush at them and distributed three defaced Bibles (shaped as if they had been unskilfully cut off the chumped end of something), more illegibly printed at the best than any curiosities of literature I have since met with, speckled all over with iron mould, and having various specimens of the insect world smashed between their leaves. This part of the course was usually lightened by several single combats between Biddy and refractory students. When the fights were over, Biddy gave out the number of a page, and then we all read aloud what we could—or what we couldn't—in a frightful chorus; Biddy leading with a high shrill monotonous voice, and none of us having the least notion of, or reverence for, what we were reading about. When this horrible din had lasted a certain time, it mechanically awoke Mr. Wopsle's great-aunt, who staggered at a boy fortuitously, and pulled his ears. This was understood to terminate the course for the evening, and we emerged into the air with shrieks of intellectual victory.

The reasons for describing this school were to renew the attack on bad private schools, conducted without any state control and no supervision or inspection by competent officers, to show the need of better appliances and text-books, and to teach the utter folly of allowing pupils to try to read any book, especially the Bible, without understanding what they were reading. Incidentally Dickens taught that to use the Bible as it was used in Mr. Wopsle's great-aunt's school develops a lack of reverence for it. The evil of corporal punishment of the indiscriminate and irregular kind comes in for a share of condemnation in this wretched school.

Dickens returned to the attack on bad private schools in Our Mutual Friend. He had made a thorough study of the evening schools conducted in London—conducted many of them by organizations with good intentions.

There are a good many Sunday schools yet which in some respects are open to the criticisms made of Charley Hexam's first school.

> The school at which young Charley Hexam had first learned from a book—the streets being, for pupils of his degree, the great preparatory establishment, in which very much that is never unlearned is learned without and before book—was a miserable loft in an unsavoury yard. Its atmosphere was oppressive and disagreeable; it was crowded, noisy, and confusing; half the pupils dropped asleep, or fell into a state of stupefaction; the other half kept them in either condition by maintaining a monotonous droning noise, as if they were performing, out of time and tune, on a ruder sort of bagpipe. The teachers, animated solely by good intentions, had no idea of execution, and a lamentable jumble was the upshot of their kind endeavours.

It was a school for all ages and for both sexes. The latter were kept apart, and the former were partitioned off into square assortments. But all the place was pervaded by a grimly ludicrous pretence that every pupil was childish and innocent. This pretence, much favoured by the lady visitors, led to the ghastliest absurdities. Young women, old in the vices of the commonest and worst life, were expected to profess themselves enthralled by the good child's book, the Adventures of Little Margery, who resided in the village cottage by the mill; severely reproved and morally squashed the miller, when she was five and he was fifty; divided her porridge with singing birds; denied herself a new nankeen bonnet, on the ground that the turnips did not wear nankeen bonnets, neither did the sheep, who ate them; who plaited straw and delivered the dreariest orations to all comers, at all sorts of unseasonable times. So unwieldy young dredgers and hulking mudlarks were referred to the experiences of Thomas Twopence, who, having resolved not to rob (under circumstances of uncommon atrocity) his particular friend and benefactor, of eighteenpence, presently came into supernatural possession of three and sixpence, and lived a shining light ever afterward. (Note, that the benefactor came to no good.) Several swaggering sinners had written their own biographies in the same strain; it always appearing from the lessons of those very boastful persons that you were to do good, not because it *was* good, but because you were to make a good thing of it. Contrariwise, the adult pupils were taught to read (if they could learn) out of the New Testament; and by dint of stumbling over the syllables and keeping their bewildered eyes on the particular syllables coming round to their turn, were as absolutely ignorant of the sublime history as if they had never seen or heard of it. An exceedingly and confoundingly perplexing jumble of a school, in fact, where black spirits and gray, red spirits and white, jumbled, jumbled, jumbled, jumbled, jumbled every night. And particularly every Sunday night. For then an inclined plane of unfortunate infants would be handed over to the prosiest and worst of all the teachers with good intentions, whom nobody older would endure. Who, taking his stand on the floor before them, as chief executioner, would be attended by a conventional volunteer boy as executioner's assistant. When and where it first became the conventional system that a weary or inattentive infant in a class must have its face smoothed downward with a hot hand, or when or where the conventional volunteer boy first beheld such system in operation, and became inflamed with a sacred zeal to administer it, matters not. It was the function of the chief executioner to hold forth, and it was the function of the acolyte to dart at sleeping infants, yawning infants, restless infants, whimpering infants, and smooth their wretched

> faces, sometimes with one hand, as if he were anointing them for a whisker; sometimes with both hands, applied after the fashion of blinkers. And so the jumble would be in action in this department for a mortal hour; the exponent drawling on to my dearerr childerrenerr, let us say for example, about the beautiful coming to the sepulchre; and repeating the word sepulchre (commonly used among infants) five hundred times and never once hinting what it meant; the conventional boy smoothing away right and left, as an infallible commentary; the whole hotbed of flushed and exhausted infants exchanging measles, rashes, whooping-cough, fever, and stomach disorders, as if they were assembled in High Market for the purpose.
>
> Even in this temple of good intentions, an exceptionally sharp boy exceptionally determined to learn, could learn something, and, having learned it, could impart it so much better than the teachers; as being more knowing than they, and not at the disadvantage in which they stood toward the shrewder pupils. In this way it had come about that Charley Hexam had risen in the jumble, taught in the jumble, and been received from the jumble into a better school.

Dickens slaughtered evils by wholesale in this brief description. The influence of the great preparatory establishment, the street, was brought to the notice of thinking people.

The need of ventilation was pointed out, and the evil of crowding a large number of pupils into poorly ventilated rooms was made very clear. "Half the pupils dropped asleep, or fell into a state of waking stupefaction."

The teachers were untrained. "They were animated solely by good intentions, and had no idea of execution." The consequence was a lamentable jumble.

The separation of the sexes was not approved.

The stupid blunder of treating all pupils alike, without regard to heredity, environment, or past experience, is aptly caricatured in giving the Adventures of Little Margery and the Experiences of Thomas Twopence to young women old in vice and to young male criminals in order to reform them.

Incidentally he disapproves of such literature for any children, and also of the autobiographies of "swaggering sinners."

The error pointed out in Pip's education of using the New Testament as a book from which pupils should be taught how to read is emphasized. "By dint of stumbling over the syllables and keeping their bewildered eyes on the particular syllables coming round to their turn, they were as absolutely ignorant of the sublime history as if they had never seen or heard of it."

He criticised severely the old custom of giving least attention to the choice of a teacher for the little ones. The old theory was: they can not learn much any way; anybody will do to teach them. "The inclined plane of unfortunate infants would be handed over to the prosiest and worst of all the teachers of good intentions, whom nobody older would endure."

The dreadful practice, still kept up in some heathen-producing Sunday schools, of having an "executioner's assistant to keep order," is severely condemned. "It was the function of the acolyte to dart at sleeping infants, restless infants, whimpering infants, and smooth, their wretched faces." The irritating influence of this operation on the suffering infants and the degrading effect on the executioner's assistant himself are clearly indicated.

But the greatest cruelty was in having the infants talked at in a droning voice for an hour by the chief executioner in a voice that would sometimes deaden, sometimes irritate their nervous systems, and in language they could not comprehend, about subjects entirely foreign to their experiences.

The danger of spreading contagious diseases in such badly ventilated schools was shown. Dickens was a leader in the department of sanitation both in homes and in schools.

The schools taught by Bradley Headstone and Miss Peecher were

> newly built, and there were so many like them all over the country, that one might have thought the whole were but one restless edifice with the locomotive gift of Aladdin's palace.
>
> All things in these schools—buildings, teachers, and pupils—were according to pattern, and engendered in the light of the latest Gospel according to Monotony.

These brief descriptions contained volumes of protest against the dead uniformity of school architecture, and against the sacrifice of individuality in schools. There are no other buildings in which there should be more care taken to have truly artistic architecture than in schools, because the children are influenced so much by their environment. Correct taste may be formed more easily and more definitely by making the places in which children spend so much of their lives truly artistic than by studying the best authorities. The child's spirits should be toned by the colouring of the walls of the schoolroom, and by the pictures, statues, and other artistic articles around them.

The phrase "Gospel according to Monotony" is one of the most effective phrases ever used to describe the destruction of individuality.

The Peecher-Headstone schools were described as one of several protests against separating little girls from little boys in schools.

Phœbe, the happy young woman, who had never been able to sit up since she had been dropped by her mother when she was in a fit, is one of the sweetest of the characters of Dickens. She lay on a couch as high as the window and enjoyed the view as she made lace. She taught a little school part of the day, and when Barbox Brothers was at Mugby Junction he heard the children singing in the school, and watched them trooping home happily till he became so interested in what was going on in the little cottage that he went in to investigate. He found a small but very clean room, with no one there but Phœbe lying on her couch. He asked her if she was learned in the new system of teaching, meaning the kindergarten system, because he had heard her children singing as he passed.

> "No," she said, "I am very fond of children, but I know nothing of teaching, beyond the interest I have in it, and the pleasure it gives me, when they learn. I have only read and been told about the new system. It seemed so pretty and pleasant, and to treat them so like the merry robins they are, that I took up with it in my little way. My school is a pleasure to me. I began it, when I was but a child, because it brought me and other children into company, don't you see? I carry it on still, because it keeps children about me. I do it as love, not as work."

What a beautiful school! What an ideal spirit for every true teacher! What a wise man Dickens was to reveal so much sweetness and trueness in the life of such a woman as Phœbe! When Phœbe had overcome her restrictions so triumphantly, surely every one who dares to teach should try to rise above personal infirmities, and treat children like the "merry robins that they are."

The Holiday Romance, in which three young children write romances for the edification of their adult friends and relatives, to show how adult treatment impresses young children, is usually regarded as merely an exquisite piece of humour. In writing to Mr. Fields about the story Dickens said: "It made me laugh to that extent, that my people here thought I was out of my wits, until I gave it to them to read, when they did likewise."

There is more philosophy than fun in these stories, however, and when carefully studied they should aid in the "education of the grown-up people"—not merely the "grown-ups" for whom they were intended, but all "grown-ups." This is especially true of the last story, written by Miss Nettie Ashford, aged "half-past-six."

The story is about Mrs. Lemon's school and Mrs. Orange's family.

"The grown-up people" were the children in Nettie's story, and the children were the managers of all things at home and at school.

Mrs. Orange went to Mrs. Lemon's and told her that "her children were getting positively too much for her." She had two parents, two intimate friends of theirs, one godfather, two godmothers, and an aunt. She wished to send them to school, because they were "getting too much for her." Many real mothers give the same reason.

> "Have you as many as eight vacancies?"
>
> "I have just eight, ma'am," said Mrs. Lemon.
>
> "Corporal punishment dispensed with?"
>
> "Why, we do occasionally shake," said Mrs. Lemon, "and we have slapped. But only in extreme cases."

Mrs. Orange was shown through the school, and had the bad "grown-ups" pointed out to her and their evil propensities explained to her in their hearing, as naturally as in a real school. She decided to send her family, and went home with her baby—which was a doll—saying, "These troublesome troubles are got rid of, please the pigs."

A small party for the grown-up children was given by Mrs. Alicumpaine, and the arrangements made for the adults, and the ways in which they were treated by their child masters, and the criticisms on the way the seniors behaved are all instructive to thoughtful parents. The real things that adult people say and do appear delightfully stupid or exquisitely silly when made to appear as said and done by children.

> When Mr. and Mrs. Orange were going home they passed the establishment of Mrs. Lemon, and necessarily thought of their eight adult pupils who were there.
>
> "I wonder, James, dear," said Mrs. Orange, looking up at the window, "whether the precious children are asleep!"
>
> "I don't care much whether they are or not, myself," said Mr. Orange.
>
> "James, dear!"
>
> "You dote upon them, you know," said Mr. Orange. "That's another thing."
>
> "I do," said Mrs. Orange rapturously. "Oh, I do!"
>
> "I don't," said Mr. Orange.
>
> "But, I was thinking, James, love," said Mrs. Orange, pressing his arm, "whether our dear, good, kind Mrs. Lemon would like them to stay the holidays with her."
>
> "If she was paid for it, I dare say she would," said Mr. Orange.
>
> "I adore them, James," said Mrs. Orange, "but *suppose* we pay her, then."
>
> This was what brought the country to such perfection, and made it such a delightful place to live in. The grown-up people (that would be in other countries) soon left off being allowed any holidays after Mr. and Mrs. Orange tried the experiment; and the children (that would be in other countries) kept them at school as long as ever they lived, and made them do whatever they were told.

This story was written about two years before the death of Dickens, so it represents his maturest thought. Its great fundamental motive was Froebel's motto, "Come, let us live with our children." It was a trenchant, though humorous criticism of the methods of treating children practised by adults, at home and at school. Mrs. Orange's adoration for children, while at the same time she was proposing to keep them at school during the holidays, is very suggestive to those mothers who in society talk so much about their "precious darlings," but who keep them in the nursery so that they have no share in the family life. The practice of calling children bad and describing their supposed evil propensities in the presence of others is also condemned in this story.

One of the very best of the stories of Dickens to show his perfect sympathy with boyhood is the story told by Jemmy Jackman Lirriper about "the boy who went to school in Rutlandshire."

It reveals the feelings of boys to the "Tartars" who teach school, as the boys, when they got control, put the Tartar into confinement and "forced him to eat the boys' dinners and drink half a cask of their beer every day."

It reveals, too, the psychological condition of a healthy boy just entering the adolescent period, if he has been fortunate enough to have had a life of love and freedom at home; with his heart filled with love for the schoolmaster's daughter Seraphina, and his mind filled with hopeful dreams of success, and triumph, and fortune, and happiness ever afterward, not excluding those who had nurtured him, but sharing all with them, and finding his greatest joy in their affectionate pride at his success. Blessed is the boy who has such glorious experiences and such hopeful dreams in his later boyhood and onward, and thrice blessed is he who finds in parenthood hearts so reverently sympathetic that it is natural for the young heart to overflow into them.

"But such dreams can never come true." They are true. Nothing is ever more true for the stage of evolution in which they naturally fill the life of the child. To stop them is a crime; to shut them up in the heart of the boy or girl makes them a source of great danger instead of an essential element in the ennoblement of character.

Let the boy dream on, and help him to dream by sympathetically sharing his visions with him. His own visions and the most wonderful visions of heroism and adventure dreamed by the best authors should fill his life during the most important stage of his growth, adolescence, when the elements of his manhood are rushing into his life and require an outlet in the ideal life as a preparation for the real life of later days.

Dickens recognises, too, in this story the great truth so little used by educators, that the child's imagination is not restricted by any conditions of impossibility or by any laws of Nature or of man. The ideal transcends the real, the desired is accomplished. Development is rapid under such conditions.

> "And was there no quarrelling," asked Mrs. Lirriper, "after the boy and his boy friend had gained high renown, and unlimited stores of gold, and had married Seraphina and her sister, and had come to live with Gran and Godfather forever, and the story was ended?"
>
> "No! Nobody ever quarrelled."
>
> "And did the money never melt away?"
>
> "No! Nobody could ever spend it all."

> "And did none of them ever grow older?"
>
> "No! Nobody ever grew older after that."
>
> "And did none of them ever die?"
>
> "O, no, no, no, Gran!" exclaimed our dear boy, laying his cheek upon her breast, and drawing her closer to him. "Nobody ever died."
>
> "Ah, Major, Major!" says Mrs. Lirriper, smiling benignly upon me, "this beats our stories. Let us end with the Boy's Story, Major, for the Boy's Story is the best that is ever told."

Miss Pupford's school in Tom Tiddler's Ground reveals the foolish conventional formalism of some teachers before their pupils; exposes the pretences of some teachers in private schools—"Miss Pupford's assistant with the Parisian accent, who never conversed with a Parisian and never was out of England"; and condemns the practice of sending mere children long distances from home to be trained and educated: "Kitty Kimmeens had to remain behind in Miss Pupford's school during the holidays, because her friends and relations were all in India, far away."

In Edwin Drood Dickens had begun a description of the school: "On the trim gate inclosing the courtyard of which is a resplendent brass plate flashing forth the legend: 'Seminary for Young Ladies. Miss Twinkleton.'"

The chief thing revealed by the brief description given of it is the formal conventionality of most teachers in such institutions, the unreality of manner and tone and character shown by most teachers in the schoolroom.

How much greater Miss Twinkleton's power would have been to help in developing human hearts and heads, if she could have been more truly human during the day! She did not deceive the young ladies either by her formalism. They merely said, "What a pretending old thing Miss Twinkleton is!"

When the rumour of the quarrel between Neville Landless and Edwin Drood reached the seminary, and began to cause dangerous excitement among the young ladies, Miss Twinkleton deemed it her duty to quiet their minds.

> It was reserved for Miss Twinkleton to tone down the public mind of the Nuns' House. That lady, therefore, entering in a stately manner what plebeians might have called the schoolroom, but what, in the patrician language of the head of the Nuns' House, was euphuistically, not to say roundaboutedly, denominated "the apartment allotted to study," and saying with a forensic air, "Ladies!" all rose. Mrs. Tisher at the same time grouped herself behind her chief, as representing Queen Elizabeth's first historical female friend at Tilbury Fort. Miss Twinkleton then proceeded to remark that Rumour, ladies, had been represented by the Bard of Avon—needless were it to mention the immortal Shakespeare, also called the Swan of his native river, not improbably with some reference to the ancient superstition that that bird of graceful

> plumage (Miss Jennings will please stand upright) sung sweetly on the approach of death, for which we have no ornithological authority—Rumour, ladies, had been represented by that bard—hem!—
>
> "Who drew
> The celebrated Jew,"
>
> as painted full of tongues. Rumour in Cloisterham (Miss Ferdinand will honour me with her attention) was no exception to the great limner's portrait of Rumour elsewhere. A slight *fracas* between two young gentlemen occurring last night within a hundred miles of these peaceful walls (Miss Ferdinand, being apparently incorrigible, will have the kindness to write out this evening, in the original language, the first four fables of our vivacious neighbour, Monsieur La Fontaine) had been very grossly exaggerated by Rumour's voice. In the first alarm and anxiety arising from our sympathy with a sweet young friend, not wholly to be dissociated from one of the gladiators in the bloodless arena in question (the impropriety of Miss Reynolds's appearing to stab herself in the hand with a pin is far too obvious, and too glaringly unladylike to be pointed out), we descended from our maiden elevation to discuss this uncongenial and this unfit theme. Responsible inquiries having assured us that it was but one of those "airy nothings" pointed at by the poet (whose name and date of birth Miss Giggles will supply within half an hour), we would now discard the subject, and concentrate our minds upon the grateful labours of the day.

The unnatural formalism of her manner and her language are properly held up to ridicule by Dickens.

He incidentally shows the great blunder of interrupting a lesson to censure a pupil, the weakness of having to demand attention, and the error of punishing by impositions to be memorized or written. What a terrible misuse it is of the literature that should always be attractive and inspiring to have it associated with punishment! He exposes the greater crime of making children commit to memory selections from the Bible as a punishment in Dombey and Son, and the association of the Bible with tasks in Our Mutual Friend.

The Schoolboy's Story deals with the problems of nutrition, coercion, robbing a boy of his holidays, the declaration of perpetual warfare between pupils and teachers in the olden days, and the surprise of the boys when they found that one of their teachers had a true and tender heart (what a commentary on teachers that boys should be surprised at their being true and good!), and how to treat children as Old Cheeseman did, when he inherited his fortune and married Jane, and took the disconsolate boys home to his own house, when they were condemned to spend their holidays at school.

In Our School the chief pedagogical lessons are: the man's remembrance of the pug dog in the entry at the first school he attended, and his utter forgetfulness of the mistress of the establishment; the folly of external polishing or memory polishing on which "the rust has long since accumulated"; the gross wrong of allowing an ignorant and brutal man to be a teacher—"The only branches of education with which the master showed the least acquaintance were ruling and corporally punishing"; the deadening injustice of showing partiality, whether on account of a boy's parentage or for any other reason; sympathy for "holiday stoppers"; the interest all children should take in keeping and training pet animals; the advantages to boys of having to construct "houses and instruments of performance" for these pets—"some of those who made houses and invented appliances for their performing mice in school have since made railroads, engines, and telegraphs, the chairman has erected mills and bridges in Australia"; the fact that "we all liked Maxby the tutor, for he had a good knowledge of boys"; and that teachers should be very particular about their personal neatness, because children note so accurately every detail of dress and manner. This is shown by the reminiscences about Maxby, the Latin master, and the dancing master. The ungenerous rivalry often existing between schools, and schools of thought, too, was pointed out: "There was another school not far off, and of course our school could have nothing to say to that school. It is mostly the way with schools, whether of boys or men."

"The world had little reason to be proud of Our School, and has done much better since in that way, and will do far better yet." This closing sentence of the sketch is very suggestive.

Dickens described one school that he visited in America in his American Notes, evidently in order to show the need of more care than was then taken in the choice of matter for the pupils to read.

> I was only present in one of these establishments during the hours of instruction. In the boys' department, which was full of little urchins (varying in their ages, I should say, from six years old to ten or twelve), the master offered to institute an extemporary examination of the pupils in algebra, a proposal which, as I was by no means confident of my ability to detect mistakes in that science, I declined with some alarm. In the girls' school reading was proposed, and as I felt tolerably equal to that art I expressed my willingness to hear a class. Books were distributed accordingly, and some half dozen girls relieved each other in reading paragraphs from English history. But it seemed to be a dry compilation, infinitely above their powers; and when they had blundered through three or four dreary passages concerning the treaty of Amiens, and other thrilling topics of the same nature (obviously without comprehending ten words), I expressed myself quite satisfied. It is very possible that they only mounted to this exalted stave in the ladder of learning for the astonishment of a visitor, and that at other times they keep upon its lower rounds; but I should have been much better pleased and satisfied if I had heard them exercised in simpler lessons, which they understood.

"The world has done better since, and will do far better yet" in the choice of reading matter for children.

The school recalled by memory in connection with the other ghosts of his childhood in The Haunted House was described briefly, but the description is full of suggestiveness.

> Then I was sent to a great cold, bare school of big boys; where everything to eat and wear was thick and clumpy, without being enough; where everybody, large and small, was cruel; where the boys knew all about the sale before I got there [his father's furniture had been sold for debt], and asked me what I had fetched, and who had bought me, and hooted at me, "Going, going, gone."

The inartistic bareness of the school, the tasteless clothing, the unattractive, unsatisfying food, the pervading atmosphere of cruelty, and the heartlessness of the boys in tearing open the wounds of the sensitive new boy—are all condemned.

CHAPTER XVI.

MISCELLANEOUS EDUCATIONAL PRINCIPLES.

The need of apperception and correlation are shown in the result of Paul Dombey's first lessons under Miss Cornelia Blimber, and in the same book in the description of the learning Briggs carried away with him. It was like an ill-arranged luggage, so tightly packed that he couldn't get at anything he wanted. The absolute necessity for fixing apperceptive centres of emotion and thought in the lives of children by experience is shown in the case of Neville Landless in Edwin Drood. His early life had been so barren that, as he told his tutor, "It has caused me to be utterly wanting in I don't know what emotions, or remembrances, or good instincts—I have not even a name for the thing, you see—that you have had to work upon in other young men to whom you have been accustomed."

Dickens emphasized the fact that the lack of apperceptive centres of an improper kind is a great advantage.

> That heart where self has found no place and raised no throne is slow to recognise its ugly presence when it looks upon it. As one possessed of an evil spirit was held in old time to be alone conscious of the lurking demon in the breasts of other men, so kindred vices know each other in their hiding places every day, when virtue is incredulous and blind.

There is no more suggestive work on the contents of children's minds than Bleak House. When Poor Jo was summoned to give evidence at the inquest he was questioned in regard to himself and his theology. The results were startling.

> Name, Jo. Nothing else that he knows on. Don't know that everybody has two names. Never heerd of sich a think. Don't know that Jo is short for a longer name. Thinks it long enough for *him*. *He* don't find no fault with it. Spell it? No. *He* can't spell it. No father, no mother, no friends. Never been to school. What's home? Knows a broom's a broom, and knows it's wicked to tell a lie. Don't recollect who told him about the broom, or about the lie, but knows both. Can't exactly say what'll be done to him after he's dead if he tells a lie to the gentlemen here, but believes it'll be something wery bad to punish him, and serve him right—and so he'll tell the truth.
>
> Jo sweeps his crossing all day long, unconscious of the link, if any link there be. He sums up his mental condition, when asked

a question, by replying that he "don't know nothink." He knows that it's hard to keep the mud off the crossing in dirty weather, and harder still to live by doing it. Nobody taught him, even that much; he found it out.

Jo comes out of Tom-all-Alone's, meeting the tardy morning, which is always late in getting down there, and munches his dirty bit of bread as he comes along. His way lying through many streets, and the houses not yet being open, he sits down to breakfast on the doorstep of the Society for the Propagation of the Gospel in Foreign Parts, and gives it a brush when he has finished, as an acknowledgment of the accommodation. He admires the size of the edifice, and wonders what it's all about. He has no idea, poor wretch, of the spiritual destitution of a coral reef in the Pacific, or what it costs to look up the precious souls among the cocoanuts and breadfruits.

He goes to his crossing, and begins to lay it out for the day. The town awakes; the great teetotum is set up for its daily spin and whirl; all that unaccountable reading and writing, which has been suspended for a few hours, recommences. Jo and the other lower animals get on in the unintelligible mess as they can. It is market day. The blinded oxen, overgoaded, overdriven, never guided, run into wrong places and are beaten out; and plunge, red-eyed and foaming, at stone walls; and often sorely hurt the innocent, and often sorely hurt themselves. Very like Jo and his order; very, very like!

A band of music comes and plays. Jo listens to it. So does a dog—a drover's dog, waiting for his master outside a butcher's shop, and evidently thinking about those sheep he has had upon his mind for some hours, and is happily rid of. He seems perplexed respecting three or four; can't remember where he left them; looks up and down the street, as half expecting to see them astray; suddenly pricks up his ears and remembers all about it. A thoroughly vagabond dog, accustomed to low company and public houses; a terrific dog to sheep; ready at a whistle to scamper over their backs, and tear out mouthfuls of their wool; but an educated, improved, developed dog, who has been taught his duties and knows how to discharge them. He and Jo listen to the music, probably with much the same amount of animal satisfaction; likewise, as to awakened association, aspiration, or regret, melancholy or joyful reference to things beyond the senses, they are probably upon a par. But, otherwise, how far above the human listener is the brute!

Turn that dog's descendants wild, like Jo, and in a very few years they will so degenerate that they will lose even their bark—but not their bite.

When Lady Dedlock met Jo, she asked him:

> "Are you the boy I've read of in the papers?"
>
> "I don't know," says Jo, staring moodily at the veil, "nothink about no papers. I don't know nothink about nothink at all."

When Guster, Mr. Snagsby's servant, got him some food, she said:

> "Are you hungry?"
>
> "Jist!" says Jo.
>
> "What's gone of your father and your mother, eh?"
>
> Jo stops in the middle of a bite, and looks petrified. For this orphan charge of the Christian saint whose shrine was at Tooting, has patted him on the shoulder; and it is the first time in his life that any decent hand had been so laid upon him.
>
> "I never know'd nothink about 'em," says Jo.
>
> "No more didn't I of mine," cries Guster.

When Allan Woodcourt took him to Mr. George's and had his wants attended to, he told Jo to be sure and tell him the truth always.

"Wishermaydie, if I don't," said Jo. "I never was in no other trouble at all, sir—'cept knowin' nothink and starvation."

When Allan saw that Jo was nearing the end, he said:

> "Jo! Did you ever know a prayer?"
>
> "Never know'd nothink, sir."
>
> "Not so much as one short prayer?"
>
> "No, sir. Nothink at all. Mr. Chadband he was a-prayin' wunst at Mr. Snagsby's and I heerd him, but he sounded as if he wos a-speakin' to hisself, and not to me. He prayed a lot, but *I* couldn't make out nothink on it. Different times, there was other genlmen come down Tom-all-Alone's a-prayin', but they all mostly sed as the t'other wuns prayed wrong, and all mostly sounded to be a-talkin' to theirselves, or a-passin' blame on the t'others, and not a-talkin' to us. *We* never know'd nothink. *I* never know'd what it wos all about."

No? Mr. Chadband, your long sermon about "the Terewth" found no place in Jo in which to rest; nothing to which it could attach itself. No wonder he went asleep. He had no apperceptive centres in his experience or his training to which your kind of religious teaching was related.

Poor Jo! He was the first great illustration, and he is still the best, of the great pedagogical truth, that we see, and hear, and understand in all that is around us only what corresponds to what we are within; that our power to see, and hear, and understand increases as our inner life is cultured and developed; and that a life as barren as that of the great class of whom Jo was made the type makes it impossible to comprehend any teaching of an abstract kind. This revelation is of course most valuable to primary teachers in cities.

Dickens showed his wonderful insight into the most profound problems of psychology in his great character sketch of poor Jo. He agreed with Herbart regarding the philosophy of apperception so far as it related to intellectual culture, but he painted Jo entirely out of harmony with Herbart's psychology in relation to soul development. After describing Mr. Chadband's sermon on "Terewth" Dickens says:

> All this time Jo has been standing on the spot where he woke up, ever picking his cap, and putting bits of fur in his mouth. He spits them out with a remorseful air, for he feels that it is in his nature to be an unimprovable reprobate, and it's no good *his* trying to keep awake, for *he* won't never know nothink. Though it may be, Jo, that there is a history so interesting and affecting even to minds as near the brutes as thine, recording deeds done on this earth for common men, that if the Chadbands, removing their own persons from the light, would but show it thee in simple reverence, would but leave it unimproved, would but regard it as being eloquent enough without their modest aid—it might hold thee awake, and thou might learn from it yet!

Jo never heard of any such book. Its compilers, and the Reverend Chadband, are all one to him—except that he knows the Reverend Chadband, and would rather run away from him for an hour than hear him talk for five minutes.

When Jo was eating at Mr. Snagsby's he stopped in the middle of his bite and looked petrified, because Guster patted him on the shoulder. "It was the first time in his life that any decent hand had been so laid upon him."

In The Haunted Man the six-year-old child was described as "a baby savage, a young monster, a child who had never been a child, a creature who might live to take the outward form of man, but who, within, would live and perish a mere beast."

Hugh, the splendid young animal who was John Willet's stable boy in Barnaby Rudge, was as deficient of most intellectual and spiritual apperceptive centres as poor Jo. When Mr. Chester asked him his name he replied:

> "I'd tell it if I could. I can't. I have always been called Hugh; nothing more. I never knew nor saw, nor thought about a father; and I was a boy of six—that's not very old—when they hung my mother up at Tyburn for a couple of thousand of men to stare at. They might have let her live. She was poor enough."

Little George Silverman's mind was almost a blank when his mother and father died. He had been brought up in a cellar at Preston. He hardly knew what sunlight was. His mother's laugh in her fever scared him, because it was the first laugh he had ever heard. When discovered alone with the bodies of his father and mother in the cellar, one of the horrified bystanders said to him:

"Do you know your father and mother are both dead of fever?" and he replied:

"I don't know what it is to be dead. I am hungry and thirsty."

After he had been supplied with food and drink he told Mr. Hawkyard that "he didn't feel cold, or hungry, or thirsty," and in relating the story in manhood he said:

> That was the whole round of human feelings, as far as I knew, except the pain of being beaten. To that time I had never had the faintest impression of duty. I had no knowledge whatever that there was anything lovely in this life. When I had occasionally slunk up the cellar steps into the street, and glared in at shop windows, I had done so with no higher feelings than we may suppose to animate a mangy young dog or wolf cub. It is equally the fact that I had never been alone, in the sense of holding unselfish converse with myself. I had been solitary often enough, but nothing better.

Redlaw, in The Haunted Man, said to the poor boy who came to his room:

> "What is your name?"
>
> "Got none."
>
> "Where do you live?"
>
> "Live! What's that?"

Such pictures were not drawn to entertain, or to add artistic effect to his stories. They were written to teach the world of wealth and culture that all around it were thousands of human souls with as little opportunity for development as young animals have; with defined apperceptive centres of cold, hunger, thirst, and pain only.

Dickens makes a strong contrast between the condition of the mental and spiritual apperceptive centres in the city boy as compared with the country boy, in a conversation between Phil Squod and Mr. George.

> "And so, Phil," says George of the Shooting Gallery, after several turns in silence, "you were dreaming of the country last night?"
>
> Phil, by the bye, said as much, in a tone of surprise, as he scrambled out of bed.
>
> "Yes, guv'ner."
>
> "What was it like?"
>
> "I hardly know what it was like, guv'ner," said Phil, considering.
>
> "How did you know it was the country?"
>
> "On account of the grass, I think. And the swans upon it," says Phil, after further consideration.

"What were the swans doing on the grass?"

"They was a-eating of it, I expect," says Phil.

"The country," says Mr. George, plying his knife and fork; "why, I suppose you never clapped your eyes on the country, Phil?"

"I see the marshes once," said Phil, contentedly eating his breakfast.

"What marshes?"

"*The* marshes, commander," returns Phil.

"Where are they?"

"I don't know where they are," says Phil; "but I see 'em, guv'ner. They was flat. And miste."

Governor and commander are interchangeable terms with Phil, expressive of the same respect and deference, and applicable to nobody but Mr. George.

"I was born in the country, Phil."

"Was you, indeed, commander?"

"Yes. And bred there."

Phil elevates his one eyebrow, and after respectfully staring at his master to express interest, swallows a great gulp of coffee, still staring at him.

"There's not a bird's note that I don't know," says Mr. George. "Not many an English leaf or berry that I couldn't name. Not many a tree that I couldn't climb yet, if I was put to it. I was a real country boy once. My good mother lived in the country. Do you want to see the country, Phil?"

"N-no, I don't know as I do, particular."

"The town's enough for you, eh?"

"Why, you see, commander," says Phil, "I ain't acquainted with anythink else, and I doubt if I ain't a-getting too old to take to novelties."

"How old are you, Phil?"

Phil's answer is intended to indicate the lack of even mathematical power in those who, like Phil, never had any training of the imagination, nor any other training to define their apperceptive centres of number beyond ten.

"I'm something with a eight in it. It can't be eighty. Nor yet eighteen. It's betwixt 'em somewheres. I was just eight, agreeable to the parish calculation, when I went with the tinker. That was April Fool Day. I was able to count up to ten; and when April Fool

> Day came round again I says to myself, 'Now, old chap, you're one and a eight in it.' April Fool Day after that I says, 'Now, old chap, you're two and a eight in it.' In course of time I come to ten and a eight in it; two tens and a eight in it. When it got so high it got the upper hand of me; but this is how I always know there's a eight in it."

The folly of trying to make a man moral by precept alone; the fact that character is developed by what we do, by true living, by what goes out in action, not by what comes in in maxims or theories, is shown in Martin Chuzzlewit.

> It has been remarked that Mr. Pecksniff was a moral man. So he was. Perhaps there never was a more moral man than Mr. Pecksniff, especially in his conversation and correspondence. It was once said of him by a homely admirer that he had a Fortunatus's purse of gold sentiments in his inside. In this particular he was like the girl in the fairy tale, except that if they were not actual diamonds which fell from his lips, they were the very brightest paste and shone prodigiously. He was a most exemplary man; fuller of virtuous precept than a copy book. Some people likened him to a direction post, which is always telling the way to a place, and never goes there.
>
> The best of architects and land surveyors kept a horse, in whom the enemies already mentioned more than once in these pages pretended to detect a fanciful resemblance to his master. Not in his outward person, for he was a raw-boned, haggard horse, always on a much shorter allowance of corn than Mr. Pecksniff; but in his moral character, wherein, said they, he was full of promise, but of no performance. He was always, in a manner, going to go, and never going.

One of the worst results that can follow a system of training is to make a man a hypocrite. It is nearly as bad to store a mind with good thoughts or fill a heart with good feelings without giving the character the tendency by practical experience to carry into effect so far as possible its good feelings and high purposes. Mr. Pecksniff was a moral monstrosity. We should create no more Pecksniffs. A different ideal is taught in the remark made by Martin Chuzzlewit to Mary, "Endeavouring to be anything that's good, and being it, is, with you, all one."

Executive training is emphasized in Nicholas Nickleby. Old Ralph Nickleby said of Nicholas: "The old story—always thinking, and never doing." The same thought is expressed very clearly in the pregnant sentence written about Sydney Carton in A Tale of Two Cities: "Sadly, sadly, the sun rose; it rose upon no sadder sight than the man of good abilities and good emotions, incapable of their directed exercise." The saddest sight in the world is a man or woman using power for evil. It is nearly as sad to see a man or woman with power, but without power to use it wisely.

In A Tale of Two Cities he caricatures admirably the class who cling to old customs and conventions, and decline even to discuss changes or improvements, in his description of Tellson's Bank.

> Tellson's Bank by Temple Bar was an old-fashioned place, even in the year one thousand seven hundred and eighty. It was very small, very dark, very ugly, very incommodious. It was an old-fashioned place, moreover, in the moral attribute that the partners in the house were proud of its smallness, proud of its darkness, proud of its ugliness, proud of its incommodiousness. They were even boastful of its eminence in those particulars, and were fired by an express conviction that, if it were less objectionable, it would be less respectable. This was no passive belief, but an active weapon which they flashed at more convenient places of business. Tellson's (they said) wanted no elbowroom, Tellson's wanted no light, Tellson's wanted no embellishment. Noakes and Co.'s might, or Snooks Brothers' might: but Tellson's, thank heaven!
>
> Any one of these partners would have disinherited his son on the question of rebuilding Tellson's. In this respect the house was much on a par with the country; which did very often disinherit its sons for suggesting improvements in laws and customs that had long been highly objectionable, but were only the more respectable.

Every child should get into his consciousness by experience, not by theory, the idea that he is expected to do his share in the improvement of his environment. The worst conception he can get is that "whatever is is right"; that things can not be improved. Every child should be encouraged to make suggestions for the improvement of his own environment and conditions in the schoolroom, in the yard, in the details of class management, or in anything else that he thinks he can improve.

The closing sentence of Our School should ring always in the minds of teachers, especially the last clause: "And will do far better yet."

Dickens had implicit faith in even weak humanity, and taught the hopeful truth, that every man and every child may be improved, if the men and women most directly associated with them are wise and loving. Harriet Carker said to Mr. Morfin:

> "Oh, sir, after what I have seen, let me conjure you, if you are in any place of power, and are ever wronged, never for any wrong inflict punishment that can not be recalled; while there is a God above us to work changes in the hearts he made."

The Goblin of the Bell said to Toby Veck in The Chimes:

> "Who turns his back upon the fallen and disfigured of his kind; abandons them as vile; and does not trace and track with pitying eyes the unfenced precipice by which they fell from good,

> grasping in their fall some tufts and shreds of that lost soil, and clinging to them still when bruised and dying in the gulf below, does wrong to Heaven and man, to time and to eternity."

The influence of Nature on the awakening mind of the child was outlined in A Child's Dream of a Star.

> These children used to wonder all day long. They wondered at the beauty of the flowers; they wondered at the height and blueness of the sky; they wondered at the depth of the bright water; they wondered at the goodness and the power of God who made the lovely world.

Nature is the great centre of interest to the child, and it may be the child's first true revealer of God, if adulthood does not impiously come between the child and God by trying to give him a word God for his intellect too soon to take the place of the true God of his imagination.

Dickens's best characters loved Nature. Esther, when recovering from her illness, said:

> I found every breath of air, and every scent, and every flower and leaf and blade of grass, and every passing cloud, and everything in Nature, more beautiful and wonderful to me than I had ever found it yet. This was my first gain from my illness. How little I had lost, when the wide world was so full of delight to me!

The deep, spiritual influences of Nature are revealed in the effects of life in the growing country on Oliver Twist.

> Who can describe the pleasure and delight, the peace of mind and soft tranquility, the sickly boy felt in the balmy air, and among the green hills and rich woods of an inland village! Who can tell how scenes of peace and quietude sink into the minds of pain-worn dwellers in close and noisy places, and carry their own freshness deep into their jaded hearts! Men who have lived in crowded, pent-up streets, through lives of toil, and who have never wished for change; men, to whom custom has indeed been second nature, and who have come almost to love each brick and stone that formed the narrow boundaries of their daily walks; even they, with the hand of death upon them, have been known to yearn at last for one short glimpse of Nature's face; and, carried from the scenes of their old pains and pleasures, have seemed to pass at once into a new state of being. Crawling forth from day to day, to some green sunny spot, they have had such memories wakened up within them by the sight of sky, and hill, and plain, and glistening water, that a foretaste of heaven itself has soothed their quick decline, and they have sunk into their tombs as peacefully as the sun, whose setting they watched from their lonely chamber window but a few hours before, faded from their dim and feeble sight! The memories which peaceful country scenes

> call up are not of this world, nor of its thoughts and hopes. Their gentle influence may teach us how to weave fresh garlands for the graves of those we love—may purify our thoughts, and bear down before it old enmity and hatred; but beneath all this there lingers, in the least reflective mind, a vague and half-formed consciousness of having held such feelings long before, in some remote and distant time, which calls up solemn thoughts of distant times to come, and bends down pride and worldliness beneath it.
>
> It was a lovely spot to which they repaired. Oliver, whose days had been spent among squalid crowds, and in the midst of noise and brawling, seemed to enter on a new existence there.

In the story of The Five Sisters of York Alice said to her sisters:

> "Nature's own blessings are the proper goods of life, and we may share them sinlessly together. To die is our heavy portion, but, oh, let us die with life about us; when our cold hearts cease to beat, let warm hearts be beating near; let our last look be upon the bounds which God has set to his own bright skies, and not on stone walls and bars of iron! Dear sisters, let us live and die, if you list, in this green garden's compass."

Dickens had very advanced opinions in regard to the importance of physical training, especially of play, as an agent not only in physical culture, but in the development of the mind and character. Doctor Blimber's school is condemned because the boys were not allowed to play, and Doctor Strong's school is highly commended because the boys "had noble games out of doors" there.

What splendid runners and jumpers and divers and swimmers those grand boys were whom Mr. Marton had the good fortune to teach in his second school in The Old Curiosity Shop!

Mrs. Crupp recommended David Copperfield to take up some game as an antidote for his despondency during his early love experience.

"If you was to take to something, sir," said Mrs. Crupp, "if you was to take to skittles, now, which is healthy, you might find it divert your mind and do you good."

Mrs. Chick told Mr. Dombey that Paul was delicate. "Our darling is not altogether as stout as we could wish. The fact is that his mind is too much for him. His soul is a great deal too large for his frame." Yet his father paid no attention to the boy's food, and sent him, when but a little sickly child, to Doctor Blimber's to learn everything—not to play. "They had nothing so vulgar as play at Doctor Blimber's."

One of the most vicious conventions is that which makes vigorous play vulgar and unladylike for girls.

He called attention in American notes to the advantages possessed by the students of Upper Canada College, Toronto, inasmuch as "the town is well adapted for wholesome exercise at all seasons." In the same book he gives his opinion that

American girls "must go more wisely clad, and take more healthful exercise."

He praised the free life of the gipsy children in Nicholas Nickleby.

In Martin Chuzzlewit, when Tom Pinch and Martin had to walk to Salisbury instead of riding in Mr. Pecksniff's gig, Dickens says it was better for them that they were compelled to walk. What a breezy enthusiasm he throws into his advocacy of walking as an exercise:

> Better! A rare strong, hearty, healthy walk—four statute miles an hour—preferable to that rumbling, tumbling, jolting, shaking, scraping, creaking, villainous old gig? Why, the two things will not admit of comparison. It is an insult to the walk to set them side by side. Where is an instance of a gig having ever circulated a man's blood, unless when, putting him in danger of his neck, it awakened in his veins and in his ears, and all along his spine, a tingling heat much more peculiar than agreeable? When did a gig ever sharpen anybody's wits and energies, unless it was when the horse bolted, and, crashing madly down a steep hill with a stone wall at the bottom, his desperate circumstances suggested to the only gentleman left inside some novel and unheard-of mode of dropping out behind? Better than the gig!
>
> Better than the gig! When were travellers by wheels and hoofs seen with such red-hot cheeks as those? when were they so good-humouredly and merrily bloused? when did their laughter ring upon the air, as they turned them round, what time the stronger gusts came sweeping up; and, facing round again as they passed by, dashed on, in such a glow of ruddy health as nothing could keep pace with, but the high spirits it engendered? Better than the gig! Why here *is* a man in a gig coming the same way now. Look at him as he passes his whip into his left hand, chafes his numbed right fingers on his granite leg, and beats those marble toes of his upon the footboard. Ha, ha, ha! Who would exchange this rapid hurry of the blood for yonder stagnant misery, though its pace were twenty miles for one?
>
> Better than the gig! No man in a gig could have such interest in the milestones. No man in a gig could see, or feel, or think, like merry users of their legs.

Dickens taught comparatively little about the subjects of instruction or the methods of teaching them. He dealt cramming its most stunning blow in Doctor Blimber's school, and he criticised sharply the methods of teaching classics and literature in the same school. He advocated the objective method of teaching number in Jemmy Lirriper's training at home by Major Jackman.

He took more interest in reading and literature than in any other department of school study, so far as can be judged from his writings. He deplored the practice of allowing children to try to read before they could recognise the words readily, and understand their meaning in the training of Pip and Charley Hexam. At the great party at Mr. Merdle's,

> the Bishop consulted the great Physician on the relaxation of the throat with which young curates were too frequently afflicted, and on the means of lessening the great prevalence of that disorder in the church. Physician, as a general rule, was of opinion that the best way to avoid it was to know how to read before you made a profession of reading. Bishop said, dubiously, did he really think so? And Physician said, decidedly, yes, he did.

He criticised, too, the reading in the school visited in an American city, because "the girls blundered through three or four dreary passages, obviously without comprehending ten words," and said "he would have been much better pleased if they had been asked to read some simpler selections which they could understand."

Mr. Wegg, when reading for Mr. Boffin in Our Mutual Friend, "read on by rote, and attached as few ideas as possible to the text."

He discusses the advantages of reading suitable books in David Copperfield, giving to David his own real experience in early boyhood. After describing the cruel treatment of the Murdstones, he says:

> The natural result of this treatment, continued, I suppose, for some six months, was to make me sullen, dull, and dogged. I was not made the less so by my sense of being daily more and more shut out and alienated from my mother. I believe I should have been almost stupefied but for one circumstance.
>
> It was this. My father had left a small collection of books in a little room upstairs, to which I had access (for it joined my own) and which nobody else in our house ever troubled. From that blessed little room, Roderick Random, Peregrine Pickle, Humphrey Clinker, Tom Jones, The Vicar of Wakefield, Don Quixote, Gil Blas, and Robinson Crusoe, came out, a glorious host to keep me company. They kept alive my fancy, and my hope of something beyond that place and time—they, and the Arabian Nights, and the tales of the Genii.

His faith in the influence of reading increased as he grew older. In Our Mutual Friend he says: "No one who can read ever looks at a book, even unopened on a shelf, like one who can not read."

Dickens taught a useful lesson in Martin Chuzzlewit regarding the way teachers used to be treated by society. Even yet there is need of a higher recognition of the teaching profession in its true dignity by a civilization that reverences wealth more than intellectual and spiritual character.

Tom Pinch's sister was engaged in the family of a wealthy brass founder. She was treated contemptuously by him and his wife, yet they complained to Tom that his sister was unable to command the respect of her pupil. Tom was naturally indignant, and he spoke his mind very clearly to the brass founder.

"Sir!" cried Tom, after regarding him in silence for some time. "If you do not understand what I mean I will tell you. My meaning is that no man can expect his children to respect what he degrades."

"When you tell me," resumed Tom, who was not the less indignant for keeping himself quiet, "that my sister has no innate power of commanding the respect of your children, I must tell you it is not so; and that she has. She is as well bred, as well taught, as well qualified by Nature to command respect as any hirer of a governess you know. But when you place her at a disadvantage in reference to every servant in your house, how can you suppose, if you have the gift of common sense, that she is not in a tenfold worse position in reference to your daughters?"

"Pretty well! Upon my word," exclaimed the gentleman, "that is pretty well!"

"It is very ill, sir," said Tom. "It is very bad and mean and wrong and cruel. Respect! I believe young people are quick enough to observe and imitate; and why or how should they respect whom no one else respects, and everybody slights? And very partial they must grow—oh, very partial!—to their studies, when they see to what a pass proficiency in those same tasks has brought their governess! Respect! Put anything the most deserving of respect before your daughters in the light in which you place her, and you will bring it down as low, no matter what it is!"

"You speak with extreme impertinence, young man," observed the gentleman.

"I speak without passion, but with extreme indignation and contempt for such a course of treatment, and for all who practise it," said Tom. "Why, how can you, as an honest gentleman, profess displeasure or surprise at your daughter telling my sister she is something beggarly and humble when you are forever telling her the same thing yourself in fifty plain, outspeaking ways, though not in words; and when your very porter and footman make the same delicate announcement to all comers?"

Dickens described a great variety of weak, and mean, and selfish, and degraded people in order to expose weakness, and meanness, and selfishness, and baseness, so that humanity might learn to overcome them, but he reserved his supreme contempt for those who oppose the general education of "the masses," because it fills their mind with ideas above their station, or disqualifies them for the work they were intended to do. This being interpreted, means in plain language that certain human beings who, because they possess wealth, or belong to what they arrogantly call the "upper classes," claim the right to dominate those who have not a sufficient amount of money to be independent of them; to fix what they selfishly call "the sphere of the lower classes"; and to prescribe the limits beyond which the children of the poor must not be educated, lest they be lifted beyond tame subserviency to their natural lords and masters, and fail to abase themselves dutifully or to be sufficiently grateful to those above them for the pittance they grudgingly give them for labouring in the menial occupations assigned them.

Dickens despised all Barnacles, and Dedlocks, and Podsnaps, and Dombeys, and Merdles; he ridiculed all who violate the sacred bond of human brotherhood; but the vials of his bitterest wrath were poured upon those who because a child was born in the home of poor parents would therefore restrict its education and dwarf its soul.

Mr. Dombey, after the christening of Paul, called Mrs. Toodle before his guests, and in a very condescending but rigidly majestic manner told her he had graciously decided to send her son to the school of the Charitable Grinders. He prefaced his announcement by a brief statement of his views regarding education:

> "I am far from being friendly," pursued Mr. Dombey, "to what is called by persons of levelling sentiments, general education. But it is necessary that the inferior classes should continue to be taught to know their position, and to conduct themselves properly. So far I approve of schools."
>
> In Mr. Dombey's eyes, as in some others that occasionally see the light, they only achieved that mighty piece of knowledge, the understanding of their own position, who showed a fitting reverence for his. It was not so much their merit that they knew themselves, as that they knew him, and bowed low before him.

There are thousands of Dombeys still. Two Canadian judges recently said in speaking of education precisely what Mr. Dombey and his class said in the time of Dickens. One objected to educating the common people because it unfitted them for positions as house servants, and made them so outrageously independent that they would not bow (bend their bodies properly, bow their heads, and look reverently at the floor) when in the presence of their mistresses. The other said that the very derivation of the word "education" meant to lead out, and it was therefore clear that "education should be used to develop a few, 'lead them out,' beyond the masses in order that they might be qualified for leadership." The necessary development to be imposed upon all but the favoured few in his system of government is willingness to follow leaders, and ignorance is the only condition that can make this possible. The glory of education is the awakening of the consciousness of freedom in the soul of the race and the revelation of the perfect law of liberty—individual right, social duty. The shackles, physical, intellectual, and spiritual, have fallen from humanity, as education has done its true work of emancipating the individual soul and revealing its own value and its responsibility for its brother souls.

The most brutal of all the characters described by Dickens is Bill Sikes. The most degraded and despicable of his characters is Dennis the hangman in Barnaby Rudge. Dickens makes Bill Sikes and Dennis use the very same arguments, from their standpoint, that the so-called upper classes have used and still do use against the education of the masses.

Bill Sikes, referring to the need of small boys in the trade of burglary, said:

> "I want a boy, and he mustn't be a big 'un. Lord!" said Mr. Sikes, reflectively, "if I'd only got that young boy of Ned, the chimbley sweeper's! He kept him small on purpose, and let him out by the job. But the father gets lagged; and then the Juvenile Delinquent Society comes and takes the boy away from a trade where he was arning money, teaches him to read and write, and in time makes a 'prentice of him. And so they go on," said Mr. Sikes, his wrath rising with the recollection of his wrongs, "so they go on; and, if they'd got money enough (which it's a Providence they haven't), we shouldn't have half a dozen boys left in the whole trade in a year or two."

And Fagin agreed with Bill Sikes.

When Hugh was formally admitted as a member of Lord Gordon's mob Dennis the hangman was much delighted at the addition of such a strong young man to the ranks, and Dickens adds:

> If anything could have exceeded Mr. Dennis's joy on the happy conclusion of this ceremony it would have been the rapture with which he received the announcement that the new member could neither read nor write: those two arts being (as Mr. Dennis swore) the greatest possible curse a civilized community could know, and militating more against the professional emoluments and usefulness of the great constitutional office he had the honour to hold than any adverse circumstances that could present themselves to his imagination.

Bill Sikes objected to education because it spoiled the boys for the trade for which he required them; Dennis the hangman objected to education because "it reduced the professional emoluments of his great constitutional office," or, in other words, reduced the number who had to be hanged; and their reasons are just as respectable as the reason given by any man in any position who objects to free education because it unfits boys for certain trades, or girls for "service," or because "it fills their minds with ideas above their station," or because they have to pay their just share of its cost, or for any other narrow and selfish reason. Selfishness is selfishness, and it is as utterly loathsome in a bishop as in Bill Sikes, in a judge as in Dennis the hangman.

Dickens never did any more artistic work than when he painted the aristocratic objectors to popular education in their natural hideousness with Bill Sikes and Dennis the hangman for a harmonious background.

CHAPTER XVII.

THE TRAINING OF POOR, NEGLECTED, AND DEFECTIVE CHILDREN.

It is a singular fact that humanity in its highest development so long neglected the poor, and the weak, and the defective. They were practically left out of consideration by educators and philanthropists. The fact that they more than any others needed education and care was not seen clearly enough to lead to definite plans for the amelioration of their misfortunes until the nineteenth century. Dickens must always have the honour of being the great English apostle of the poor—especially of neglected childhood.

He wrote in the Uncommercial Traveller:

> I can find—*must* find, whether I will or no—in the open streets, shameful instances of neglect of children, intolerable toleration of the engenderment of paupers, idlers, thieves, races of wretched and destructive cripples both in body and mind; a misery to themselves, a misery to the community, a disgrace to civilization, and an outrage on Christianity. I know it to be a fact as easy of demonstration as any sum in any of the elementary rules of arithmetic, that if the State would begin its work and duty at the beginning, and would with the strong hand take those children out of the streets while they are yet children, and wisely train them, it would make them a part of England's glory, not its shame—of England's strength, not its weakness—would raise good soldiers and sailors, and good citizens, and many great men out of the seeds of its criminal population; it would clear London streets of the most terrible objects they smite the sight with—myriads of little children who awfully reverse our Saviour's words, and are not of the Kingdom of Heaven, but of the Kingdom of Hell.

He sympathized with childhood on account of every form of coercion and abuse practised upon it by tyrannical, selfish, or ignorant adulthood, under the most favourable conditions; but his great heart was especially tender toward the little ones who, in addition to coercion and abuse, and bad training by the selfish, the ignorant, and the careless, were compelled to endure the terrible sufferings and deprivations of poverty. He was conscious not only of the material and physical evils to which the children of the very poor were exposed, but of the mental and spiritual barrenness of their lives, and one of his most manifest educational purposes was to improve social conditions, to arouse the spirit of truly sympathetic brotherhood (not merely considerate altruism, but genuine brotherhood) to place the poorest children in conditions that would develop by experience the apperceptive centres of intellectual and spiritual growth, and to direct special attention to the urgent need of education for the blind, the deaf, and the mentally defective.

No other American touched his heart and won his reverence quite so thoroughly as Dr. Howe, of Boston, who will undoubtedly be recognised as one of the greatest men yet produced by American civilization when men are tested by their purposes, and by their unselfish work for humanity in hitherto untrodden paths. After describing Dr. Howe's work for the blind, he reverently says: "There are not many persons, I hope and believe, who, after reading these passages, can ever hear that name with indifference."

Dickens charged on humanity, on society, the crime of making criminals. He said with great force and truth in the preface to Martin Chuzzlewit:

> Nothing is more common in real life than a want of profitable reflection on the causes of many vices and crimes that awaken general horror. What is substantially true of families in this respect, is true of a whole commonwealth. As we sow, we reap. Let the reader go into the children's side of any prison in England, or, I grieve to add, of many workhouses, and judge whether those are monsters who disgrace our streets, people our hulks and penitentiaries, and overcrowd our penal colonies, or are creatures whom we have deliberately suffered to be bred for misery and ruin.

This thought was the motive that led him throughout his whole life to try to arouse sympathetic interest of the most active kind in the conditions and circumstances of the poor.

One of his most striking appeals to thoughtful people is made in Martin Chuzzlewit. These profound words will always be worthy of careful study by teachers and reformers:

> Oh, moralists, who treat of happiness and self-respect, innate in every sphere of life, and shedding light on every grain of dust in God's highway, so smooth below your carriage wheels, so rough beneath the tread of naked feet, bethink yourselves in looking on the swift descent of men who *have* lived in their own esteem, that there are scores of thousands breathing now, and breathing thick with painful toil, who in that high respect have never lived at all, nor had a chance of life! Go ye, who rest so placidly upon the sacred bard who had been young, and when he strung his harp was old, and had never seen the righteous forsaken, or his seed begging their bread; go, teachers of content and honest pride, into the mine, the mill, the forge, the squalid depths of deepest ignorance, and uttermost abyss of man's neglect, and say can any hopeful plant spring up in air so foul that it extinguishes the soul's bright torch as fast as it is kindled! And, oh! ye Pharisees of the nineteen

> hundredth year of Christian knowledge, who soundingly appeal to human nature, see that it be human first. Take heed it has not been transformed, during your slumber and the sleep of generations, into the nature of the beasts.

Dickens saw clearly the depravity of human nature, but he looked beyond the depravity to its cause, and he found a natural cause for the degradation, but not the cause that had been commonly assigned. He taught that the highest and holiest elements in human nature were the causes of its swiftest deterioration when misused, perverted, or neglected.

Alice Marwood, in Dombey and Son, was introduced to teach parents and society in general the duties they owe to childhood, and to show how lives are wrecked by neglect and by a false use of power. When she returned, an outcast, to her mother, and her mother upbraided her, the young woman said:

> "I tell you, mother, for the second time, there have been years for me as well as you. Come back harder? Of course I have come back harder. What else did you expect?"
>
> "Harder to me! To her own dear mother!" cried the old woman.
>
> "I don't know who began to harden me, if my own dear mother didn't," she returned, sitting with her folded arms, and knitted brows, and compressed lips, as if she were bent on excluding, by force, every softer feeling from her breast. "Listen, mother, to a word or two. If we understand each other now, we shall not fall out any more, perhaps. I went away a girl, and have come back a woman. I went away undutiful enough, and have come back no better, you may swear. But have you been very dutiful to me?"
>
> "I!" cried the old woman. "To my own gal! A mother dutiful to her own child!"
>
> "It sounds unnatural, don't it?" returned the daughter, looking coldly on her with her stern, regardless, hardy, beautiful face; "but I have thought of it sometimes, in the course of *my* lone years, till I have got used to it. I have heard some talk about duty first and last; but it has always been of my duty to other people. I have wondered now and then—to pass away the time—whether no one ever owed any duty to me."
>
> Her mother sat mowing, and mumbling, and shaking her head, but whether angrily, or remorsefully, or in denial, or only in her physical infirmity, did not appear.
>
> "There was a child called Alice Marwood," said the daughter with a laugh, and looking down at herself in terrible derision of herself, "born among poverty and neglect, and nurtured in it. Nobody taught her, nobody stepped forward to help her, nobody cared for her."

"Nobody!" echoed the mother, pointing to herself and striking her breast.

"The only care she knew," returned the daughter, "was to be beaten, and stinted, and abused sometimes; and she might have done better without that. She lived in homes like this, and in the streets, with a crowd of little wretches like herself; and yet she brought good looks out of this childhood. So much the worse for her. She had better have been hunted and worried to death for ugliness."

"Go on! go on!" exclaimed the mother.

"She'll soon have ended," said the daughter. "There was a criminal called Alice Marwood—a girl still, but deserted and an outcast. And she was tried, and she was sentenced. And Lord, how the gentlemen in the court talked about it! and how grave the judge was on her duty, and on her having perverted the gifts of Nature—as if he didn't know better than anybody there that they had been made curses to her!—and how he preached about the strong arm of the Law—so very strong to save her, when she was an innocent and helpless little wretch! and how solemn and religious it all was! I have thought of that many times since, to be sure!"

She folded her arms tightly on her breast, and laughed in a tone that made the howl of the old woman musical.

"So Alice Marwood was transported, mother," she pursued, "and was sent to learn her duty where there was twenty times less duty, and more wickedness, and wrong, and infamy, than here. And Alice Marwood is come back a woman. Such a woman as she ought to be, after all this. In good time, there will be more solemnity, and more fine talk, and more strong arm, most likely, and there will be an end of her; but the gentlemen needn't be afraid of being thrown out of work. There's crowds of little wretches, boy and girl, growing up in any of the streets they live in, that'll keep them to it till they've made their fortunes."

Bleak House is one of the greatest of the educational works of Dickens. One of its chief aims was to arouse a sympathetic interest in the lives of poor children. The Neckett children, Charlotte, and Tom, and Emma, revealed a new world to many thousands of good people.

"Charley, Charley!" said my guardian. "How old are you?"

"Over thirteen, sir," replied the child.

"Oh! what a great age," said my guardian. "What a great age, Charley!"

"And do you live alone here with these babies, Charley?" said my guardian.

"Yes, sir," returned the child, looking up into his face with perfect confidence, "since father died."

"And how do you live, Charley? Oh! Charley," said my guardian, turning his face away for a moment, "how do you live?"

"Since my father died, sir, I've gone out to work. I'm out washing to-day."

"God help you, Charley!" said my guardian. "You're not tall enough to reach the tub!"

"In pattens I am, sir," she said, quickly. "I've got a high pair as belonged to mother."

"And when did mother die? Poor mother!"

"Mother died just after Emma was born," said the child, glancing at the face upon her bosom. "Then father said I was to be as good a mother to her as I could. And so I tried. And so I worked at home, and did cleaning and nursing and washing, for a long time before I began to go out. And that's how I know how; don't you see, sir?"

"And do you often go out?"

"As often as I can," said Charley, opening her eyes, and smiling, "because of earning sixpences and shillings!"

"And do you always lock the babies up when you go out?"

"To keep 'em safe, sir, don't you see?" said Charley. "Mrs. Blinder comes up now and then, and Mr. Gridley comes up sometimes, and perhaps I can run in sometimes, and they can play, you know, and Tom ain't afraid of being locked up, are you, Tom?"

"No-o!" said Tom stoutly.

"When it comes on dark the lamps are lighted down in the court, and they show up here quite bright—almost quite bright. Don't they, Tom?"

"Yes, Charley," said Tom; "almost quite bright."

The hearts must be hard that are not moved to a deeper and more practical interest in the children of the poor by this pathetic story, and others of a kindred character which Dickens told over and over again for the Christian world to study. And the study led to feeling and thought and co-operative action.

The fruits of these wonderful stories are the splendid homes, and organizations for children, and the laws to protect them from cruelty by parents or teachers, or employers, and the free public schools to educate them, and the joy, and happiness, and freedom, that are taking the place of the sorrow, and tears, and coercion of the time when Dickens began his noble work.

The tragic story of poor Jo illustrated the poverty, the ignorance, the destitution, the hopelessness, the barrenness, and the dreadful environment of a London street boy. The world has done much better since, as Dickens prophesied it would do, and the good work is going on. Hundreds of thousands of the poor Joes of London are now in the public schools of London alone of whom the Christian philanthropy of the world thought little till Dickens told his stories.

In Nobody's Story Dickens returns to his special purpose of changing the attitude of civilization toward the education of the poor. The Bigwigs represent society, and "the man" means the poor man.

> But the Bigwig family broke out into violent family quarrels concerning what it was lawful to teach to this man's children. Some of the family insisted on such a thing being primary and indispensable above all other things; and others of the family insisted on such another thing being primary and indispensable above all other things; and the Bigwig family, rent into factions, wrote pamphlets, held convocations, delivered charges, orations, and all varieties of discourses; impounded one another in courts Lay and courts Ecclesiastical; threw dirt, exchanged pummellings, and fell together by the ears in unintelligible animosity. Meanwhile, this man, in his short evening snatches at his fireside, saw the demon Ignorance arise there, and take his children to itself. He saw his daughter perverted into a heavy slatternly drudge; he saw his son go moping down the ways of low sensuality, to brutality and crime; he saw the dawning light of intelligence in the eyes of his babies so changing into cunning and suspicion, that he could have rather wished them idiots.

Dickens objected to a certain kind of sentimentality exhibited in his day toward criminals, and draws a very suggestive picture full of elements for psychological study in David Copperfield, in which he makes the brutal schoolmaster Creakle a very considerate Middlesex magistrate, with an unfailing system for a quick and effective method of converting the wickedest scoundrels into the most submissive, Scripture-quoting saints by solitary confinement. Dickens did not approve of the system, and he did not approve either of the plan of the spending of so much money by the state in erecting splendid buildings for criminals, while the honest poor were in hovels, and especially while the state allowed the boys and girls, through neglect, to be transformed into criminals by thousands every year. Dickens would have made criminals earn their own living, and he urged the establishment of industrial schools for the boys and girls of the streets, so that they might become respectable, intelligent, self-reliant, law-abiding citizens instead of criminals.

David said:

> Traddles and I repaired to the prison where Mr. Creakle was powerful. It was an immense and solid building, erected at a vast expense. I could not help thinking, as we approached the gate, what an uproar would have been made in the country if any de-

> luded man had proposed to spend one half the money it had cost, on the erection of an industrial school for the young, or a house of refuge for the deserving old.

As usual with great reformers, the philanthropists of his own day refused to accept the theories of Dickens, but succeeding generations adopted them. The reforms for which he pleaded began to be practised so soon because he winged his thought with living appeals to the deepest, truest feelings of the human heart.

Dickens said truly of Barnaby Rudge:

> "The absence of the soul is far more terrible in a living man than in a dead one; and in this unfortunate being its noblest powers were wanting."

He pleaded again for those who are weak-minded in Mr. Dick's case in David Copperfield. Mr. Dick was evidently introduced into the story to show the effect of kind treatment on those who are defective in intellect. The insane were flogged and put in strait-jackets in the time of Dickens. His teaching is now the practice of the civilized world. The insane are kindly treated, and weak-minded children are taught in good schools by the best teachers that can be obtained for them.

Betsy Trotwood, David's aunt, was an embodiment of a good heart united with an eminently practical head. She did not talk about religion, as did the Murdstones, but she showed her religious life in good, reasonable, self-sacrificing, helpful living. David asked her for an explanation of Mr. Dick's case.

> "He has been *called* mad," said my aunt. "I have a selfish pleasure in saying he has been called mad, or I should not have had the benefit of his society and advice for these last ten years and upward—in fact, ever since your sister, Betsy Trotwood, disappointed me."
>
> "So long as that?" I said.
>
> "And nice people they were, who had the audacity to call him mad," pursued my aunt. "Mr. Dick is a sort of distant connection of mine—it doesn't matter how; I needn't enter into that. If it hadn't been for me, his own brother would have shut him up for life. That's all."
>
> I am afraid it was hypocritical in me, but seeing that my aunt felt strongly on the subject, I tried to look as if I felt strongly too.
>
> "A proud fool!" said my aunt. "Because his brother was a little eccentric—though he is not half so eccentric as a good many people—he didn't like to have him visible about the house, and sent him away to some private asylum place; though he had been left to his particular care by their deceased father, who thought him almost a natural. And a wise man *he* must have been to think so! Mad himself, no doubt."
>
> Again, as my aunt looked quite convinced, I endeavoured to

look quite convinced also.

"So I stepped in," said my aunt, "and made him an offer. I said, 'Your brother's sane—a great deal more sane than you are, or ever will be, it is to be hoped. Let him have his little income, and come and live with me. *I* am not afraid of him; *I* am not proud; *I* am ready to take care of him, and shall not ill treat him as some people (besides the asylum folks) have done.' After a good deal of squabbling," said my aunt, "I got him; and he has been here ever since. He is the most friendly and amenable creature in existence; and as for advice!—but nobody knows what that man's mind is, except myself."

Dickens was greatly delighted with the asylums of the United States, and he strongly advocated the adoption in England of American methods of treating the insane. He says, in American Notes:

> At South Boston, as it is called, in a situation excellently adapted for the purpose, several charitable institutions are clustered together. One of these is the State Hospital for the Insane; admirably conducted on those enlightened principles of conciliation and kindness, which twenty years ago would have been worse than heretical, and which have been acted upon with so much success in our own pauper asylum at Hanwell. "Evince a desire to show some confidence, and repose some trust, even in mad people," said the resident physician, as we walked along the galleries, his patients flocking round us unrestrained. Of those who deny or doubt the wisdom of this maxim after witnessing its effects, if there be such people still alive, I can only say that I hope I may never be summoned as a juryman on a commission of lunacy whereof they are the subjects; for I should certainly find them out of their senses, on such evidence alone.
>
> Each ward in this institution is shaped like a long gallery or hall, with the dormitories of the patients opening from it on either hand. Here they work, read, play at skittles, and other games; and, when the weather does not admit of their taking exercise out of doors, pass the day together. In one of these rooms, seated, calmly, and quite as a matter of course, among a throng of mad women, black and white, were the physician's wife and another lady, with a couple of children. These ladies were graceful and handsome; and it was not difficult to perceive at a glance that even their presence there had a highly beneficial influence on the patients who were grouped about them.
>
> Every patient in this asylum sits down to dinner every day with a knife and fork; and in the midst of them sits the gentleman whose manner of dealing with his charges I have just described. At every meal, moral influence alone restrains the more violent

> among them from cutting the throats of the rest; but the effect of that influence is reduced to an absolute certainty, and is found, even as a means of restraint, to say nothing of it as a means of cure, a hundred times more efficacious than all the strait-waist-coats, fetters, and handcuffs, that ignorance, prejudice, and cruelty have manufactured since the creation of the world.

How much those benighted teachers who so tragically ask "What *can* you do with bad boys, if you do *not* use corporal punishment?" might learn from the last sentence!

Blinded by old ideals, these teachers whip away, admitting that they fail to reform many of the best boys, and quieting their consciences with the horrible thought that the evil course was the natural one for the boys, and that they are not responsible for their blighted lives. They comfort themselves with the thought that it is God's business, and if he made a boy so bad that flogging would not reform him, they at any rate are free from blame, because they "have beaten, and beaten, and beaten him, and it did him no good." Having beaten him, and beaten him, and beaten him, they rest contented with the sure conviction that they have faithfully done their duty; and when, perchance, the poor boy becomes a criminal, they solemnly say without a blush or a pang: "I knew he would come to a bad end, but I am so thankful that I did my duty to him."

Ignominious failure to save the brave boys who are not cowardly enough to be deterred from doing wrong by beating has taught nothing to some teachers. Even yet they placidly beat on, and get angry if they are requested to try freedom as a substitute for coercion in the training of beings created in God's image. They even question the sanity and the theology of those who dare to doubt the efficiency of the sacred rod. They do not deem it possible that by studying the child and their own higher powers they could find easier, pleasanter, and infinitely more successful methods of guiding a boy to a true, strong life than by beating, and beating, and beating him.

The keepers of asylums in the time of Dickens were equally severe on the wise friends of the insane. They honestly believed that terrible evils would necessarily result from giving greater freedom to the afflicted patients in asylums. Dickens took the side of freedom and common sense, and the strait-jackets, and handcuffs, and fetters have been taken off, and, *even as a means of restraint*, kindness and freedom have done better work than all the coercive fetters that "ignorance, prejudice, and cruelty have manufactured since the creation of the world."

So all teachers who have grown wise enough have found that kindness and freedom are much better even as restraining agents, and infinitely better in the development of true, independent, positive, progressive characters than all the coercive terrors of rod, rule, strap, rawhide, or any form of cruelty ever practised on helpless childhood by ignorance, prejudice, and perverted theology since the creation of the world.

In American Notes Dickens gave a long description of Laura Bridgman written by Dr. Howe, and showed his intense interest in what was then a new movement in favour of the education of the blind.

Speaking of Laura Bridgman, Dickens himself wrote:

> The thought occurred to me as I sat down in another room before a girl, blind, deaf, and dumb; destitute of smell, and nearly so of taste; before a fair young creature with every human faculty, and hope, and power of goodness and affection inclosed within her delicate frame, and but one outward sense—the sense of touch. There she was before me; built up, as it were, in a marble cell, impervious to any ray of light, or particle of sound; with her poor white hand peeping through a chink in the wall, beckoning to some good man for help, that an immortal soul might be awakened.
>
> Long before I looked upon her the help had come. Her face was radiant with intelligence and pleasure. Her hair, braided by her own hands, was bound about her head, whose intellectual capacity and development were beautifully expressed in its graceful outline, and its broad open brow; her dress, arranged by herself, was a pattern of neatness and simplicity; the work she had knitted lay beside her; her writing book was on the desk she leaned upon. From the mournful ruin of such bereavement there had slowly risen up this gentle, tender, guileless, grateful-hearted being.

The touching story of Caleb Plummer and his blind daughter was intended to arouse interest in blind children.

Doctor Marigold should be one of the best beloved of all the beautiful characters of Dickens. If any kind of language could awaken an intense interest in the education of deaf-mutes, the story of the dear old Cheap Jack must surely do it.

The sad picture of the cruel treatment of his own little Sophy by her mother; of her dying on his shoulder while he was selling his wares to the crowd, whispering fondly to her between his jokes; and the suicide of the mother, when she afterward saw another woman beating her child, and heard the child cry piteously, "Don't beat me! Oh, mother, mother, mother!"—these prepare the heart for full appreciation of the tender, considerate, and intelligent treatment of the deaf-mute child adopted by Doctor Marigold in Sophy's place.

> I went to that Fair as a mere civilian, leaving the cart outside the town, and I looked about the back of the Vans while the performing was going on, and at last, sitting dozing against a muddy cart wheel, I come upon the poor girl who was deaf and dumb. At the first look I might almost have judged that she had escaped from the Wild Beast Show; but at the second I thought better of her, and thought that if she was more cared for and more kindly used she would be like my child. She was just the same age that my own daughter would have been, if her pretty head had not fell down upon my shoulder that unfortunate night.

It was happy days for both of us when Sophy and me began to travel in the cart. I at once gave her the name of Sophy, to put her ever toward me in the attitude of my own daughter. We soon made out to begin to understand one another, through the goodness of the Heavens, when she knowed that I meant true and kind by her. In a very little time she was wonderful fond of me. You have no idea what it is to have anybody wonderful fond of you, unless you have been got down and rolled upon by the lonely feelings that I have mentioned as having once got the better of me.

You'd have laughed—or the rewerse—it's according to your disposition—if you could have seen me trying to teach Sophy. At first I was helped—you'd never guess by what—milestones. I got some large alphabets in a box, all the letters separate on bits of bone, and say we was going to WINDSOR; I gave her those letters in that order, and then at every milestone I showed her those same letters in that same order again, and pointed toward the abode of royalty. Another time I give her CART, and then chalked the same upon the cart. Another time I give her DOCTOR MARIGOLD, and hung a corresponding inscription outside my waistcoat. People that met us might stare a bit and laugh, but what did *I* care if she caught the idea? She caught it after long patience and trouble, and then we did begin to get on swimmingly, I believe you! At first she was a little given to consider me the cart, and the cart the abode of royalty, but that soon wore off.

The way she learned to understand any look of mine was truly surprising. When I sold of a night, she would sit in the cart, unseen by them outside, and would give a eager look into my eyes when I looked in, and would hand me straight the precise article or articles I wanted. And then she would clap her hands, and laugh for joy. And as for me, seeing her so bright, and remembering what she was when I first lighted on her, starved and beaten and ragged, leaning asleep against the muddy cart wheel, it give me such heart that I gained a greater height of reputation than ever.

This happiness went on in the cart till she was sixteen years old. By which time I began to feel not satisfied that I had done my whole duty by her, and to consider that she ought to have better teaching than I could give her. It drew a many tears on both sides when I commenced explaining my views to her; but what's right is right, and you can't neither by tears nor laughter do away with its character.

So I took her hand in mine, and I went with her one day to the Deaf and Dumb Establishment in London, and when the gentleman come to speak to us, I says to him: "Now, I'll tell you what I'll do with you, sir. I am nothing but a Cheap Jack, but of late

> years I have laid by for a rainy day notwithstanding. This is my only daughter (adopted), and you can't produce a deafer nor a dumber. Teach her the most that can be taught her in the shortest separation that can be named—state the figure for it—and I am game to put the money down. I won't bate you single farthing, sir, but I'll put down the money here and now, and I'll thankfully throw you in a pound to take it. There!" The gentleman smiled, and then, "Well, well," says he, "I must first know what she has learned already. How do you communicate with her?" Then I showed him, and she wrote in printed writing many names of things and so forth; and we held some sprightly conversation, Sophy and me, about a little story in a book which the gentleman showed her, and which she was able to read. "This is most extraordinary," says the gentleman; "is it possible that you have been her only teacher?" "I have been her only teacher, sir," I says, "besides herself." "Then," says the gentleman, and more acceptable words was never spoke to me, "you're a clever fellow, and a good fellow." This he makes known to Sophy, who kisses his hands, claps her own, and laughs and cries upon it.
>
> "Now, Marigold, tell me what more do you want your adopted daughter to know?"
>
> "I want her, sir, to be cut off from the world as little as can be, considering her deprivations, and therefore to be able to read whatever is wrote with perfect ease and pleasure."

No one ever read this story and its delightful closing without being more deeply interested in deaf-mutes and their education.

All the children, especially poor and defective children, should be taught how much they owe to Dickens, that they might reverently love his memory.

One of the most awful pictures shown to Scrooge by the Phantom was the picture of the two "wretched, abject, frightful, hideous, miserable children."

> They were a boy and a girl. Yellow, meagre, ragged, scowling, wolfish; but prostrate, too, in their humility. Where graceful youth should have filled their features out, and touched them with its freshest tints, a stale and shrivelled hand, like that of age, had pinched, and twisted them, and pulled them into shreds. Where angels might have sat enthroned, devils lurked, and glared out menacing. No change, no degradation, no perversion of humanity, in any grade, through all the mysteries of wonderful creation, has monsters half so horrible and dread.
>
> "They are Man's," said the Spirit, looking down upon them. "And they cling to me, appealing from their fathers. This boy is Ignorance. This girl is Want. Beware them both, and all of their degree, but most of all beware this boy, for on his brow I see that written which is Doom, unless the writing be erased. Deny it!"

> cried the Spirit, stretching out its hand toward the city. "Slander those who tell it ye! Admit it for your factious purposes, and make it worse. And abide the end!"

Dickens bravely fought the battle against the enemies of the children, and helped to win the grandest victories of Christian civilization.

THE END.

Printed by Libri Plureos GmbH in Hamburg, Germany